The Complete
Decorated Journal

The Complete
Decorated Journal

A COMPENDIUM OF JOURNALING TECHNIQUES

Gwen Diehn

LARK CRAFTS
Asheville

for JACOB, TALLIS, LUCA, MAYA, BARNABY, AND NATE DIEHN

Editor: Linda Kopp

Art Director: Travis Medford

Illustrator: Gwen Diehn

Photographers: Stewart O'Shields,
  Keith Wright, Evan Bracken

Supplementary Photography: Aleia Woolsey,
  Elyse Weingarten

Cover Designer: Kristi Pfeffer

An Imprint of Sterling Publishing
387 Park Avenue South
New York, NY 10016

ISBN 978-1-4547-0203-0

Library of Congress Cataloging-in-Publication Data

Diehn, Gwen, 1943-
  The complete decorated journal : a compendium of journaling techniques / Gwen Diehn.
    p. cm.
  "Revised and combined edition of The decorated page and The decorated journal."
  Includes index.
  ISBN 978-1-4547-0203-0 (pb-trade pbk. : alk. paper)
  1. Photograph albums. 2. Scrapbook journaling. I. Diehn, Gwen, 1943- Decorated page.
II. Diehn, Gwen, 1943- Decorated journal. III. Title. IV. Title: Compendium of journaling
techniques.
  TR465.D5295 2011
  745.593'8--dc23

                      2011030851

Distributed in Canada by Sterling Publishing
c/o Canadian Manda Group, 165 Dufferin Street
Toronto, Ontario, Canada M6K 3H6
Distributed in the United Kingdom by GMC Distribution Services
Castle Place, 166 High Street, Lewes, East Sussex, England BN7 1XU
Distributed in Australia by Capricorn Link (Australia) Pty. Ltd.
P.O. Box 704, Windsor, NSW 2756, Australia

For information about custom editions, special sales, and premium and
corporate purchases, please contact Sterling Special Sales at 800-805-5489 or
specialsales@sterlingpublishing.com.

Email academic@larkbooks.com for information about desk and examination
copies. The complete policy can be found at larkcrafts.com.

Manufactured in China

2 4 6 8 10 9 7 5 3

larkcrafts.com

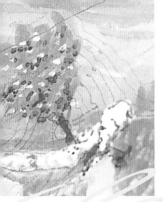
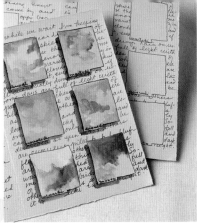

CONTENTS

Introduction

Keeping a journal is truly a journey. The very words come from a common root: the Old French word *journée*, meaning "day." A journey originally meant the distance traveled in a day; a journal was a book in which one would record a day's events.

I first kept a journal during fifth grade, when I received a little green plastic-covered diary with a golden key plugged into a tiny lock. However, my first experiment with combining images with text didn't come until my second year of college, when my biology teacher required us to keep a journal detailing the ecology of a particular tree on campus. I selected an orange tree growing outside the library that I had often admired for its glossy leaves and sweet smell even when it was not in bloom.

This journaling experience began in a predictable way: I devoted an early page to recording the tree's scientific name and to describing its leaf form and the texture of its bark. Each day I sat in front of the tree and made entries that included date, time, weather conditions, and sightings of any insects or birds. By the third week of the semester, I was bored with the project and had cut down my daily journal period to a brief five- or ten-minute stop on my way home from the library. The journal reflected my boredom. Its bland pages were densely filled with writing. The only variety was the occasional change in ink color—from blue to black to brown.

One day, however, my journaling took a surprising turn. While waiting in the checkout line at the college bookstore, I spotted some wrapping paper that was the exact color as the newest leaves on my tree. It was glossy and delicate with hints of lime green, just like the tiny leaves. On impulse I bought a sheet, and that night I cut out a shape from the luscious green paper and pasted it to the next blank page of my journal. "This is the color of the leaves when they first open," I wrote across the top of the page. The next day, I sat in front of the tree and sketched an image of a leaf on the green page.

A door in my imagination had swung open. Soon I began drawing the pattern of the leaf veins and noticed that they were in the same pattern as the tree's branches. Once I began drawing patterns, I saw more and more of them. I still wrote my observations, but I drew small charts along the margins of the pages to make this information easier to record and read. I also began making bark rubbings, lists, and visual collections. One day I sketched every insect in the vicinity. Then I used my sketches to identify them in an insect book. I drew details of the holes insects made in the tree. I made a map of a trail of ants and discovered where they came from and where they were headed. I began looking at the tree as a habitat, the environment of insects and birds. And then I began to look more broadly at the tree's own environment.

Ann Turkle's careful attention to detail is expressed in her closely observed and annotated sketches and narrative accounts of sheep in the Irish countryside.

Some information was difficult to write about, so I found purely visual means of explaining it. I used a small set of watercolors to paint a color swatch of the weather each day. I huddled under the tree during a spring storm and painted the swaying movements of its branches in the wind. As time passed, I became more and more curious about the tree. I talked to the groundskeeper and learned its history. During this time I learned that the tree was in the way of a new path that was to be built that summer. I worried that the tree would be cut down, and wrote its story on a piece of fragile tissue paper that I slipped into an envelope and glued inside the back of the journal.

On the last day of the project, I went out to make my final journal entry. The book was now fat and splayed open, spilling its rich insides. I arrived at the library eager to record some final comments, but the tree was gone, cut off a few inches above the ground. Sadly, I painted a black page that day, and glued some of the tree's sawdust around the edges.

My tree journal taught me that keeping a record of both written and visual elements opened new processes of thinking, feeling, observing, focusing, and experiencing life. If I had limited myself only to writing about the tree, I would never have been able to show what it felt like to be with the tree in a storm. I could never have expressed the beauty of the tree's patterns or the exact color of its leaves and bark. I would never have followed the ants or discovered the reason for their journey. I would not have known what to do with my feelings the day I discovered the tree cut down.

What can we call this deeper kind of journal with its richly layered pages that integrate writing with visual elements? "Visual-verbal" comes close, but sounds a little dry and academic. "Annotated sketchbook" places the value of the visual elements above the written ones. "Art journaling" misses the boat entirely, implying that the work in the journal is artwork, done with an audience in mind, rather than the personal, tentative, and unself-conscious work one does in a true journal. I prefer nature journalist Hannah Hinchman's use of the term "the illuminated journal" as well as Bruce Kremer's term "the textured diary."

Joseph Osina uses this page of his journal to visually represent a memory of his grandfather. The colors, textures, and shapes evoke a particular state of mind far more effectively than a written description could.

Kerstin Vogdes sums up a day at the beach with loose, lively sketches and brief notes, and then includes an envelope of tiny shells and fragments that bring to life the colors, textures, and spirit of the beach.

In truth, this kind of journal is a marriage of form and content, of text or writing and visual elements. In this kind of journal, the way a page looks is determined by the thoughts and reflections expressed on the page. A certain idea or image will seem to need a certain kind of layout or design, and particular materials will allow you to express yourself more powerfully. Each element, visual and verbal, informs the other and in turn informs your own understanding of the events, ideas, and reflections that you record. Painting in watercolors, for example, might make it easier to express feelings; using collage elements might help you recall an experience more vividly; writing might help you analyze a thought.

The good news is that journaling in this way doesn't have to be time-consuming or difficult, even if you haven't touched paints since kindergarten. The "Materials" section at the beginning of this book will introduce you to a variety of easy-to-use materials that can help you express your ideas and feelings in a different way. This materials section takes the position that less is more, provided that the less is of good quality and that you understand how it works. Because this section tells how materials work and

interact, it can help you make informed choices when buying adhesives, paints, papers, and other materials.

The next major section of the book, "Pages in Stages," strips away the mystery behind pages that look complicated and difficult. There are many different styles of pages represented in this section, some very simple, others many-layered and seemingly complex. Once you see how they are done, you can easily try out your own combinations and approaches.

In the following section, "Layouts," you will learn a variety of ways to compose the elements of a page in order to organize your thoughts and express your ideas clearly. You'll learn exactly how to get from a blank page to a rich page, brimming with meaning and delightful for you to look back at.

The next section, titled "How Does Your Journal See the World?," relates the ways different people throughout history and around the world have interpreted what they call reality by representing the world in images and text. While layered pages can be great fun and are very popular today, they don't represent the only possibility for working in a journal. This section discusses many ideas for using your journal to explore as well as express different worldviews. It includes, among other ideas, a look at symbolic, naturalistic, and creative journal keeping, as well as some ideas for processes that are frequently used in these different kinds of journals.

The next-to-last section of the book, the "Applications" section, explores several ways to jump-start the verbal or written aspect of journal keeping. There are prompts in this section for various kinds of entries that lend themselves to visual embellishments and integration with visual elements. You'll find examples of 10 different types of journal entries that will inspire you and help you organize your thoughts. This section of the book will not only show you how, but it will help you make your own journal (and not expire from the effort), even if you are most definitely not interested in becoming a fine bookbinder. Being able to whip together your own journal will enable you to have the exact kind of paper you love, exactly the right size and shape of book, and even special little touches that can never be found in purchased journals. Best of all, you will need no more sophisticated equipment than what you can find in the junk drawer in your kitchen.

The final section of the book, the "The Reluctant Bookbinder," answers one of the most persistent questions I've encountered: Where can I find a blank book that has [fill in your own exacting specifications as to paper type, size, shape, cover material, price, etc.]? In my experience, the answer to this question is, sadly, "Nowhere, because there just aren't that many people who love to write and draw on flattened-out lunch bags bound into a nice little soft leather cover with a pocket added to the second-to-last section. So manufacturers can't afford to produce these things." But you can afford to make these wonderfully eccentric, perfect-for-you journals.

Bruce Kremer's complex arrangement of stamps, drawings, painting, typewritten text, and collage invites the viewer to meander around the page at a leisurely pace.

Throughout the book are short essays that introduce you to journal keepers and journal lore in order to build a context for the practice of keeping a journal. Reading about the widely varying uses that have been made of illustrated journals and the myriad contexts in which they have been created can jump-start explorations of your own. Personally, I was delighted to learn that Francis Galton considered keeping a journal right up there in importance with procuring a team of good strong camels to get himself across a desert. I felt very close to Muriel Foster when I saw that she disregarded the printed lines of her fishing diary and painted a lovely scene of the stream in which she was fishing right across the middle of two pages. And I was positively enraptured by Jennifer Bartlett's ability to not only make the best of a bad situation when she painted and drew the same really rather pedestrian garden scene every day for almost a whole rainy year, but to transform this base material into a spectacular body of artwork afterward.

I think these examples from journaling luminaries will inspire you as they did me. They teach us all how to look and look again, and then look yet again. These journal keepers' patient looking and recording opens our eyes to the richness that is everywhere.

In this revised and combined edition of *The Decorated Page* and *The Decorated Journal*, you'll find pages placed throughout the book that feature the words and selected pages of 13 contemporary people who keep what seem to me to be real live journals. As you read their statements about how keeping a journal makes their lives richer, more entertaining, more reflective, and more focused, you'll perhaps gain ideas for expanding the use you make of your own journals. Documenting information about your life and the world around you should not be just another burden, another place to compare yourself unfavorably with other people. If your journal isn't a pleasure, a solace, a refuge, a playground, why impose the keeping of it on yourself? In *The Complete Decorated Journal* you'll learn new ways of making your journal your home away from home, your room of your own, your pleasure palace, your private kingdom. Let the fun begin!

Gwen Diehn. 6 x 9 inches (15.2 x 22.9 cm). Watercolor, gouache, fluid acrylic, pen on handmade paper.
Photo by Aleia Woolsey.

Susan Saling's page communicates facts as well as the feeling of the Pere Lachaise cemetery in Paris. She combines her train ticket, parts of a cemetery brochure, her own sketch and painting, and a few written notes to summarize a day spent at this Paris attraction.

Gwen Diehn. 6 x 9 inches (15.2 x 22.9 cm). Gouache, acrylic, watercolor, and colored markers on handmade paper. *Photo by Aleia Woolsey.*

While riding the train north from New York to New Hampshire in late December, I passed the time by making a collage of a train timetable, some birch bark, and a map by Jacob Diehn.

Materials & How to Use Them

The difficult truth about art materials is that the materials themselves are not as important as what you do with them. Another hard fact, which you already know, is that art is a practice, and as such it needs to be tended and nurtured by engaging in it on a regular basis. No product is going to make your journal or other artwork come alive and be inspired. Only you can do that by working and playing every day with your small supply of excellent materials.

Less is More: On Selecting Materials

"Less is more," said architect Mies van der Rohe when explaining one of the basic principles underlying his spare and elegant work. And even before Mies, back in the 14th century, a philosopher named William of Occam insisted that, "What can be done with fewer is done in vain with more." These are good thoughts to keep in mind when buying art materials. "That may be,"

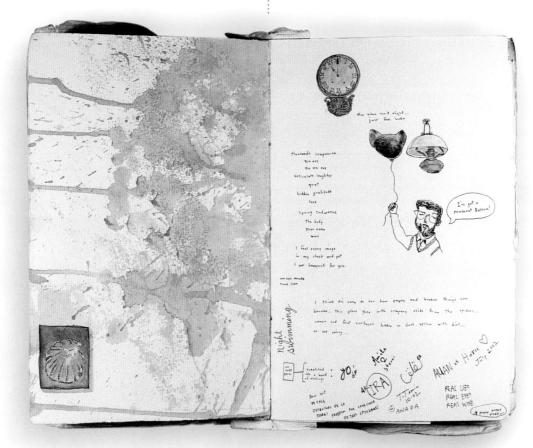

Ivy Smith, *Shell and Muskrat Balloon*, 2004. 11¼ x 9 inches (28.6 x 22.9 cm). Bound Journal, ink, watercolor. *Photo by Aleia Woolsey.*

Materials for journal keeping.

you protest, "but if I can only find out what kind of paint was used to do the background of this page, my own work would take off and might look just as good." So off you go in search of the magic paint. But when you find it, you have to buy five jars because it only comes in sets labeled "Autumn Colors Collection" and "Spring Colors Collection." And, it's so thinly pigmented and filled with chalky stuff that you can't use it to mix anything, making it necessary for you to buy a separate bottle if you want a slightly more yellowish orange.

When the buying crazies hit you, when your confidence in your own work slips, try holding on to the idea that less really can be more. Try sticking to a small range of high-quality materials and practice with them to learn how they work. Once you can use these few materials well, you *will* be able to produce every effect you want. Adopting such an approach frees you from wasting time and money chasing after every new product that comes along, and it keeps you from becoming dependent on manufacturers who are only too willing to sell you more and more stuff—much of it good for doing only one thing.

DETERMINED & NEUTRAL MATERIALS

Making any kind of art is basically the process of making a series of choices that carries out your intentions for a particular piece of work. Choosing materials and supplies is usually the first of all of these choices. Art materials can be described as falling along a continuum from neutral materials—those that don't have any meaning or much connotation of their own—to strongly determined materials—those that do carry meaning and connotations of their own.

Neutral materials include white or lightly tinted sheets of paper, standard colors of paint, blank rubber stamp-making material, ordinary black ink, colored and graphite pencils, as well as any other materials that do not assert themselves. Neutral materials will become in a sense transparent once they've been incorporated into a piece of artwork because your own expression will easily dominate them.

Strongly determined materials, at the other end of the continuum, already carry messages and connotations, and these meanings severely limit their usefulness. Consider all the nostalgic reproductions of Victorian women, children, and Renaissance angels that are sold in packages of ready-made collage materials. Originally, collage involved incorporating ephemera—the small things from everyday life that are of short-lived use or interest—into artwork. These clippings, ticket stubs, pieces of wrapping paper, and other incidental materials took on new meaning in the context of the artwork. At the same time, they brought to the work traces and hints of the original meanings and connotations that they held for the artist.

Using real ephemera from daily life can add richness to a journal. But packaged images—which might well be called pseudo-ephemera—besides not really being related to our lives have become ubiquitous, and like anything too often repeated, these images have become clichés. As such, this material weakens any artwork in which it's used unless it's radically changed or used very deliberately and for reasons that relate clearly to the concept of the piece.

WHAT TO BUY

When buying art materials, you want to know how flexible and adaptable each material will be. Are the paints of good enough quality that a few basic colors will yield good mixes? Or, must you buy the entire 30-bottle, pre-selected set because the colors are so lightly pigmented and adulterated by additives that they turn to mud when mixed? Neutral materials can be used in infinite ways and situations to do whatever needs to be done. If you decide to buy some strongly determined materials, such as pre-carved rubber stamps or stencils and printed or other decorative papers, be sure to use the meaning of the material to carry out your own intention in the artwork. Keep this material to a minimum so that it doesn't leap out— "There's that great rubber stamp of the flying fish again!"—and use it in good balance with more neutral materials.

You can, however, sometimes use determined materials ironically to great effect. For example, there's an artist's book in which the artist has used excessively cute, pre-carved rubber stamps of kittens and puppies to construct a graph of the population explosion of unwanted kittens and puppies due to failure to spay and neuter.

Following is a discussion of some basic art materials to use in your bookwork and journals. Once you understand how they work, you can decide when to buy the best and when to cut some corners. You'll also understand why materials act the way they do, so you can use them in ways that ensure they'll do what you want. As you experiment and discover new media to use in your work, always apply these tests to the materials:

- Are they of good enough quality to mix well?

- Do they result in a stable surface that won't rub off or smear?

- Will they not bleed through the particular paper you'll be using? If that's not the effect you want— don't use them.

- Are they acid free or archival?

Paper, the Substratum

Keep in mind that every material will act upon the paper to which it is applied. Therefore, before thinking about the materials you'll use on the paper, it's good to understand exactly what paper is and how it works. Knowing a few basic facts can save you a lot of time when choosing or making journals, and can help you select materials that will work well with the paper you're using.

All paper is made by first macerating, or bruising, cellulose fibers so that they will attract the water that's mixed with them to make pulp. The pulp is then formed into a sheet, and the water pressed out. Pressing causes the cellulose fibers to form hydrogen bonds with each other. The paper is then dried, and sometimes the surface is treated by pressing. Somewhere along the way, sizing is usually added, either to the pulp before the sheets are formed or to the surface of the finished sheet. Sizing is glue that stops the fibers from attracting water. The addition of sizing makes it possible to write or draw on the paper with liquid media without its bleeding through. Sometimes other chemicals are added to the paper pulp, either to improve the finish of the paper or to make it easier to form into sheets.

KIND of PAPER	SOURCE of CELLULOSE	PRODUCTION PROCESS	ADDITIVES/ SURFACE TREATMENT
inexpensive machine-made, such as newsprint or construction paper	wood pulp with impurities and high acid content; paper deteriorates quickly	large paper mill used to bruise fibers, then sheet formation by large machine and machine drying	sizing, pressing, fillers
expensive machine-made, such as good offset printing papers	100% cotton or cotton rag	same as above	sizing, hot- or cold-pressing with metal plates to give smooth or very smooth finish for some papers; calcium carbonate or other chemicals added to some to improve opacity and receptivity to ink
mold-made artists' papers	the best are 100% cotton or cotton rag yielding very strong long-lasting paper	paper mill such as Hollander beater to bruise fiber, then a cylinder-mold to form sheets	sizing; maybe cold- or hot-pressing; maybe calcium carbonate to improve opacity and to give a smooth finish for some papers
handmade decorative and artists' papers	cotton, flax, abaca, jute, hemp, sisal, kenaf, esparto, mulberry, cotton, and linen rags— many sources, all cleaned of impurities so that the paper is long-lasting	hand beaten with a mallet or stick or in a machine such as a Hollander beater; some people use kitchen blenders, but these chop and shorten fibers rather than bruise them, making the resulting paper weak	sizing; maybe pressing on variously textured blankets or surfaces or with hot irons to alter surface; maybe pigments or dyes; maybe flower parts for textural interest

Kerstin Vogdes, *Travel Journal: Thailand and Cambodia*, 2004. 4 x 6 inches (10.2 x 15.2 cm) Hand-bound journal, PVA glue, vellum, ink, shells. *Photo by Aleia Woolsey.*

Paper is always somewhat fragile and easily affected by what happens on its surface and even by the air around it. With this in mind, it is important to respect each sheet's limitations. Paper must be matched to the media you'll use on it. Wet media are particularly hard on paper. When you apply anything containing water to paper, you're in a sense reversing the papermaking process; the fibers of the sheet take on water to a greater or lesser degree and begin to swell, the bonds between the individual fibers weaken, and surface finishes, such as pressing, are undone to a degree.

WATERCOLOR PAPER

Whether it's mold-made, handmade, or machine-made, watercolor paper is made to withstand being wet and rewet without undue stretching and buckling. It's usually a heavier-bodied paper with sufficient sizing to control absorbency and help the matting of surface fibers stand up to scrubbing and even scratching. It comes in three main surfaces: hot-pressed, cold-pressed (also designated as "not," as in "not hot-pressed"), and rough or toothy. Hot-pressed has the smoothest, hardest surface. Cold-pressed (or not) has a slightly toothy or rough surface and is the most versatile of the three. Rough paper has a more pronounced texture. It's especially good for making bright, sparkling washes since the brush skips over some of the crevices between the bumps in the surface, leaving the white of the paper to sparkle through.

DRAWING PAPER

In addition to watercolor paper, there are a number of good-quality drawing papers sold in art supply stores made for use with pen and graphite, that also work very well with light watercolor work, such as watercolor sketching. But you must respect the limitations of this paper by not asking it to absorb as much water as watercolor paper. You can't expect a lighter paper to stand up under repeated washes, for example. But, if you just want to add light washes to pen drawings, or sketch lightly in color, drawing paper can be useful. Single-ply and double-ply bristol, a relatively inexpensive paper, is an example. Some relatively inexpensive handmade papers, such as lokta paper which originates in Nepal, are also very interesting to use for drawing as well as painting and light collage.

PAPER FOR COLLAGE

Paper that will become the base of collage needs to be heavy enough to support the weight of the elements attached to it plus the adhesive used. Lightweight paper will curl and buckle when wet adhesives are applied to it. As mentioned above, when paper is rewet, either by watercolor washes, wet adhesive, or a liquid ground, the fibers will absorb water and swell. The fibers in machine-made paper (and to some extent mold-made paper) are lined up more or less parallel to each other due to the directional movement of the papermaking machine during sheet formation. The direction of the paper fibers is referred to as the grain of the paper. (Most handmade paper does not have grain because it is shaken in all directions during sheet formation.)

When fibers in grained papers swell, they do so in a sideways direction, so that the piece of paper actually increases in size slightly in a direction perpendicular to

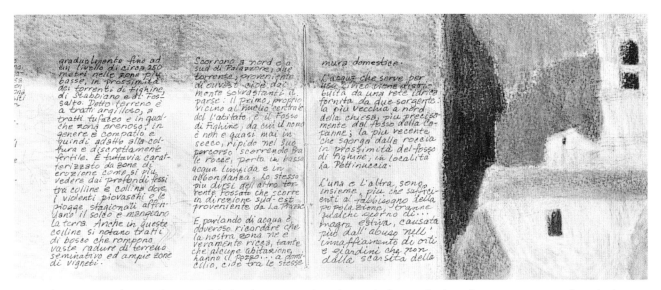

Watercolor crayons can be turned into a wash by brushing over marks with water. In this page by the author, some texture was drawn back into the wash after it was dry. *Photo by Elyse Weingarten.*

the grain when it is wet. Then, as the paper dries and the fibers lose water to evaporation, the sheet shrinks. When paper is wet unevenly, such as when it is painted or has adhesive applied to a small part of it, it curls, buckles, and wrinkles (known as cockling) because of uneven swelling and drying. The heavier the paper and the dryer the adhesive, the flatter the paper will dry in general, unless it's stretched and dried under restraint (which is difficult to impossible to do when the paper is bound into a book). See Adhesives on page 40.

VELLUM

Translucent vellum paper is an interesting alternative to opaque sheets, but it requires some special considerations. It is made by over beating cellulose fibers to form a jelly. The pulp is then tinted, formed into sheets, and drained. The resulting paper is translucent with a smooth, low-porous surface. This paper is more reactive to moisture and temperature than conventional papers. It buckles and curls very easily when wet, so it's best to use drier adhesives on it, such as glue sticks. It can be printed on an ink-jet printer but will curl from the heat of a laser printer. You can write on it with all kinds of inks, but when you use water-based, non-permanent inks it will take a little longer to dry due to the low porosity of the paper. Watercolor, gouache, fluid acrylics, and tube acrylics will adhere to translucent paper, but they all cause some buckling and cockling. You can buy envelopes made of translucent paper, which are best glued into a journal using a glue stick.

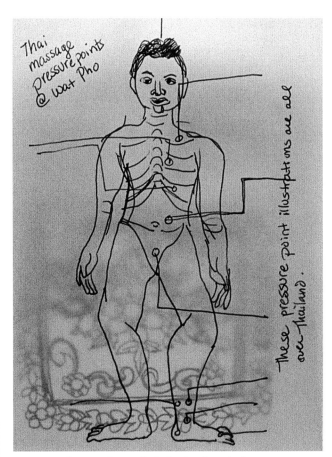

Kerstin Vogdes, *Travel Journal: Thailand and Cambodia*, 2004. 4 x 6 inches (10.2 x 15.2 cm). Hand-bound journal, PVA glue, vellum, ink, shells. *Photo by Aleia Woolsey.*

Keeping a Creative History

by Laura Ladendorf

*"I've made art since
I could hold a pencil.
Writing comes less easily,
but journals give my words
a place. I keep them all,
and, while there is little
order or overall purpose,
they do form a bit of my
own creative history."*

Haiti Journal Pages. 9 x 12 inches (22.9 x 30.5 cm). Pen; collage.

8 x 11 inches (20.3 x 27.9 cm). Pen.

My journals and sketchbooks provide an informal way to record ideas and thoughts. I use my books both as personal history and to develop art projects. The personal pages are rants or sketches of events or some fleeting vision—usually drawn in a hurry with feeling—and I'm less concerned with the art of it.

Art pages usually relate to projects that will evolve into some other form. I'll work out color or compositions in small spaces so I can see them as thumbnails. I often like the small sketches as well as the finished work. It may be that the lack of finality makes them more free-form and appealing.

I've made art since I could hold a pencil. Writing comes less easily, but journals give my words a place. I keep them all, and, while there is little order or overall purpose, they do form a bit of my own creative history.

An Artistic and Human Practice

by Becca Johnson

8½ x 12 inches (21.6 x 30.5 cm). Pen, pencil, watercolor; taped-on elements.

> *"...journals, like dreams, can serve as some sort of aperture to one's brilliantly strange subconscious mind."*

8 x 14 inches (20.3 x 35.6 cm). Pen, marker, painted paper fragment.

It's been a struggle not to judge myself when looking back through old journals. There is absolutely a place for one's harsh self-critique, for high standards, and cold judgment. But it seems to me, the great importance of a journal is a respite from those things—to give myself one small place in the world where I'm allowed to be unpolished and awkward, and to make naïve and/or uncensored attempts at explaining the great, complicated business of being alive.

I find there's often a nervy lack of sophistication, a rough-hewn honesty, and freshness to the work in my journals that simply can't be manufactured or mimicked in the work that's done with public exhibition or critique in mind. But, alas, side B of this story is that, when allowing for completely uncensored, unsorted, loose, and cloddish thoughts and sketches to be recorded and preserved, one runs the risk of not only facing but having cold, hard proof of one's faults, one's utter lack of brilliance.

That's why keeping a journal requires a great deal of humility as well, for it takes discipline to remain nonjudgmental and to allow space for risk taking. But if one is successful, then journals, like dreams, can serve as some sort of aperture to one's brilliantly strange subconscious mind. They can be the place where rubber meets the road, where ideas might make fire.

Drawing Closer: Nature Journaling

W hat I have not drawn, I have never really seen," writes Frederick Franck in his book *The Zen of Seeing* (1973, Random House). Franck's statement is in many ways the basis of the practice of nature journaling. From ancient people who drew carefully observed animals on the walls of caves, to 19th-century amateur naturalists who avidly drew their collections of insects and plants, drawing has long been a primary way to learn about and record the natural world.

Interestingly, photography has never really replaced drawing as a way of knowing or as a way of accurately representing nature. Certainly nature has been extensively photographed, and the resulting images have been used in many ways. But photography is too fast to replace the process of drawing; the same kind of slow, intimate, developmental seeing does not take place. It's still true that if you want to learn about the buds on your night-blooming cereus plant, drawing is one of the best ways to do so. A drawing records them with greater clarity because it lets you omit background clutter while emphasizing details such as the little spurs that barely show against the side of the bud stem. Drawings are still often used for identification manuals because of their clarity and ability to isolate certain elements while eliminating the extraneous.

Keeping a nature journal will enhance your enjoyment of nature, and you don't have to be an artist to keep one. Hannah Hinchman, a long-time nature journaler and the author of *A Trail Through Leaves: The Journal as a Path to Place* (1997, W. W. Norton & Co.), believes that drawing should be taught to every child alongside reading and writing and given equal emphasis. In Betty Edwards's groundbreaking book *Drawing on the Right Side of the Brain* (1999, JP Tarcher), Edwards says that in our culture we act as though visual skills were rare and mysterious and only available to a few highly gifted "artists." In reality, Edwards, Hinchman, and others maintain that everyone can and should learn to draw; and everyone would do so if they were given good materials (instead of markers, blunt crayons, and cheap paper), and were asked simple questions that would help them see and draw what they see.

I know from my own experience of teaching drawing for many years that everyone can learn to draw. The tools that most help me teach students to draw are, actually, a few questions. It helps to have a teacher, but you can simply ask them of yourself as you set out to draw that night-blooming cereus bud before it does its one-night-stand-blooming performance and disappears forever.

Here are the questions:

1. What, actually, do I see? (What is its general shape? What does this shape remind me of? How much of it do I want to draw?)

2. How wide is it compared to its height?

3. How big is this part compared to that part?

4. Is this part a true vertical or horizontal, and if not, how far off the vertical or horizontal is it?

5. If I dropped a plumb line (a string with a weight tied to the end) from this point, what would it hit lower down? If I ran a straight horizontal across from this point, where would it intersect this part?

Hannah Hinchman, *Wind River, Number 13*, June 1989.
Printed with permission of the artist.

To answer these questions, which you will ask over and over again, whenever something looks wrong or even slightly off, and especially when you start a new drawing, you'll need a pencil or other straight stick at least 6 inches (15.2 cm) long. To make comparative measures, you will hold the stick in one hand with your elbow straight. (This is important, as you need to keep the relative distance between the object, your eye, and the stick the same throughout measuring.) Close one eye. Place the tip of the stick so that it appears to touch one edge of the object, then place your thumbnail at the apparent other edge of the object. Holding this unit of measurement—and keeping your elbow straight—see how many of these units fit across the expanse you're measuring. For example, I might determine the size of the width of a stem, and then see how many stem-widths (the unit) long the bud is.

To determine how far off a vertical or horizontal something is, hold the stick horizontally beneath or vertically alongside the object, close one eye, and estimate how far off the vertical or horizontal the object (or the part of the object) is.

To use a plumb line or horizontal straight lines, use the stick in either a vertical or horizontal orientation.

With practice you'll get better and better at estimating measures and will soon no longer need to actually measure so often. But even after years of practice you'll from time to time look at a drawing in progress and say, "It looks funny. Something's off." That's when you need to measure, and you'll easily discover what you need to do to fix things.

Of course there is more that you can learn about drawing, but these few tools will get you started. The key to learning is practice. If you find that you really like to draw and you want to learn more refinements, I highly recommend Hannah Hinchman's and Betty Edwards's books.

Hannah Hinchman, *Torrey Valley and Torrey Rim*, May 1990. Printed with permission of the artist.

Blank Books

Blank books, like other art materials, range from the neutral to the strongly determined. Neutral ones are generally plain and unadorned, and they pose no great challenge other than that of being blank. They can easily be made to blend with the expression of a wide variety of feelings and ideas. They can be changed, as described in the section on Customizing a Blank Book (see page 212), or they can be left as they are—whatever suits your ideas for a particular journal.

Strongly determined blank books, those made with a high level of craft, often carry much meaning of their own. They almost seem to challenge you to deface them.

Don't let them terrorize you! Always carefully consider whether a particular blank book can be made to express the feelings and ideas that you want your book to express. For example, a leather-bound book might connote traditional values of craftsmanship, elegance, and a certain formal restraint. It also offers great protection for the pages within because leather is such a strong and durable material.

This book might be the perfect book to turn into a travel journal, since traditional travel journals were often bound in leather. Though they were usually rather plain, travel journals were extremely durable and able to withstand being pulled in and out of a pocket or pack many times. They could also withstand the heat of the sun, desert sand, seawater, and dirt from a forest floor. And travel journals have a long tradition, making them very compatible with a traditional-looking book.

This same plain-leather book, on the other hand, could also be a great foil to a collection of riotously colored, very emotional pages that burst from within when the book is opened. The contrast between the restrained exterior and the unbridled interior can be exciting and full of meaning.

A blank book that has a cover decorated with natural materials would be an obvious good fit for a garden or wildlife journal. But its earthy-looking cover could also be an interesting juxtaposition to an interior that deals with the process of building a house, which is an example of keeping nature at bay.

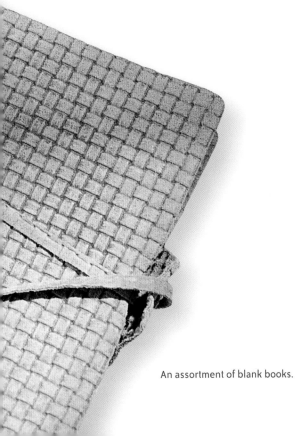

An assortment of blank books.

Archival Quality

There are a few other considerations to keep in mind when selecting a blank book. If you want the book to last for a long time, buy a book with acid-free or archival paper. Paper that's made from wood pulp is full of acid, and will begin to deteriorate within a few months. Look for books with labels that say they're made from 100% cotton or rag paper or acid-free paper. Some recycled paper is acid-free, but some is not, so don't assume that recycled paper is the best paper to use. Recently some manufacturers have been labeling paper "lignin free." Lignin is a natural adhesive that holds plant fibers together and gives woody plants their rigidity. Lignin is removed from fibers when fibers are cooked and cleaned prior to being beaten into pulp. But the absence of lignin doesn't itself guarantee a neutral pH. You can buy a pH-testing pen in some art supply stores. This inexpensive pen lets you make a small mark on the paper that will turn a certain color if the paper is acidic, and another color if it is neutral. This pen is a good

A pH pen determines that papers are acidic.

investment because many papers are not marked as to their acidity. You can use the test pen on all kinds of papers and cardboard, including paper elements for collage.

Gwen Diehn. 6 x 9 inches (15.2 x 22.9 cm). Pen and watercolor on handmade paper. *Photo by Aleia Woolsey.*

BINDING STYLES

Consider, also, the way the book is bound. Sewn bindings last a great deal longer than glued bindings. You'll be opening and closing this book often, and it needs to withstand this frequent stress on the binding.

TRADITIONAL BINDINGS

Traditional sewn bindings will stay open flat if the pages are relatively large and made of a paper that is light enough to drape. Books with closed-spine bindings afford good protection to pages as well as to other elements incorporated into the book. If you glue elements onto the pages, you can modify these books to prevent them from splaying out. (See Modifying The Book Form on pages 212 to 214.)

SPIRAL BINDINGS

Spiral or plastic comb bindings are relatively durable. They also allow the book to remain flat when open—an advantage if you work in watercolor or other wet media that must dry in an open position. The natural springiness of these bindings is also rather forgiving when you add elements to pages. When you adhere elements onto many pages, the book will still close flat instead of splaying out as it would with a tighter binding.

A stab bound journal.

These bindings, however, do not afford as much protection to pages as closed-spine bindings. Because spiral bindings create a gap that separates facing pages, you may find them difficult to work with if you enjoy doing two-page spreads.

Julie Wagner, 2001. 12 x 9 x 1 inches (30.5 x 22.9 x 2.5 cm).
Spiral-bound sketchbook, ink, watercolor. *Photo by artist.*

JAPANESE STAB BINDING

Books that are sewn in the Japanese stab-binding manner (see the photo on page 24) are durable, but do not remain flat when open.

ALBUM BINDINGS

These strong bindings are related to Japanese stab bindings. They usually have some spine-thickening modifications so that they do not splay out when you glue elements to pages. They have the advantage of being able to be unbound and re-bound easily so that pages can be removed or added. These books do not generally stay flat when open.

PAPER REVISITED

The thickness and finish of the paper in a blank book should be a major concern. If you've skipped the section on paper, go back and read it now. The very thin, light-weight paper in many blank books will not accept wet media, such as acrylic or watercolor, without wrinkling and possibly tearing. Some inks and stamp pad dyes can bleed through the backs of these pages. Thin papers can also be problematic if you want to attach items to the pages. Ideally, the paper to which you glue something should be equally heavy or heavier than the elements that are attached to the page. However, in certain cases, you may prefer a thin paper. For example, you might want to emphasize the delicacy of the wildflowers you plan to draw in a nature journal. Just be aware of the limitations of thin paper, and choose the media you use with consideration of the paper's weight and delicacy.

Some blank books are made with heavy watercolor paper, and are useful if you plan to do a lot of painting in your journal. But if you want pages that drape nicely and feel soft, and you don't need all the pages to be watercolor paper, you might prefer adding some sheets of watercolor paper to a book with lighter, more graceful pages. (See Customizing a Blank Book on page 212.)

The finish of a sheet of paper refers to how smooth or rough it feels and whether or not it has had sizing added to it. Most blank books have sized paper, but if you buy one with unsized paper, you'll need to use a ballpoint, gel pen, or pencil to write in it instead of using a liquid-ink pen. In general, very smooth, hard-finished paper is not as receptive to drawing media as softer, rougher (or toothier) paper. Pigment-based stamp pad inks take a very long time to dry on hard, smooth paper, as it is not very absorbent. Experience will teach you what kinds of paper work best with the media you prefer.

Paints

All paints are made of finely ground pigments mixed in a liquid, such as water or oil, with some kind of binder added that makes the pigment adhere to a surface. Depending on the kind and quality of the paint, various other substances may be added to increase opacity or to improve the way the paint flows from a brush. In my experience, the most useful paints for bookwork are watercolor, gouache (opaque watercolors), and fluid acrylics. These are all water-based paints that dry quickly and completely, with no surface stickiness.

A spiral binding is helpful if you want the pages to lie flat when the book is open, as in this journal by Ann Turkle. *Photo by Aleia Woolsey.*

KIND of PAINT	BINDER	HOW IT WORKS
watercolor	gum arabic	The water evaporates, leaving a delicate film of fine grains of pigment held to the paper by a water-soluble, relatively weak glue called gum arabic, which is the sap of a species of acacia tree. Depending on the pigment, watercolors are more or less transparent. Can be rewet after drying.
gouache	gum arabic	Works exactly like watercolor. Regardless of the pigment, gouache is opaque due to the addition of China clay, talc, zinc white, or other opacifiers. Can be rewet after drying.
fluid acrylic	polymer resin	The water evaporates, leaving behind a tough film of polymer in which particles of pigment are trapped. Once dry, the polymer resin is not water soluble. Fluid acrylics are more heavily pigmented than tube acrylics. They dry completely, without the somewhat sticky surface of other acrylics, because they do not have the waxy opacifiers that are added to other acrylic paints. They are also more transparent than other acrylics, and this fact, plus their heavy pigment load, causes them to yield clean color mixes. They dilute with water and can be used to pour, drip, and stain as well as to paint.

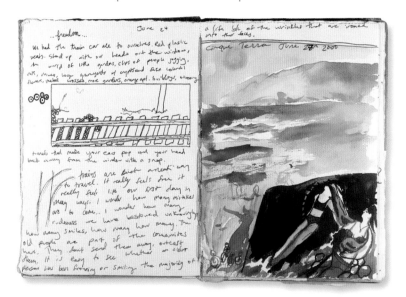

Gouache is more opaque than watercolor and is capable of giving very bright colors, as in this page by Kelcey Loomer. *Photo by Elyse Weingarten.*

PIGMENTS

Pigments are the coloring material in paints. They come from a variety of mineral, vegetable, and animal sources. Some are synthetic. Pigments vary in more ways than in the obvious hue or color. Some pigments, such as ultramarine, which is ground from a semi-precious stone called lapis lazuli, are rare and therefore more expensive. Others, such as yellow ochre, which comes from yellowish-brown earth or clay, are easy to find and process and are, therefore, less expensive. Some pigments are transparent and make good, clear glazes and mixes, while others are opaque and not suitable for glazing. Some are permanent and lightfast; others fade rather quickly and are referred to as fugitive.

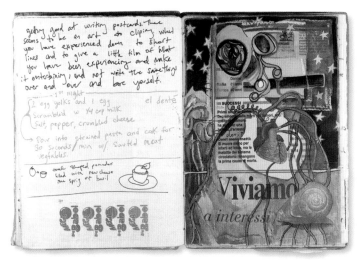

Kelcey Loomer, *Untitled Journal Page*, 2000. Photo by Elyse Weingarten.

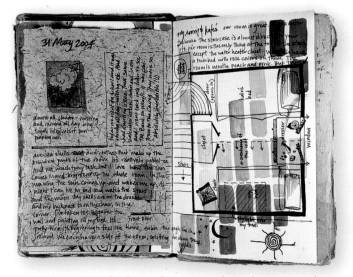

Sarah Bourne, *Ireland Journal Page*, 2004. 8½ x 11 (21.6 x 27.9 cm). Hand-bound journal, handmade paper, watercolor, and ink. Photo by Aleia Woolsey.

Brown ink gives this page by Dusty Benedict a soft look.

WATERCOLORS

Watercolors are manufactured in two general classes: student grade and artist's or professional grade. Artist's grade contains more pigment and fewer additives than student grade paint. The level of transparency for artist's grade is related to the transparency or opacity of the pigment, not to the addition of opacifiers or other fillers. In order to keep the price down for student grade paints, manufacturers often mix an expensive pigment, such as ultramarine, with a less expensive pigment to make a color that's similar to the pure pigment color even though it isn't an exact match. They also add opacifiers and other thickeners to student grade paint to increase the body of the paint, thereby compensating for the reduced amount of pigment.

Even if the label doesn't say artist's grade or student grade, you can tell by the price. Artist's grade paint is more expensive. It's also priced in categories determined by the cost of the pigments. Student grade paints are usually uniformly priced and contain more pigment mixes (usually labeled "hues") than pure pigment paints. Student grade paints are fine for starting out, but they don't give you the flexibility of use of artist's grade.

Watercolors come in tubes or cakes, and both are sold individually as well as in sets. If you buy tubes, you can make your own set with just the colors you want by squeezing the paint into empty pans or even into empty tin boxes such as candy tins. When you run out of a color, simply squeeze in more paint. You can mix tube paint and cake paint. If you start out with a set of cake paint and some colors run out, buy tubes of those colors and replace them as needed. Watercolors can be rewet as long as they aren't so old that the gum arabic has hardened. Even if you let watercolors dry on a palette or in their pans, they're ready to use the next time you need them by just adding water.

If you want to follow the principle of "less is more," buy only a few tubes or cakes of artist's grade watercolors. Following is a good starter list. Because artist's grade paints contain more pure pigment, these few colors will yield clear mixes and you won't have to buy lots of colors. If you buy cheap watercolors, which mix poorly, you'll need to buy many more paints in order to get a range of colors. Keep in mind that it doesn't take much paint to change a color when mixing, so mix slowly, always beginning with the lighter color and slowly adding the darker one.

WATERCOLOR STARTER PALETTE

- Cadmium yellow medium
  (an opaque, bright yellow)

- Cadmium red medium
  (an opaque, bright vermillion red)

- Permanent rose
  (a transparent, bluish-red, excellent for mixing)

- Ultramarine blue
  (a transparent, deep blue with a violet undertone)

- Cobalt blue
  (a transparent, deep blue, cooler than ultramarine)

- Raw sienna (a transparent yellowish-brown, good for glazes and mixing)

- Burnt sienna (a transparent, warm reddish-brown, good for glazing and mixing)

- Burnt umber (a warm brown, more transparent than burnt sienna, good for mixing)

Watercolors come in tubes as well as pans. The small tin shown here is an old chewing gum tin that I filled with daubs of tube watercolors to use as a small travel set. The blue-handled brushes are water brushes, an excellent tool for journal keepers on the move.

Local Pigments

A number of tailgate markets have sprung up lately in the town where I live. People seem to love eating locally for good reason—the produce is fresher, eating what's in season when it's in season gives a nice rhythm and variety to our diets, and it supports the local economy. When I travel, I especially enjoy shopping for and eating locally grown food; it's a good way to get to know a place and to feel a part of a culture, if only for a short while.

Art supplies made out of local materials can be thought of in the same way. A number of years ago I read an article about a potter who, when she traveled, always gathered a small amount of clay to make a pinch pot out of to represent the place. Journal keepers can use this idea, too. By making paints and inks out of local materials and using them in your journals, you can help represent a particular place and your experiences there.

Every place has some material that can be used to make paint, and many places have materials for making both inks and paint. Soil, especially clay-rich soil, is one almost universally available material for making paint. Take a look around; the soil in your garden may be the color of cinnamon. Across town, my friend's creek bed yields red clay, more or less the color of red bricks. There are deposits of grayish-white clay in a park near the waterfront in the village where another friend lives. In some places the local clay is so famous that it has a name. The Siena area of Italy gives its name to the colors burnt and raw sienna, while the Umbria Province of Italy gives its name to burnt and raw umber.

The word *ochre* is generally associated with a dull brownish-yellow pigment, but in fact it refers to all earth pigments. The element that all earth pigments have in common is hydrated iron oxide. It's the amount of iron oxide present that determines the color of the pigment. Ochre is, as far as we know, the most ancient pigment and the first paint. Traces of it have been found in 250,000-year-old cave paintings and in burials from thousands of years ago. Red ochres seem to have been especially prized and used for special ceremonies.

To make your own earth-pigment watercolor, begin by collecting a jar full of clay-rich soil. You can often find it near creek and riverbanks but also in road cuts as well as other places. You'll recognize clay from other soil components because its particles cling to each other, and it feels slippery and somewhat sticky when you rub it between your fingers.

Mix the clay with at least an equal amount of water. Strain the watery mix into a second container by pouring it through a layer of screen. Clean out the

Amber Maloy, *Galway Bay*, 2004. 8½ x 11 inches (21.6 x 27.9 cm). Watercolor, watercolor pencils, pen, feather, shrimp, beach sand, rope; glued. *Photo by Aleia Woolsey.*

first container, throw away the large particles that have collected on the screen, and pour the clay-rich water (called slip) back into the first container by straining it through two layers of screen turned so that the two meshes form a finer mesh. Repeat this straining process, using finer and finer meshes. Old pantyhose are also very useful for this process.

The final straining should be done through a couple of layers of an old T-shirt. Afterward, you'll have a container of what looks like colored water. Let this stand for a few hours until you notice fine sediment settled on the bottom. Gently pour or scoop off the water, being careful to avoid stirring up the sediment. When you have poured off as much water as possible, scoop out the sediment, which is mostly pigment, onto a few layers of old newspaper. Let the remaining water evaporate. You can keep the dried lumps of pigment in a plastic bag or small bottle until you've collected enough for your project. You can store dried ochres indefinitely until you're ready to mix them with binders.

When you're ready to make paint, pour the pigment onto a smooth, hard surface (a piece of glass or marble, as well as a mortar, work very well for this process), and add enough water to make a thick paste. Grind the pigment with a blunt smooth instrument such as a pestle, the bowl of a spoon, or a dull knife until it is completely mixed with the water. Add a few drops of liquid gum arabic (available in art supply stores) as a binder to give an adhesive quality to the paint. You can store this watercolor in a regular watercolor pan. When it dries out, simply rewet it for use like any other watercolor paint.

You can also make egg tempera or casein paint out of dried pigment, depending on the binder you use. To make egg tempera, carefully separate the yolk of an egg from the white. Gently lay the intact yolk on a piece of paper towel. Lift the edges of the paper towel and carefully roll the yolk back and forth to remove all traces of egg white. When the yolk is clean, pinch a small bit of the yolk sack between your thumb and index finger and hold tightly while lifting the yolk. Now, feeling very Medieval, hold the yolk over a small bowl and pierce the bottom of the sack with a pin. The yolk will flow out of the sack into the bowl. To paint, dip your brush first in

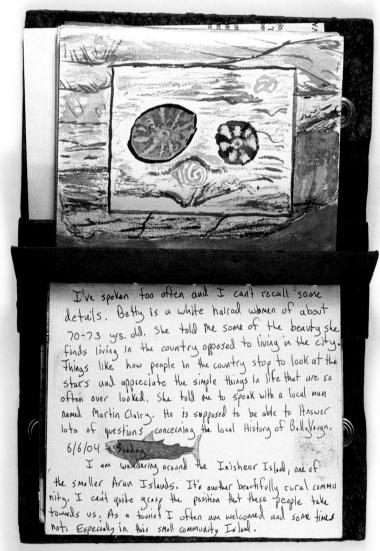

Matt Rogers, 2004. Watercolor, pen. *Photo by Aleia Woosley.*

pigment and then in the egg yolk, being careful to avoid touching the sides of the container that has the egg yolk in it. Egg tempera has a nice, eggshell finish, giving a slightly different surface to a painting than watercolor. Be patient. You'll have to proceed slowly to build up layers of this transparent color. You can't store egg tempera, so mix just as much as you need each time you paint.

The protein in milk is called casein, and that is the part that provides the adhesive or binder in casein paint. Casein has a slight sheen, similar to egg tempera.

To make casein paint, you can mix the pigment into a little milk until the viscosity feels right for the kind of painting you want to do. Evaporated milk creates a heavy bodied paint, while skim milk will yield a more watery one.

You can also make very fine ink from tannin and it ages beautifully. This local material comes from several vegetable sources, among them black walnut hulls and also the insect galls that you find on certain plants. The most tannin-rich materials are oak galls, which can be found in many locations.

Oak galls are round growths found mainly on the leaves and twigs of oak trees. They form around a growing larva after a gall wasp lays its eggs in the tissue of the plant. When the larva hatches, it drills its way out of the gall and leaves a tiny round hole, which tells you the gall is empty and the left-behind nut is rich in tannic acids. The photograph below shows a drawing of an oak gall colored with ochre. The very best galls are reputedly from shrub oaks imported from Aleppo in the Levant area of France. Perhaps you'll be going there to journal? If not, you can try galls from other oak trees to make ink. In addition to the oak galls, you'll need a half-cup or so of mild acid, such as vinegar, and a small amount of gum arabic powder or liquid.

A Medieval recipe says to crush the galls to a powder, then boil the powder in rainwater for as long as it takes to recite the *Pater Noster* three times (the whole prayer, I would assume). The vinegar is then added slowly, a few drops at a time,

until the liquid turns from pale brown to black. The original recipe calls for stirring with a fig stick, but a wooden spoon or some other kind of stick works fine in my experience. The final step is to add a little gum arabic as a binder and thickener.

Another recipe for ink makes use of charcoal from your campfire or fireplace or from an oil or kerosene lantern. Collect lampblack from the glass covers of lamps (such as hurricane lanterns) or else gather a handful of charcoal. Grind the charcoal or lampblack with a mortar and pestle or with the bowl of a spoon or a spatula or table knife until it is a fine consistency. Make a solution of gum arabic and water, and grind the charcoal or lampblack into it. Dilute with more water until the ink is of the right consistency to flow from a pen. This ink darkens on the page to a beautiful bluish-black over time.

Matt Rogers, 2004.
Watercolor, pen. *Photo by Aleia Woosley.*

As you gain experience, you may want to add a few more colors:

- Viridian green (a cool, transparent bluish-green)

- Yellow ochre (a transparent, golden yellow)

- Payne's Gray (a cool, transparent blue-gray)
  Note: Payne's gray is a hue or mix, and as such it varies from brand to brand. Experiment with different brands to find one that you like.

- Davy's Gray (a warmer, opaque green-gray; also a hue or mix)

- New Gamboge Hue (a warm, bright yellow, excellent for mixing greens; another hue or mix)

- Alizarin crimson (deep bluish-red transparent, excellent for mixing but fugitive)

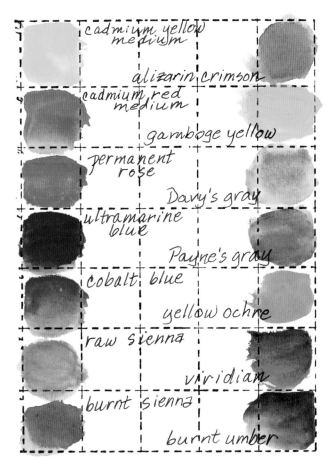

cadmium yellow medium

alizarin crimson

cadmium red medium

gamboge yellow

permanent rose

Davy's gray

ultramarine blue

Payne's gray

cobalt blue

yellow ochre

raw sienna

viridian

burnt sienna

burnt umber

A basic watercolor palette with the starter colors to the left.

GOUACHE

Gouache is an opaque to semiopaque watercolor. It comes in tubes, jars, and bottles, and in a large range of colors, some of them very brilliant, but they are sometimes fugitive. For a long time, gouache was a popular medium for graphic designers who needed bright colors and a matte finish. They weren't concerned with permanence, because their work was to be photographed. Today it's relatively easy to find high-quality gouache in small sets of primary colors made for mixing—magenta (a violet-red), cyan (a greenish-blue) and yellow, as well as white and black.

Gouache varies in permanence, color, covering power, and flow from one manufacturer to another. The best quality of gouache is permanent as well as densely pigmented, which results in good covering power or opacity. The colors are pure, and good mixes are possible. It's a good idea to try out a small amount of several different brands before investing in a supply of gouache. Cheaper gouache is less heavily pigmented and relies on a white pigment, such as chalk, for its opacity and smoothness. It's difficult to get good mixes with cheap gouache, and it's often sold in sets of many colors.

Bleed-proof white is another graphic designer's paint that's sold as gouache. This very dense white paint works well as a block-out layer. It has excellent covering power, but can be rewet. If you paint on top of bleed-proof white, you'll notice some chalkiness and lightening of the color you're using as the overpaint. If you want to create a layer that won't be disturbed after it's dried, mix bleed-proof white (and any other gouache) with acrylic medium. (See Pages in Stages, page 56.)

Even if you're mainly interested in watercolors, a tube of white gouache is a good addition to your watercolor palette. White gouache mixes with watercolor to make pastels that can add nice contrast to watercolors. White gouache by itself is useful for adding highlights to watercolor sketches.

CASEIN

Casein is a water-based paint that's made with pigment, water, and extracted milk protein as the binder. It's one of the oldest types of paint, used both for artwork and for decorating.

Casein owes its permanence (and paint-over ability) to the fact that the longer it dries, the tougher its film grows. It most resembles gouache in that it's opaque when painted with little dilution, and its dry surface is a velvety matte. But, unlike gouache, it can also be thinned to lovely transparent washes.

USING CASEIN IN JOURNALS

Why would you use casein for your journals rather than other paints and pigments? I spent an afternoon experimenting with casein with two artist friends who had never used it before. As you can see from their paintings (at the top of this page), you can achieve an enormous variety of effects when using it:

- You can draw over casein with pen or pencil (figures 1 and 2).

- You can paint back into it because its stability allows overpainting (figures 1, 2, and 3).

- It's easy to mix and makes interesting shifts and changes on the paper (figures 1 and 3).

- You can paint casein over China marker as well as oil-based printing ink, and it won't obscure the printed or drawn line (figure 2).

- It relates well to other materials. You can make transparent washes with it and great mixes (figure 3).

- It works well on a variety of papers (figures 1, 2, and 3).

WORKING WITH CASEIN

Casein dries quickly. When you paint with it, use lots of water and keep brushes wet as long as you're using them. Note: If the paint dries in a brush, it will ruin it. You can clean brushes with water and either detergent, an abrading soap, or borax.

You can more easily correct casein than watercolor. Unlike watercolor, it's capable of opacity as well as transparency. And unlike watercolor and gouache, it can be overpainted without disturbing the layer underneath as long as the first layer is dry.

Figure 1

Kore Loy Wildrekinde-McWhirter
Untitled Journal Page, 2011. 6 x 5 inches
(15.2 x 12.7 cm). Casein, ink. *Photo by artist.*

Figure 2

Bette Bates *Untitled Journal Page,*
2011. 8 x 10 inches (20.3 x 25.4 cm). Casein,
lithographic marker. *Photo by artist.*

Figure 3

Bette Bates, *Untitled Journal Page*, 2011. 7½ x 6 inches (19 x 15.2 cm).
Casein over collagraph. *Photo by artist.*

You can easily transport casein in a little tin or plastic box. You can make your own using a mint tin with plastic water bottle caps to hold each color.

Slip the tin and a small brush, favorite pen, small pencil and sharpener, a piece of rubber eraser, a small paper towel, and small jar full of water with oxgall into a plastic bag, and you're ready to go.

No Pressure

by Benedicte Caneill

"This loose way of working enables me to be non-judgmental and have fun with the process—in other words, no pressure. As my pages record a moment in time, they're great memory keepers, and I love going back to look at them."

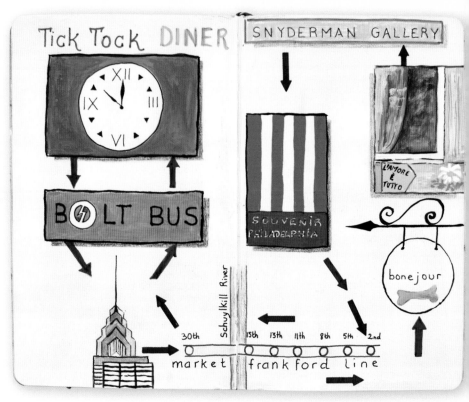

Philly Trip. 8½ x 10¼ inches (21 x 26 cm). Felt tip markers, gouache, watercolor pencils. *Photo by artist.*

Stormy Weather. 10¼ x 8¼ inches (26 x 21 cm). Acrylic paints, black and white gesso, pen, gel medium, tissue paper. *Photo by artist.*

As a field botanist and naturalist, my journals were a way to record observations and data. Over the years, however, my way of keeping a journal has become unconventional. My journaling practice is not a rigorous discipline. I have multiple notebooks of various sizes. The most important thing is to have an available format when I need it.

My journal pages are not meant to be works of art. They're notes taken at a museum, sketches done at home, in nature, or in the street. As an artist, I sometimes work out a design idea for a large piece, jot down a drawing from my imagination, or do a collage or small composition.

This loose way of working enables me to be nonjudgmental and have fun with the process—in other words, no pressure. As my pages record a moment in time, they're great memory keepers, and I love going back to look at them. When I beg my Muse, "Please give me inspiration!" she answers, "Go back to your journals. I already spoke to you a long time ago!"

Gwen Diehn. 6 x 9 inches (15.2 x 22.9 cm). Gouache, pen, and watercolor on handmade paper.

FLUID ACRYLICS

Acrylics come in several forms. The most popular form is in a tube and has a consistency like oil paint. You can modify it by mixing it with various acrylic mediums and gels. Over the past few years, one manufacturer of acrylics started producing a fluid form of acrylic in response to artists who wanted a pigment-saturated acrylic that could be poured, dripped, and even sprayed. The artists had been thinning traditional acrylics with water, but the resulting mix yielded weak colors. The result of the manufacturer's experiments was the finest fluid acrylics that are made today. They are so densely pigmented that they remain brilliant even when further diluted for pouring thin veils of color. Good fluid acrylics, with no added opacifiers, are the purest form of acrylic paint and are therefore excellent for mixing.

One consideration for bookwork is whether or not the surface of a dried paint is truly dry or if it's sticky. Unlike most other artwork, bookwork involves pressing paper on top of a worked surface over and over again. If a particular medium rubs off or is tacky or sticky, the artwork will eventually be harmed. Tube acrylics, depending on a number of factors, are more or less sticky even after they're completely dry. Fluid acrylics, however, dry hard and stay that way because they contain fewer additives in the basic mix of pigment, water, and polymer resin.

All acrylics are relatively transparent, but fluid acrylics are the most transparent. You might want to buy some tube acrylics to mix with your fluid acrylics when you want more dense coverage and opacity. You can reduce the stickiness of the tube acrylics by sealing the page with a polymer varnish or by rubbing the page with a piece of waxed paper after the paint is dry.

All fluid acrylics aren't equal, and the price is largely dependent on how much actual pigment is used in the paint. There are cheap brands of fluid acrylic that are filled with additives and are made by mixing inexpensive synthetic pigments in with the more expensive pigments. In buying paint, you get what you pay for, so if you're looking for excellent color and mixing ability, buy a few bottles of the highest quality fluid acrylics and use them to mix every color you can dream of.

ACRYLIC STARTER PALETTE

- Quinacridone crimson (similar to the more fugitive alizarin crimson, a traditional violet-red mixing color; all the quinacridone colors are brilliant with vibrant undertones and excellent transparency and permanence.)

- Quinacridone gold (similar to burnt sienna yet with a golden undertone that is more brilliant than the siennas)

- Quinacridone red (a very intense mixing primary red)

- Phthalo Green/Blue Shade (transparent, deep, intense green with bluish undertones; mixed with quinacridone crimson, it yields the deepest, richest black imaginable)

- Phthalo Blue/Green Shade and Red Shade (both are transparent, vibrant blues, one cooler and the other with warm reddish undertones)

- Pyrrole Red (excellent opacity and lightfastness, similar to cadmium red, but better for mixing)

- Hansa Yellow (similar to cadmium yellow but yields clearer mixes)

- Yellow Ochre (good lightfastness; good coverage, transparent, warm brownish-yellow)

- Payne's gray (cool, bluish-gray, very dark)

To the basic palette you might enjoy adding some of the excellent metallic and iridescent fluid acrylics. The better brands of fluid acrylics include coppers, golds, and other shimmering metallics that retain their strength even when diluted with water and poured in extremely thin washes.

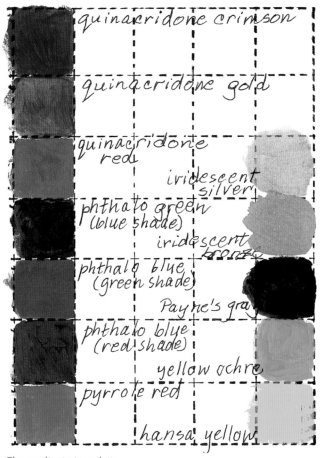

The acrylic starter palette.

Gwen Diehn. 6 x 9 inches (15.2 x 22.9 cm). Gouache, pen, and watercolor on handmade paper. *Photo by Aleia Woolsey.*

Brushes

A brush has a handle, bristles, and a ferrule, which is the band that holds the bristles to the handle. The bristles of the brush form a belly, which holds water, and a tip through which the water is released. A good brush has a tip that stays pointed and a well-made ferrule that prevents hairs from falling out as you work. Buying cheap brushes is a false economy. They're frustrating to work with for many reasons, but mainly because their bristles don't hold a point or even stay flat. Although good brushes can be very expensive, fortunately, as with paint, the concept of "less is more" holds true when buying them.

Two or three good brushes will serve almost any purpose for painting in a journal. You can use the same kinds of brushes for acrylics as you do for watercolor. Brushes come in rounds and flats as well as various specialty brushes such as fans, riggers, and mops. However, you don't need an array of brushes for your journal work. Just buy a #5 and a #2 round brush of good quality, such as Kolinsky sable. Over time, you can add to your collection of brushes, but you will probably find that you keep returning to your one or two old favorites.

There are three exceptions to the "good-brushes-are-expensive" rule. One of these is a recently marketed plastic-handled water brush with synthetic bristles. This very useful brush has a hollow handle for carrying water. The water is slowly released through the bristles, and, if you need a stronger flow of water, you just squeeze gently on the handle. These brushes are excellent for travel journaling because you don't need to carry extra water to use them. To clean the brush between colors, you simply wipe the bristles on a rag, paper towel, or your jeans. They come in three sizes: small, medium, and large, and also in a flat.

(Right to left:) round brushes, #2 and #5, and sumi brush.

You'll find a mini version (with a medium tip) for travel painting, and there's one that comes apart and can fit into a small box of watercolors. The tips are all interchangeable, so that if you want a mini with a fine tip, buy a mini and a fine and reverse the tips. The synthetic tips hold a point beautifully, and the large version of the brush is fine for laying the relatively small areas of wash that you generally do in a journal. Best of all, water brushes are reasonably priced.

Another exception is the Asian brush. Sometimes called a sumi brush, these are made with bamboo handles and are extremely inexpensive. They are wonderfully versatile, with bellies that hold a large amount of water, and tips that hold a point beautifully as long as the brush has been completely saturated prior to painting. As with any paintbrush, you must wet the entire length of the bristles when you begin to paint so that they will hold a point and not split and splay at the tip. Finally, one other inexpensive and useful brush is a 1-inch (2.5 cm) flat paintbrush that you can buy in a hardware store. It works well for laying in washes and usually costs less than a can of soda.

Water brushes.

Pen and Ink

Pen and ink is a basic medium for sketchbooks and journals. The range of available pens and inks is enormous. Rather than try to describe to you what is best learned by your own experience, I will present some categories of pens and inks. Take time to find out which feel best and will make the kind of marks you want to make.

PENS

This tool is indispensable for writing, as well as for making quick sketches. Pens are capable of producing a variety of textures and tones and can be used very successfully in careful drawing. **Note:** Conventional ballpoint pens are not recommended here because they are very acidic and the ink never completely dries.

Some of the wide variety of pens and inks available.

BASIC BLACK EXTRA-FINE STEEL OR PLASTIC-TIP WATERPROOF PEN

Most of these are inexpensive, last a long time, and reliably make fine, dense black lines. They produce crisp, clean lines that are useful when you want to make a precise illustration or discuss a cool, logical idea. Because the ink is waterproof, they won't bleed when you brush watercolors over them. Some brands also come in brown (sepia), blue, red, purple, and green, but usually colored inks are not waterproof.

GEL PENS

Similar to ballpoint pens, but with opaque pastel or metallic ink, these work especially well on dark papers. Most have fine tips, and many have inks that are acid-free or archival.

METALLIC PENS

All metallic pens will add a luminous quality to your pages. In the Middle Ages, silver and gold were used extensively on manuscripts to bring light into the texts they illuminated. Metallics have always carried the aura of the precious metals from which they are made. These pens come in various tip widths. The best of them—the most convincingly gold, silver, or bronze—are solvent-based and require a few minutes of shaking to mix them before use. Some will stain paper if they are incompletely mixed. Many will blot at the beginning of a line, leaving you with a glob of ink. To avoid this, keep some scratch paper at hand, and take a few strokes on it before beginning work in your journal.

Kelcey Loomer, 2002.12 x 11¾ inches (30.5 x 30 cm). Coptic bound journal, marker, silver pen, waxed linen thread, neo-pastel. *Photo by Aleia Woolsey.*

Kelcey Loomer, *Bronze Woman*, 2004. 9¼ x 6¼ inches (23.5 x 15.9 cm). Journal, acrylic paint, colored pencil, pen, email from a friend, cut-out window; collaged. *Photo by Aleia Woolsey.*

DIP PENS

In addition to drawing and writing with pens that have metal nibs in holders, you can use sticks, twigs, feathers, coffee stirrers, and many other objects. The marks made by this type of tool tend to be less controlled and predictable, making them more spontaneous, emotional, and lively. Experiment with Italian glass pens, thin-line crow quill pens, hand-carved bamboo reed pens. Make pens out of sticks and reeds you find at the place you're writing or drawing about. And when you discover which are best for you, keep experimenting—you'll find there's a perfect pen for every use.

INKS

There are several different kinds of ink for use with pens as well as brushes. Inks are made of ground pigments or dyes mixed in water with gum arabic added to improve flow as well as to allow the pigment to adhere to the paper after the water has evaporated. They are either waterproof or not, permanent or not.

Art supply stores sell vibrant, transparent inks in glowing colors, luminous pearlescent inks, crackling metallics, as well as jet black and smoky gray inks. Search further and you can find inks made of walnuts, wine, and oak galls. You can even make your own inks from strong coffee, teas, and beet juice. (See Local Pigments on pages 29 to 31.)

WATERPROOF INKS

Waterproof inks have shellac added to them. Beware of refilling ink cartridges or fillable pens with waterproof ink because they may clog. Waterproof inks, such as India ink and some colored inks, are fine for use with dip pens, but clean the pen with water after each use. You can paint over waterproof ink with watercolor or colored ink without the waterproof-ink layer being affected.

NON-WATERPROOF INK

This ink will sink into the page more than waterproof ink and will dry to a matte finish. It's fine for line work, but you can't paint over it or it will run.

COLORED INK

Because it's made with water-soluble dyes, colored ink is not permanent or lightfast. This fugitive ink is not as problematic for bookwork as it is for work that will be exposed to light for long periods of time. However, even inside a book, colored ink will fade over time. You can dilute ink with distilled water to make washes. Inks can be mixed with each other to create new colors.

Adhesives

When you apply an adhesive to a material, the adhesive's long chain of molecules seeps into and mixes with the surface of the material, causing the adhesive to stick to the surface. When you place a second material on the material with adhesive on it, the adhesive molecules move closer together allowing the molecules of the two surfaces to attract each other and mingle, causing a strong bond between materials. While this is a very simplistic explanation of a complicated process, the important thing to realize is that using an adhesive changes the surface of the materials you're adhering. With this fact in mind, you need to approach the use of adhesives with care, since it is scarily easy to ruin a project by mishandling or choosing the wrong adhesive.

NATURAL & SYNTHETIC ADHESIVES

Natural adhesives are either plant-derived (pastes) or animal-derived (glues). Synthetic adhesives are made from polymers. Natural adhesives are made by breaking down organic substances into carbohydrates and proteins and then mixing them with water. Plant-based adhesives are more commonly used by book artists than protein- or animal-based adhesives which have largely been replaced by PVA today. Plant adhesives come in the form of pastes made from flours or starches.

Synthetic adhesives are made by manipulating single-strand molecules into multiple-strand, tacky molecules called synthetic resins. There are many kinds of synthetic resins, but the ones most useful to most book artists are polymer resins in the form of water-based polymer emulsions (PVA).

WET OR DRY?

The first thing to consider when you're choosing an adhesive is how the paper is likely to react to the water in the adhesive and whether or not you can live with the resulting changes. Since the adhesive mixes with the molecules of the paper, the paper itself becomes wet, and as it dries it cockles and buckles to a greater or lesser degree. Some papers, such as translucent papers (vellum) react strongly to water and wrinkle extensively when wet. Very thin papers tend to wrinkle

and even tear in the presence of wet adhesive. Heavier papers hardly react at all. Cardboards can swell and buckle. If you've done work in water media on one side of a page, including using ink-jet ink, applying very wet adhesives to the other side of the page can cause this work to run.

As you can see on the chart on page 41, the wettest adhesives are pastes and methylcellulose, followed by PVAs (synthetic polymer-resin adhesives) and acrylic mediums (which are very similar to PVAs), followed by glue sticks (which are PVAs with much less water in them), then tape-like rolls. The driest adhesive is drymount tissue, a hot-melt adhesive tissue originally developed for use by photographers for adhering water-sensitive photographic paper to mounting boards.

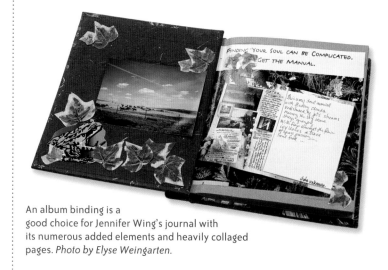

An album binding is a good choice for Jennifer Wing's journal with its numerous added elements and heavily collaged pages. *Photo by Elyse Weingarten.*

Christine Toriello used train tickets as a base for this ink, color, and watercolor page. Its grid nicely echoes the repetition of the train cars. *Photo by Elyse Weingarten.*

ADHESIVE	WETNESS	GOOD FOR	DRAWBACKS
wheat or rice flour paste	very wet	relatively strong bond, non-staining, long-lasting, archival, good track record among book conservators, reversible, repositionable while wet, and it stays wet a long time, inexpensive	the gluten in wheat can attract bugs, not good for use on very thin papers and vellum, does not grab fast, very wet
wheat or rice starch paste	very wet	strong bond, non-staining, long-lasting, archival, not as attractive to insects as wheat or rice flour, smoother, reversible, repositionable while wet, slow drying	very slow drying, slightly acidic, does not grab fast, very wet
methylcellulose (made by treating wood or cotton with an alkali and then with methyl chloride)	very wet	archival, dries flexible, long shelf life in granular form, does not grow mold, non-toxic, reversible, doesn't attract pests, inexpensive, sold in granules at craft and art supply stores	weaker than flour and starch pastes, shorter track-record with conservators, very wet
PVA (comes in many forms and brands)	wet	low-odor, acid-free, non-toxic, dries flexible, strong, relatively quick bond, cleans up with water, better brands tend not to wrinkle most papers	stains leather and book cloth as well as paper, difficult to impossible to reposition or reverse, wrinkles vellum and thin papers
acrylic mediums/gels/ varnishes	wet	archival, permanent, most dry flexible, relatively strong bond, low odor, good for adhering small papers as well as top-coating and sealing items such as pressed leaves and flower parts that are adhered to pages, can be used to texture	can wrinkle thin paper and vellum, stains, can't be reversed in most cases, not good under water media, many dry tacky, use varnish only for top coating and sealing as it dries hard
glue sticks	dry	long-lasting or temporary (check the label), won't wrinkle paper, fast-drying, can adhere porous paper to non-porous surface such as mica or glass, inexpensive, doesn't attract insects, repositionable while wet	some are acidic so check labels, weak bond, some very alkaline, especially those with a strong ammonia smell
double-stick tapes	dry	some are acid-free, some are permanent, and some are repositionable (check labels); won't wrinkle paper, even vellum	very narrow band, not good for adhering large areas, expensive
drymount tissue	dry	the best are archival (these are the most expensive), non-acidic, long-lasting, can be used at home with an iron, doesn't wrinkle or cockle most papers, but the heat of the iron wrinkles vellum	can be awkward to use, requires use of a hot iron or drymount press, can't be used on heat-sensitive paper such as vellum

What is PVA?

PVA (polyvinyl acetate) is the thick white liquid adhesive that comes in plastic bottles. It's marketed under a variety of names and can be school quality, craft quality, or high quality. You can tell the difference by the price. School quality PVAs are cheap. They're the kind you see sold in grocery stores in the school-supply aisle. They're low-strength and are also the most likely to wrinkle paper. They're not useful for bookwork. Craft quality PVAs are sold in craft and art supply stores and are strong, medium-quality adhesives, generally difficult to reverse, and fairly likely to wrinkle thinner papers. High-quality PVAs are usually only sold in art supply stores or outlets that specialize in bookbinders' supplies. They're usually about four times as expensive as craft-quality PVAs. They're the strongest PVAs, dry the most flexible, are the easiest to spread, and are also the least likely to wrinkle most papers. But remember that all PVAs tend to cause wrinkles when papers of unlike size, thickness, and strength are adhered to each other. All PVAs can be thinned with a little distilled water or methylcellulose to improve the way they flow from a brush, but strength is lost when these adhesives are thinned, and of course they become wetter when thinned.

PVA can also be mixed with paste. A small amount of paste increases the drying time, allowing easier repositioning.

HOW STRONG AND HOW FAST?

An important consideration when choosing an adhesive is how strong the bond needs to be. If you're just attaching a thin piece of paper to another piece of paper, you won't need a very strong bond. If you're attaching an envelope to a page, you'll need something stronger to accommodate the greater weight of the envelope as well as the stress you'll place on the adhesive bond every time you manipulate the envelope.

Related to strength is how quickly the adhesive grabs or bonds the surfaces. Some jobs, such as adhering stiff book cloth to a book cover, are much easier to do with an adhesive that grabs fast and holds tight. In other cases it's easier to use a wetter adhesive, such as paste, one that allows you to reposition several times without damaging the papers. Paste is usually used when adhering leather to boards.

OTHER CONSIDERATIONS

There are other factors to take into consideration when choosing an adhesive to use in your journal. Here are some of the most common questions to ask yourself:

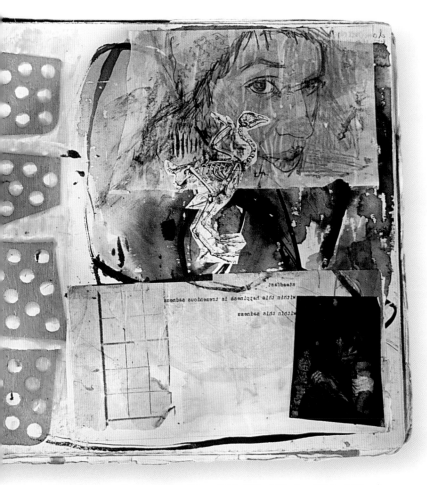

Becca Johnson, *Untitled Journal Page*, 2004. 11½ x 12 inches (29.2 x 30.5 cm). Handmade journal, collage with photographs, paper scraps, book pages, packaging scraps, beeswax, ink.

- How quickly do I want this to dry? How tolerant of wetness are the materials to be adhered?

- Do I need a strong quick bond or will a slower one do?

- Does the adhesive attract insects, which can, of course, eventually ruin the book?

- How large are the pieces that need bonding? (PVA works best on smaller pieces.)

- How convenient is the adhesive to use? If you're trying to attach things to your journal while you're flying over the ocean, a glue stick is a lot easier to use than drymount tissue (see page 44)!

- Do I need the adhesive to be forgiving of occasional clumsiness? Can it be cleaned up without staining?

- Is the adhesive reversible? Can you unattach something after the adhesive has dried?

Make Your Own Paste

Here's a good recipe for paste: Mix 1 part flour or starch with 1 part water. Stir to a smooth paste. Then add 4 more parts water. Heat while stirring constantly with a wooden spoon over medium heat (a double boiler is usually suggested, but not necessary if you keep the heat low enough and stir constantly). When the paste first comes to a boil, count to 30 and then remove it from the heat. Option: Add a few drops of essential oil such as lavender or rosemary to make it a little less attractive to molds and insects and to give it a good smell as well as the vibrations of the plants from which the oil was made. Store the paste in a covered jar, labeled with the date, in a refrigerator. Keeps for about a week. Best used when fresh and still warm.

It can be rewarmed by sitting it in the sun or near a heater.

PVA AND PASTE

Mixing PVA (white craft glue) with paste offers you the best of all possible adhesive worlds. You'll find the mixture grabs more quickly than paste alone, making it better for adhering stiff materials. And the mixture won't go bad as paste tends to do—it can sit on your workbench for months. You can reposition with the mixture as easily as you can when using paste. And you'll find it's easier to clean off bookcloth, leather, or heavy paper than PVA alone. You can make your own mixture by simply combining equal amounts of each. Any PVA works well for this recipe, even the least expensive brands.

Drymount Tissue

Drymount tissue can be found at photographic supply stores. It comes in several grades, with the most expensive being the thinnest with the best archival qualities. When you use it to laminate two sheets of paper together, the resulting laminate will be stiffer and more like card stock than the individual pieces. This can be an advantage or a disadvantage, depending on the project. Originally designed to be used in a drymount press, it works fine if you place it between the two sheets to be adhered and iron the papers for a few seconds to a minute with a warm (not hot) iron with no steam. It's a good idea to cover the top sheet with scrap paper. The piece of drymount tissue should be cut to fit ⅛ inch (3 mm) inside the perimeter of the papers being laminated. (See Laminating Pages on page 213.)

Coral Jensen, *Untitled Journal Cover*, 2000. *Photo by artist.*

APPLICATION OF ADHESIVES

Liquid PVAs and pastes are applied with brushes, and you'll want to keep one brush for PVAs and a different one for pastes—PVAs are harder on brushes and will stiffen them over time. Ideally, paste brushes should be softer, more tapered, and more flexible than PVA brushes. To apply paste, stroke the paste onto the paper to be adhered for several minutes to allow the paste to penetrate and soak the paper. At first the paper will curl. Continue brushing until it lies flat again. Then apply the item to the dry page. To apply PVA, use a stiff, blunt brush to push the PVA into the paper. You don't need a lot of force, but will need more of a pounding motion than the stroking motion you use for paste. Work as quickly as possible, as the PVA dries much faster than paste.

BASIC ADHESIVE SELECTION

Depending on the kind of paper you generally use, a basic adhesive kit would include a bag of wheat or rice flour (ground very fine) or starch for making paste (which you can use as both adhesive and sizing), a pH-neutral glue stick, and a bottle of the best PVA you can afford. To that add one paste brush and one PVA brush and an old telephone directory to use as scrap paper when you use your adhesives. From time to time you may want or need one of the other adhesives, but you can go for a long time with the basics.

RUBBER CEMENT AND TAPES

You'll notice that rubber cement and tapes of all kinds were not included in this discussion. Rubber cement is a solvent-based wet adhesive. It forms a strong, flexible bond and doesn't wrinkle papers. But it was not designed to be permanent, and the bond weakens with age (and not very much age at that). Its solvent base is toxic and damages paper over time—the solvent base can harm some papers and photographs immediately. It's not recommended for permanent work.

Tapes are a form of pressure-sensitive adhesive. These are generally not very strong, and they lose their adhesive qualities as they dry out over time. Even if they are sold as "acid free," they eventually discolor and deteriorate paper. There are a few tapes, such as linen tape, that are archival and approved by some conservators, and if you feel that you must use tape, look for these in bookbinding- and matting and framing supply catalogues.

Does this mean you should never indulge in the fun of using masking tape or Band-Aids or duct tape in your journal? Of course not!

Pencils and Crayons

What could be easier to buy and use? While you might be thinking of more sophisticated art supplies, don't overlook these versatile and simple tools that can create many wonderful effects on their own.

GRAPHITE PENCILS

These are excellent for rendering subtle differences of dark or light as well as a variety of textures. They can make very gentle, graceful marks or crisp, precise ones depending on the technique used.

Graphite pencils are graded and sold according to the ratio of graphite to binder that determines their range of hardness. Softer pencils that have a less waxy binder make darker marks and smear easily. The softer pencils are the "B" pencils, and the higher the number before the B, the softer the pencil. Harder pencils are called "H" pencils, and the higher the number the harder the pencil. Since you want to avoid using materials that will smear for journal work, stay away from extremely soft pencils. A good range is between 3B and 2H. Keep a pencil sharpener and sandpaper block handy to sharpen your pencils.

Some graphite pencils are made with a water-soluble binder. These will make a wash when you brush the pencil lines with water. Even regular graphite pencil lines can be turned into washes by using mineral spirits and a brush.

Watercolor pencils.

WATER-SOLUBLE COLORED PENCILS

Although water-soluble colored pencils tend to be slightly lower in intensity and brightness than waxy colored pencils, they dry hard and won't smear or rub off onto facing pages like the waxy ones do. You can use them for writing and drawing, or you can apply them on a page using broad strokes to create layers of color. These layers can then be turned into washes by brushing them with a wet brush. You can then apply more color if you wish or create textures on top of the washes. If you must use waxy colored pencils, place tracing paper or vellum between the pages to interleaf them to prevent the colors from smearing or rubbing off on the facing page. You can also try waxing the page with balled-up waxed paper.

The roughness of a wax crayon rubbing helps this page by Colleen Stanton shout its message. *Photo by Elyse Weingarten.*

Wendy Hale Davis, *Sabado/Leap*, 2004. (8 x 17½ inches, 20.3 x 44.5 cm).
Ink, watercolor, crayons, acrylic paint. *Photo by Anne Butler.*

CRAYONS

Because crayons aren't good for rendering small detail, they're always a somewhat abstract medium. For the best effect, use them to communicate generalized information with bold strokes or to create fields of color.

In addition to your basic wax crayons, art supply stores also sell water-soluble crayons. Both kinds are useful to the journaler. You can use regular wax crayons for the process of wax resist. To do this, first use a light colored crayon to draw a shape or shapes. Then brush watercolor washes over the shape and its background. The watercolor will adhere only to the non-waxy areas of the paper, yielding an interesting surface that can look something like batik.

Water-soluble crayons work just like water-soluble colored pencils but they have thicker points. They also deposit a heavier layer of pigment onto the paper, and when you brush over them with water, the resulting surface is somewhat grainy, which adds an interesting texture. Oil pastels are also fun. Their soft creamy texture allows you to use your fingers for mixing right on the page.

Other Useful Tools

STENCILS

Because text is an important design and communicative element, you can broaden the range of lettering on your pages by using various guides or stencils. You can find these at craft, drafting, or office supply stores. Choose different fonts or letter styles so that you'll have ones that suit a variety of moods or purposes. You can also use the stencil for the basic letter shape, and then tailor the letters to the project at hand.

MATT KNIVES

These are useful for removing pages, shaping pages and corners, and trimming ephemera for use in collage. The heavy-duty kind with break-off blades is the most flexible and therefore useful. Invest in one of these rather than buying the smaller, flimsier ones sold in most craft stores.

You may have to go to a hardware store for it. Get a few extra packs of blades while you're at it.

STRAIGHTEDGES

If you plan to make your own journals, a good steel straightedge is a worthwhile investment. Steel is harder than aluminum and will resist cuts that result from slips of the blade. Although these straightedges are expensive, they last forever and are useful for tearing as well as cutting paper and board. If you can get a 36-inch-long (1 m) steel one with one beveled edge and one straight edge, you'll be in business. If you want a good, general-use straightedge first for drawing lines, get a 12-inch (30.5 cm) aluminum one. This is an inexpensive item, but also one that will last forever.

Andrea A. Peterson, *Ox Bow*, 2003. 12 x 18 inches (30.5 x 45.7 cm). Coptic hand-bound journal, cotton rag handmade paper, pastel chalk, toothpicks, colored pencil, handmade paper; glue. *Photo by artist.*

Grounds

Book artists, especially people who make altered books or who use old books as journals, are always looking for ways to (1) opaque out material already printed or written on the page; (2) transform flimsy paper into something substantial enough to support wet media; and (3) improve the paper's surface so watercolors will spread better and look brighter, and pen and strange experimental media (such as shellac) won't bleed through and stain the other side.

I would love to be able to write that you can easily turn flimsy or aged paper into strong, useful paper by applying one of the many grounds available to artists. But acrylic gesso, absorbent ground, wheat paste, gelatin, even traditional animal-glue gesso, as well as acrylic mediums and gels all have limited use in transforming paper. I have spent a lot of time trying out all of these substances on a variety of papers, both single sheets and in journals and old books. So far what I've learned is that all of these substances are wet, and they all make the papers curl and crinkle to some degree. Some papers dry flatter than others (but these are always the heavier papers that don't need transforming in the first place). In no case have I been able to turn a flimsy piece of paper into a good page for water media.

Absorbent white ground provides an opaque covering.

However, in trying to find solutions to this problem, I've come up with a few things that do work. Wheat paste and gelatin sizing, especially when applied to heavy-weight paper, can reduce the absorbency of the paper to a degree and thereby make watercolors and inks look a little brighter. This is because the pigments are not sinking into the paper as much, but are sitting more on the surface and therefore are showing up more.

Colleen Stanton, 2000.
Photo by Elyse Weingarten.

Tara Chickey, *Untitled Journal Page*, 2003. 10 x 20 inches (25.4 x 50.8 cm). Spiral-bound journal, handmade silk paper, watercolor paper, gesso, acrylic paint, 24-gauge copper wire, pen, alphabet rubber stamps, alphabet stickers. *Photo by artist.*

Absorbent ground is an acrylic product that I've found is the best for blocking out. It dries to a porous, paper-like surface and even turns glossy surfaces into surfaces that can receive any media that paper can hold. You can use acrylic absorbent ground to block out the print in a book you're altering, but sadly the resulting surface is not as good for watercolor or pen as plain paper. The absorbent ground can be an interesting surface, by appying it thickly and then engraving it after it's almost dry. Water-based media adhere to it better than they do to acrylic gesso, but don't expect to be able to create a true paper-like surface for delicate work. Acrylic gesso is also an acrylic-based product, but it produces a slightly glossy surface that is not as good for wet media as absorbent ground. Acrylic gesso is of limited use in blocking out underlying text because it's relatively transparent. It also produces a non-porous surface that's not a suitable ground for watercolors or pen and inks. However, it can be used under fluid acrylics provided the paper is heavy enough to support the heavy surface that will result from the layers of denser medium. Another material that blocks out an underlayer is gouache (see page 32). But because it's water soluble, the resulting surface is subject to being rewet and anything you paint over it will mix with the gouache.

If the old page is very thin and subject to wrinkling with wet adhesive, you can laminate other paper (see page 213) over the print in an old book using glue stick; if the page is heavier, try laminating and collaging with PVA.

Setting Up a Work Station

Once you've assembled all your supplies, find two boxes to keep them in. If you're going to keep your everyday supplies out on a desk or table, the box doesn't need to have a lid. Keep the water jar full of clean water, ready for action. Refill it after using it and put the lid on it, and it'll always be ready. You'll be surprised at how much more often you'll use watercolors if you don't have to get up first to fill the jar with water! If you don't have a permanent workplace, get a box with a lid and store it on a convenient shelf, under a bed, or in a centrally located closet.

Keep the supplies for customizing books and preparing pages in a separate, lidded box, as you won't use these as often as the everyday supplies.

TRAVEL SUPPLY KIT

If you're going to work on your book outside or away from your house, you'll need to streamline your supplies and keep the ones you use on a daily basis in a small travel case, such as the one shown. Select your favorite supplies, perhaps buying smaller than usual sizes of some items. Even a traveling supply kit—if it includes watercolors—needs a plastic jar full of water; a small shampoo bottle and the outer lid from a can of shaving cream work very well.

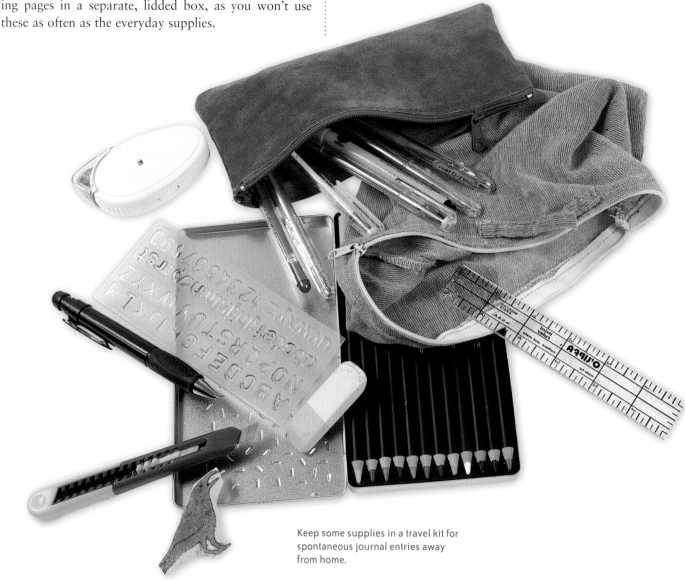

Keep some supplies in a travel kit for spontaneous journal entries away from home.

Everyday Supply Kit

All the page preparation materials you'll use everyday can be kept in one small box.

- Small jar (with a screw-on lid) full of clean water

- Small watercolor set, either tubes or pans, including the basic colors: alizarin crimson, pthalo or ultramarine blue, gamboge yellow, yellow ochre, raw sienna, pthalo green, Payne's gray*

- #12 round watercolor brush**

- Mixing tray (old pie tin or an inexpensive watercolor mixing pan)

- Scissors

- Small set of watercolor pencils

- Small set of water-soluble pastel crayons

- Plain lettering guide (stencil)***

- Rubber stamp letters, commercial or handcarved

- Rubber stamp carving material, corks, erasers

- Linoleum carving tool set

- Dye-based and pigment-based stamp pads, black and multicolored

- Small box of regular wax crayons

- Pens and inks (black, colored, metallics, but preferably not ballpoint pens with acidic ink)

- Waterproof black fine-line pen

- Graphite pencils and erasers

- Small container of citrus-based gel-type paint stripper for solvent transfers

- Collage items—labels, stamps, old letters, wrapping papers, magazine images, other memorabilia and ephemera from your life

- Color and black-and-white photocopies for transfers (photos, maps, etc.)

- Flat, soft 1-inch-wide (2.5 cm) brush

- Rag

- PVA or acid-free, permanent roll-on adhesive

- Glue brush (if using PVA)

- White gouache (opaque watercolor, either a tube or a jar)

- Small self-healing cutting mat

*You can add other colors if you want to, but these will get you started. Also, don't worry if the set you buy doesn't have exactly these colors. Just get a basic set.
**This is a good starter brush. Add others as you need them.
***Choose one sized to fit the pages you're working on.

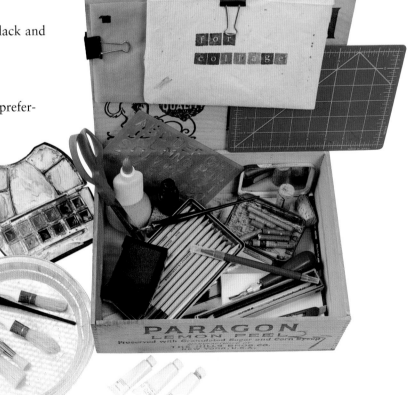

SUPPLY KIT FOR CUSTOMIZING BOOKS AND PREPARING PAGES

- Stencil brush

- Matte knife or craft knife

- Masking tape

- Fluid or liquid acrylics*

- Small empty liquid detergent bottle or other squeeze bottles or medicine droppers

- Sponge with flat sides

- Blotter paper

- Old newspaper

- Plastic needlepoint canvas, #7 or bigger holes

- Thin metal sheets, paper, or cloth with patterns of holes cut out of them

- Decorative edge scissors, one or two pairs

- Envelopes for gluing into journal

- Tracing paper

- Graph paper or other kinds of drawing or writing paper

- Watercolor paper or set of blank watercolor postcards or note cards

- Small ruler, 12 inches long (30.5 cm) or shorter

- Cotton make-up removal pads

- Cling-style plastic wrap

- Table salt in a shaker

- Acrylic matte medium

- Polymer varnish (either satin, matte, or gloss finish)

- Sand, seeds, talcum powder, shells, etc. (for encrustation)

- Scraps of mat board or other lightweight cardboard

*Get small bottles in several colors. Be sure to include some metallics if you like their look.

Materials for customizing books and preparing pages should be kept in a separate box.

Illogical Illuminations

rom inside its glass museum case, the page glows with life. The handwritten text, beautifully lettered and embellished with graceful flourishes and ornate initials, surrounds a tranquil scene of praying women. Gold illuminates the halos around their bowed heads. The tendrils of vines form an intricate border that gently leads the eye to the margins of the page. But there the serious religious mood is abruptly shattered. The margins are the site of romping monsters, a monkey riding backwards on a donkey, a hooded person glancing skeptically at the text, and a hedgehog munching on the vines themselves. The margins seem to poke fun at the central part of the page, yet they are drawn with as much care as the central illustration. What is going on here?

The book is an illuminated manuscript, one of many that were made from the sixth through the mid-15th centuries in Europe. Created before the invention of printing, these books were hand-copied and hand-painted, mostly by monastic scribes. In later years, such books were made by artisans working on commission. Technically, the word "illumination" refers to the gold and silver that were used on most of these books to bring light into the manuscripts.

Illuminated manuscripts were produced throughout Europe by diverse groups of scribes and artisans over a long period of time. All of them have a few things in common. They were all done on prepared animal skins (parchment) at first and later handmade rag paper. Most of the earlier manuscripts have religious subject matter. The production of these books involved different people doing different parts of the job. Often, several scribes copied different parts of an original onto prepared parchment.

"Saint Bartholomew Apostle," from *The Book of Hours of Catherine of Cleves*, Netherlands (Utrecht), c. 1435. *Courtesy of The Pierpont Morgan Library/Art Resource NY.*

Illuminated Margin, *Royal Manuscript 10 E IV*, folio 245.
©*The British Library.*

Usually someone else compared the copies to the original and made corrections in the margins. Finally, an artist or artists embellished the manuscript by adding initials, chapter headings, illustrations, and marginal drawings. Often, several artists worked on the same page at different times. One might draw a cartoon or sketch, another would lay gold or silver leaf onto areas that were to be illuminated, and still another would paint in colors, sometimes following directions given by the sketcher. Finally, a binder gathered the sheets and sewed the book together.

The presence of several artisans working on the same page may account for the strange things that happen on some pages. There are, of course, many manuscript pages featuring mostly text with a few simple flourishes (perhaps in a second color) on the initials and a plain ruled border. There are also many

pages on which text and a central illustration support one another and tell the same story. But there are some pages in which, while text and central illustration support one another, the illustrations in the margins tell a totally contradictory story. The margins of some pages are filled with monkeys, acrobats, monsters, jugglers, thieves, knights and ladies, nuns and monks, all in a variety of often bawdy scenes.

Occasionally, a margin figure points at a line of text and makes a face, showing disagreement. In one page from *The Book of Hours of Catherine of Cleves*, the sober figure of St. Bartholomew the apostle is the central image, but the margins are lined with a border of pretzels and biscuits. Hooded men and monks sit in each corner of the page, tugging on the pretzel twists, as if trying to keep the page together (see page 53).

"Wildman Carries the Damoysele," from the *Yates Thompson Manuscript.* 13, folio 62v. ©*The British Library.*

On some illuminated pages, blank spaces after a line of text are filled with the elongated bodies of monsters, some of which communicate with each other and with the marginal figures (who are busily going about acting out a scene that has nothing to do with the text). The activities in the margins often deal with subject matter that was marginalized by society, pushed from the center of daily life, or even pushed to the edges of general awareness.

In later manuscripts, a different kind of play between text and various images began to happen. In northern Europe in the 15th century, a new kind of margin begins to take the place of cavorting monkeys and monsters. On these pages the margins are filled with extremely realistic *trompe l'oeil* (literally "fool the eye") objects from everyday life. The margins become three-dimensional architectural elements, cupboard-like structures framing the deep space of the miniature painting and the text. Three systems of seeing collide on these pages. The viewer's eye travels between the deep space of the miniature scene (which was supposed to enhance meditation on the prayer contained in the text), the flatness of the text, and the objects in the margins, which seem to project forward and beg to be lifted from the page. These realistic margins create a distraction from the main business of the page, while the careful perspective drawing of the miniature exerts a pull back to prayer.

It is only possible to touch on the complicated subject of medieval page design here. For a thorough discussion and a wealth of examples, see Michael Camille's book *Images on the Edge: The Margins of Medieval Art* (1992, Harvard University Press).

Pages in Stages: Ways of Working

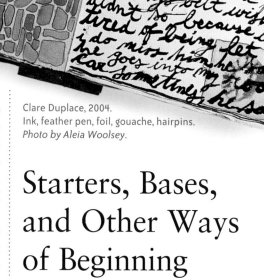

Whether you're interested in working in many overlapping layers or in composing clear, concise pages with a minimum of visual noise, it's useful to work in stages. A visual journal, at its most simple, is an interplay between text and image that conveys meaning. However, if you take this too seriously, you can build a certain amount of anxiety over facing the blank page—and this is the exact opposite feeling you want to bring to your work. It might help you to think in terms of beginning processes (starters), middle processes (middles), and final processes (toppings). Working this way can give you enough of a structure to start your practices flowing. When you work in stages, you'll find your pages will pull together in a whole new way.

In this chapter, you'll find ideas for carrying your pages to completion. Working in stages is a mix-and-match exercise with no right or wrong answers. You can combine starters, middles, and toppers any way you please. Write or draw on a map, use metallic pens for text in a collage, flow a watercolor wash over writing, use an opaque ground to "erase" your work and start again, make your own stamps to create a border, remove pages or laminate them—the combinations are endless.

Clare Duplace, 2004.
Ink, feather pen, foil, gouache, hairpins.
Photo by Aleia Woolsey.

Starters, Bases, and Other Ways of Beginning

Where to begin? Ideas you want to convey and feelings you want to portray and evoke are bubbling inside you. The choices seem limitless, if not daunting, when you're facing a new page. The ideas presented here will give you a nudge to get you started.

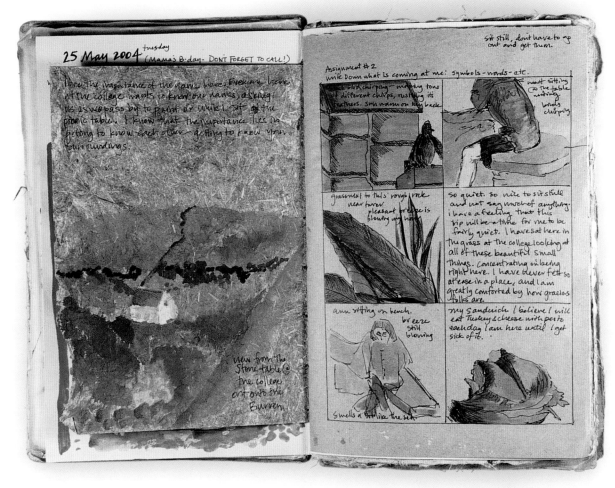

Sarah A. Bourne, *Ireland Journal Page*, 2004. 8½ x 11 inches (21.6 x 27.9 cm).
Bound journal, handmade paper, drawing paper, watercolor, ink. *Photo by Aleia Woolsey.*

PAPER

When you begin to incorporate images into a journal, suddenly the very paper on which you're working takes on new importance and actually becomes the first stage. It's a great boon if the paper is sufficiently alluring to make you look forward to putting down some marks. If it provides you, the journal keeper, with the impetus to work, an interesting paper may be all the starter that you need.

In a very real way, the paper itself is a part of every image, in some cases forming a ground that reflects its own whiteness and adds sparkle and light to the drawn or painted images. In other instances the paper acts as a foil or counterpoint to the work that is done on it, thus creating a nice tension and edginess. Sometimes the paper provides a wash of color, an emotional tone, or a sense of the past. Sometimes the paper lends a sense of order or control.

You may be lucky enough to find enticing paper already bound in a journal that you fall in love with. Its heavy pages with just a hint of a creamy peachy color invite your pen to stroke them. You love the shape and size of the pages—best of all, the book fits perfectly in your coat pocket. But even if you can't find a journal that you love, you can usually find paper that you love, and you can easily make a journal out of this paper (see The Reluctant Bookbinder, pages 195 to 210) or modify a blank book to include this paper (see Customizing a Blank Book on page 212).

POURED COLORS

Sometimes beautiful paper isn't sufficient to get you going. If you need more of an invitation, try pouring colors or tints on the paper. The random patterns that result can make whatever you put on top of them more interesting. The shapes, moreover, can be the basis for a layout or page design that you would have never thought of on your own. The only caveat is that the paper needs to be substantial enough to handle getting wet. Thin, inexpensive paper wrinkles badly, and unless that's the look you want to achieve, you might want to reserve this technique for heavier pieces of paper (which you can add to a purchased journal if it has thin paper). If you're binding your own journal, simply pour the pages before cutting or tearing them and binding the book.

To pour the color, you'll need fluid acrylic paints or acrylic inks in a few colors that suit your mood for the journal. You can also use strong tea or coffee. Metallic or iridescent colors make a nice addition if you like to work on pages that sparkle or glow. Gather together a couple of old plastic squeeze bottles such as dish detergent bottles, some blotting paper or old newspaper, a piece of plastic, such as a drop cloth or a large plastic garbage bag, and water.

Begin by spreading the plastic on the floor or a table-top, and lay a sheet of watercolor or other slightly heavy to heavy paper on it. There are several brands of text or cover paper that are wonderful choices for this process, but other multi-media papers work well, too. Pour 1 to 3 inches (2.5 to 7.6 cm) of

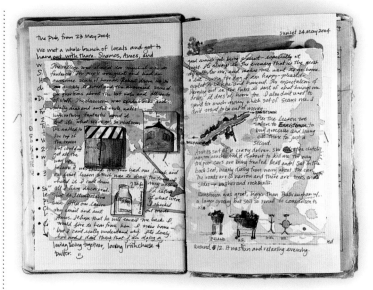

Sarah A. Bourne, *Ireland Journal Page*, 2004. 8½ x 11 inches (21.6 x 27.9 cm). Hand-bound journal, handmade paper, watercolor, ink. *Photo by Aleia Woolsey.*

water in each bottle, then add a couple of drops of paint or ink, and shake the bottle to mix. If the colors seem too dark and heavy, add more water. If the colors are too light or thin, add more paint. If you're using tea or coffee, there's no need to dilute.

Materials for pouring color onto a page.

Gwen Diehn. 6 x 9 inches (15.2 x 22.9 cm). Watercolor on handmade paper page with poured fluid acylic.
Photo by Aleia Woolsey.

Now simply squirt or dribble the watery paint onto the paper. You can:

- move the paint around on the page by rolling the paper or by gently folding (but not creasing) each corner into the center and then back out

- press another piece of the same kind of paper on top of the first sheet, thereby making two sheets at once

- blot the color to lighten it

- add layers of color, letting colors dry between layers

- hold it up so that rivers of color trickle down toward the edges

- spread the paint with your hands or a sponge or a brush

- do anything else that makes the kinds of marks you want to make.

When you're finished with one side, turn the page over and do the other side. Hang the sheet up on a clothesline to dry or drape it over the back of a chair or a drying rack. After it dries, the paper will look even more spectacular. You can then cut or tear it down to the size you need it to be. You can't go wrong with this process!

As mentioned, you can do the same process using watercolors, strong coffee or tea, or water-based inks. However, these media can be rewet, and painting over them with more water media will move the dye or pigment around and change the shapes they form on the paper. Because acrylics dry to a permanent state and can't be rewet, they'll remain in the shapes they were when they dried, even when you paint over them with water media. If you want to modify the hues or colors of acrylic poured paint, overlay them with thin washes of watercolor, fluid acrylics, or transparent inks.

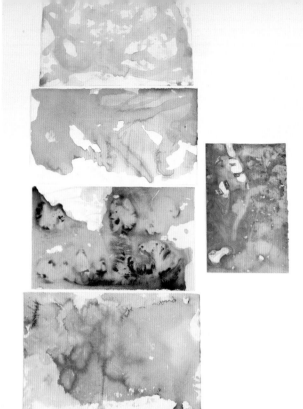

BAKED PAPER

This impossible-to-get-wrong process yields improbable and lovely effects. My friend, Becca Johnson (page 19), taught me how to do this, and I've improvised on it a bit. I encourage you to do the same

Before you begin, you'll need: paper; tea; a teapot or saucepan for brewing strong tea; a cookie sheet with a shallow lip to contain the liquid; onion skins and cut grass or leaves as desired; an oven, pre-heated to 250°F (121°C); and an arrangement for drying the papers (see Ink Washing on page 61). Set up your work area near a sink for easy rinsing.

The best papers for this process are on the heavy side, although I tried a piece of computer paper and that yielded very lovely effects. Lighter paper will wrinkle more than heavier paper. My favorite papers for this process are Arches cover or text wove, Annigoni, Velata, and white drawing paper. Because the paper needs to fit completely on the cookie sheet, you'll need to first cut or tear the paper to the size needed for the folios.

Begin by brewing a pot of very strong tea. I used six or seven tea bags or a generous handful of loose tea in about 1 pint (.5 L) of water. Experiment with different varieties of tea for different colors. I used a black English breakfast tea for these sample pages.

Lay a piece of cut or torn paper on the baking sheet. (My cookie sheet was old and dark. Because I suspect the condition of the sheet is a variable in this process, it's best to experiment.) Then lay the onion skins and pieces of grass or leaves on the paper. Pour in enough tea to wet the bottom of the pan and to have it puddle a bit on top of the paper. There's no need to strain the tea; it's fine if the tea leaves land on the paper.

Place the cookie sheet inside the oven and bake for approximately 10 minutes (another variable). When the sheet comes out of the oven, you may notice some inky blackish tea in the pan. This chemically changed tea makes a gorgeous dark color on the paper, so you may want to flip the page over to pick up some of that color on the other side. Experiment for best results. When the page looks sufficiently covered with color, hold it under running water to rinse off the tea as well as any vegetable remains.

Hang the papers to dry. You'll find that drying further changes things. For one, the edges become more defined and fragile. You can bake a page again to improve the color or add more interesting tones. It isn't necessary to dry the paper before re-baking it, but you can re-bake a page that has dried.

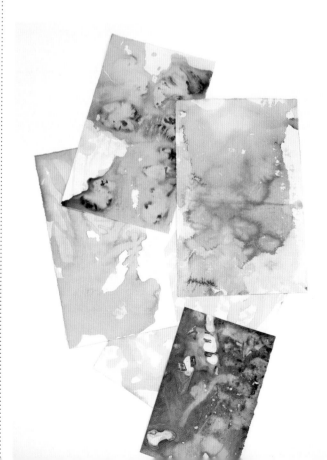

INK WASHING

An ink wash can create a lovely or lively base for your page. In this process you brush waterproof ink over parts of a page, let it dry for a few minutes, and then wash out the ink that has not yet dried. This leaves fragile marks at the edges of the shapes made by the ink.

You want to use relatively heavyweight, sized paper for this process. The sizing keeps the ink from penetrating too quickly and slows the drying time of the ink so you can wash the ink out. Very thin, fragile paper will wrinkle more, but if you don't mind that, it can produce some nice effects. Just make sure to always use sized paper regardless of its weight. If you use paper that is unsized, the ink will penetrate below the surface and stain the paper, which defeats the washed effect you seek.

Begin by gathering your paper. (My favorites for this process are Arches cover and Arches text wove, Velata, and Annigoni.) You can leave the pieces full size, or pre-cut or tear them to the size folios you'll use in your book. You'll also need a jar of India ink—which is waterproof black drawing ink made with some form of carbon, water, and shellac—and a few paintbrushes.

Set up your workstation close to a sink where you can wash out the ink as soon as it begins to dry. Also arrange a place for drying the wet paper, either on a small clothes rack, a clothesline with clothespins, or a stack of blotters. You can also lay the wet pages on a countertop, but they'll take much longer to dry that way.

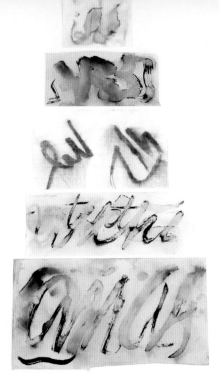

Dip a brush in either full-strength or diluted India ink and make your marks on the paper. Calligraphic lines are good, as are patterns of dots, swirls, or abstract shapes. Be random and playful. Now watch the ink marks carefully. As soon as the edges become matte or look dry, carefully rinse off the remaining ink.

Keep in mind that this ink-drying stage takes practice. Some people prefer leaving greater amounts of ink on the paper than others. There's no perfect way to do this, so it's best to experiment. Whatever looks good to you at the time is the right amount of drying. If you think you've washed off too much ink the first time, let it dry longer the next time.

Once the ink is dried to your satisfaction, turn on a light stream of water, and hold the paper under the tap. You'll immediately see lots of ink washing off. You can lightly rub some areas with your fingers to encourage more to wash off, or just let whatever happens happen.

Hang the page to dry, or lay it on a blotter. You can speed the process along by using a hair dryer. Repeat the process on the other side of the page if you want an ink wash on both sides. For a variation, start out with diluted ink and then brush on a darker layer for a second round of washing. Always wait until the paper is completely dry before brushing on a second round of ink. If you don't, the marks will be fuzzy. However, some people prefer the fuzzy edges, so again experiment to find your own preferences.

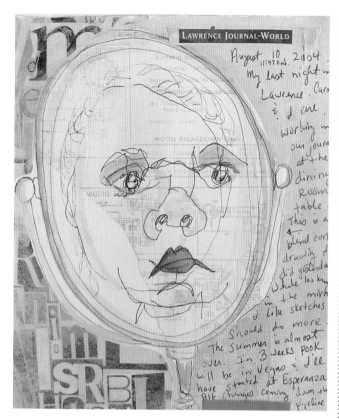

Mary Ann Moss, 2004. 8 x 6 inches (20.3 x 15.2 cm). Handmade journal, gesso, acrylic paint, ink, watercolor markers, ephemera, magazine and newspaper scraps, packing tape; glued, collaged, painted, and illustrated. *Photo by artist.*

PRINTED FORMS

Another interesting way to get started is to use printed forms for your journal paper. Grid paper or quadrille paper, lined paper, ledger sheets, and other pre-printed forms impose order on information. Their very orderliness and fussiness invite your comments, your splashes of color, and your out-of-the-lines drawing. See what happens when you disregard the prescribed spaces and draw, paint, and write wherever you want. The order is still there, in the background, on a bottom layer, and it forms a stage on which emotion and impetuous expression are heightened by the contrast.

Search office supply stores, antique stores, and school supply stores for forms. If the paper is too flimsy for heavy, wet media, you can either laminate it to heavier paper (see Laminating Pages on page 213), or use colored pencils, pens, crayons, pencils, or light watercolor sketching when you work on those pages. An interesting example of the use of this starter is in Patterns Found and Lost (see page 79), in which the journal keeper began with pre-printed forms made specifically for recording the results of a day's fishing.

MAPS AND DIAGRAMS

Maps and other kinds of diagrams impose a different kind of order on a page. Unlike forms, these carry some content and meaning themselves and are not simply blank matrices for organizing content. They also carry connotative meaning that can enhance or act as a foil against the content you add.

There are several ways to turn a map or diagram into a first stage for a journal page. One way is to use a computer to scan the map or diagram and then print it on the paper you want to use in your journal. This method offers the most flexibility in that you can modify the color, the darkness or lightness of the print, as well as its size.

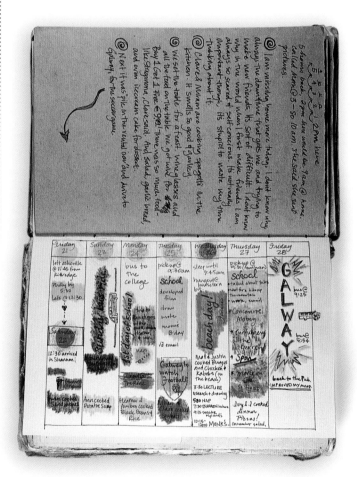

Sarah A. Bourne, *Ireland Journal Page*, 2004. 8½ x 11 inches (21.6 x 27.9 cm). Hand-bound journal, handmade paper, watercolor, ink. *Photo by Aleia Woolsey.*

I started with a map that I had transferred onto the page before I made the journal.

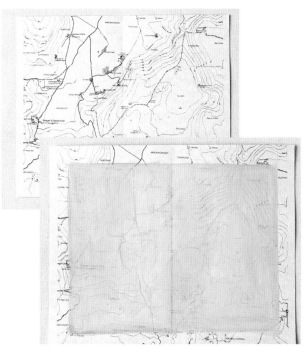

I painted out the central part of the map with white gouache to which I had added a little bit of blue watercolor.

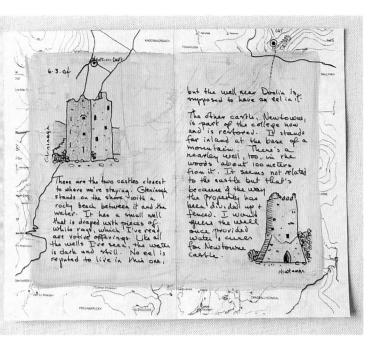

I drew and wrote, then later added watercolor to the drawing.

Gwen Diehn. 6 x 9 inches (15.2 x 22.9 cm). Watercolor, gouache, and pen over a copier transfer map. *Photo by Aleia Woolsey.*

Another way is to glue or bind the actual map or diagram into the book. While this is the most authentic use of the item, the paper it's printed on may not be the best for the medium you'll be using on top of it. If the paper is slick and non-porous, use waterproof pens and inks, gel pens, permanent markers, and acrylic paints on it. A process that helps when painting on slick paper is to mix watercolor with a little soap or dish detergent. The soap helps break the surface tension of the water so that it adheres better to the non-porous paper.

COPIER TRANSFER

Another starter process is to make a copier transfer. This is done by making a color or black-and-white photocopy of an image, enlarging or reducing it as needed, and then brushing gel style citrus-based paint stripper on the back of the copy and burnishing with a wooden spoon to transfer the map or diagram to the paper in the journal. Fresh new photocopies work better than old ones. As shown in the photo on page 64, begin by laying the copy facedown on the journal page. To keep it from moving, you might want to tape it lightly to the page with drafting tape. Then generously brush the back of the copy with citrus-based gel-style paint stripper. Wait about 30 seconds for the gel to penetrate the paper, and then rub or burnish the back of the page with the rounded bowl of a wooden or metal spoon. Be very careful not to shift the copy as you burnish.

You can see how well the image is transferring by holding the copy in place and carefully lifting one corner at a time. If the transfer isn't dark enough, either burnish some more while applying more pressure or apply more gel before continuing to burnish. If you're still having trouble transferring the image, it may be the age of the gel stripper. If you're using stripper that's been in your workshop awhile, purchase a new container of fresh stripper.

Once the copy is transferred, you can draw or paint right on top of it, add color, and otherwise alter the image to suit your purposes. Copier transfers are a good way to introduce appropriated imagery to your work.

Kelcey Loomer, 2004. 5 x 4 inches (12.7 x 10.2 cm). Copier transfer, watercolor. *Photo by Aleia Woolsey.*

Materials and tools needed for making a copier transfer.

COLLAGE

At the heart of many journals today are the scraps, the ephemera of a journey, of an experience, of a project, or of daily life. These are logical starters for use as the base of a page, or as the point of departure for drawings. Collage is equally effective as a starter, a top layer of a layered page, or as a stand-alone, simpler page. Using collage as a starter sets a context for the page that is derived from the meaning of the collaged item or items. Placing an item in the background will quietly set a tone for whatever work you put on top. If you highlight the collaged item, it can be the base for the whole page.

Some flat items to collect are photographs, computer printouts of scanned drawings and photographs, tickets, receipts, notes, napkin sketches, wrapping paper, scraps of handwriting, sugar packets, maps, seed packages, labels, magazine and newspaper clippings, pressed flowers, stamps, paper bags, and fortune-cookie fortunes.

You want to attach these objects to the page using an adhesive that's appropriate to the supporting paper as well as to the collage items (see Adhesives on page 40).

Scott Gordon, 2004. 14 x 21½ inches (35.6 x 54.6 cm). Bound journal, acrylic paint, found paper; collage. *Photo by Rick Wells.*

Consider tearing or cutting objects into strips or small pieces as well as using the whole item. Keep in mind that the supporting paper should ideally be as heavy or heavier than the collage items. Also, if you want your journal pages to lie flat, avoid attaching large collage items that are made of a different kind of paper than the supporting page. When you adhere a piece of grained paper (and all machine-made paper is grained) to another paper, the grain pulls against the support as it dries. If the support has no grain (handmade paper) or a weak grain (light, thin machine-made paper), the result is going to be warping and curling. You can, to some degree, counteract the warping by laminating a sheet of comparable paper to the back of the collaged journal page. Doing this will equalize the pull of the grain from the heavy collage.

Collage materials.

Keep in mind that heavily collaged pages fatten the fore edge of a book. You will need to compensate for this by removing a page or two immediately in front of the collage (see Removing Pages on page 212). If some items are too bulky to attach to the book itself, make scans or photocopies of them, and attach or transfer the copy to the journal instead of using the original object. Pressed leaves and flower petals can be preserved and protected by brushing them with matte or satin finish polymer varnish. The varnish glues the flattened organic material to the page and seals out air and moisture.

Like copier transfers, collage makes use of appropriated images and words. These will bring their own accumulated meanings and connotations with them into their new configurations on your pages. These items are marks, and as such should contribute to the overall meaning of the work and not dominate the piece. Work that is basically an enshrinement of an appropriated image fails on many levels.

Manufactured images, specially packaged for collage, are a poor substitute for authentic ephemera and do nothing to further the art or the progress of the artist. You can save a lot of money by walking right past the aisle that sells packages labeled "Nostalgia" and "Beauty" and "Cute Animals," just as you avoid paint-by-numbers and coloring books when you want to engage in authentic expression. Remember that less is more.

Kristin A. Livelsberger, *Rest*, 2003. 10 x 10 x 2¾ inches (25.4 x 25.4 x 7 cm). Spiral- bound journal, mounting paste, acrylic paint, found paper and paper scraps, paint swatches, pen, charcoal, tape; painted, layered, glued, and taped. *Photo by Fine Art Photo Portrait Studio.*

WATERCOLOR WASH

A watercolor wash, unlike an acrylic wash, can be rewet after it has dried. This means that if you're painting on top of watercolor, there will be some mixing of colors. You can exploit this quality to good effect, or you can work faster and with a light touch to minimize color mixing.

YOU WILL NEED

- Watercolors
- Water
- Mixing jar
- Watercolor brush
- Mixing tray (any smooth, flat, non-porous surface will do: an old dinner plate, an old pie tin, etc.)
- Blotter or stack of newspapers

INSTRUCTIONS

1 Mix up a watery batch of watercolor paint and water on the mixing tray.

2 Put a blotter or some sheets of newspaper beneath the page you're going to prepare. Paint the color smoothly onto the page. You can add a border, as in the photo below, do a plain wash (add another color or layer after the first dries for more depth), paint an overall pattern, or extend your pattern over two pages.

3 Prepare pages one after the other, following the instructions for drying on page 70.

VARIATION

For a subtle texture, dab paint on one page in a random pattern, then touch it with the opposite page, spreading the paint (see photo, right).

WATERCOLOR WASH WITH PLASTIC WRAP

There are several effects that you can get from manipulating wet watercolor washes. The next two processes will change ordinary watercolor washes into mysterious surfaces with elegant, spontaneous passages.

YOU WILL NEED

- Blotters or newspapers
- Watercolors
- Watercolor brush
- Mixing tray
- Sponge
- Plastic wrap

INSTRUCTIONS

1 Place a blotter or some sheets of newspaper beneath the page you're going to prepare.

2 Mix up a batch of watercolor and water in a mixing tray.

3 Sponge clean water over the entire page to dampen it.

4 Working quickly, paint the page with the wash. You can also pour on a couple of different colored puddles and let them flow together.

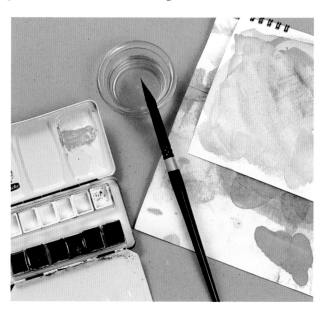

5 Before the paint dries, lay a sheet of plastic wrap over the entire painted surface, scrunching the plastic wrap into wrinkles. Leave the plastic wrap in place for about 5 minutes.

6 Peel off the plastic wrap. The resulting design is caused by paint darkening in the places where it was in contact with the plastic wrap. Follow the directions on page 70 for drying and pressing the book.

VARIATION

You can achieve interesting effects by adding table salt to a wet watercolor wash.

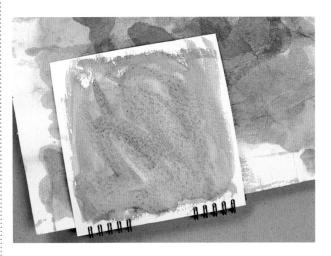

Working quickly before the paint dries, sprinkle table salt in a random arrangement over the painting. Wherever the salt lands, it will absorb water in such a way that the area around the salt crystal will be lighter than the surrounding area.

Dry Processes

These are actually *relatively* dry processes. They work well for thin paper that can't withstand the large amount of water used in the wet processes, and equally well for heavier papers. None of these processes warp or cockle paper.

Because these are only relatively dry processes, you should treat them as you do wet processes until your book is dry. To dry pages, keep sheets of newspaper or blotters between all wet sheets while you're working. When you finish, stand the book up to dry with the pages fanned out. Once they're dry, press them flat by closing the book and placing it under a pile of heavy books or bricks. As an alternative, you can speed the drying process by using a hair dryer to blow-dry individual pages.

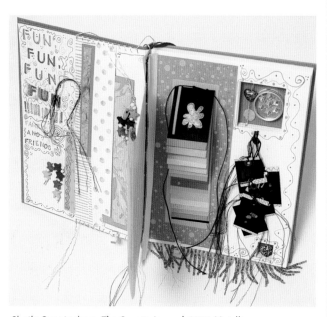

Sheila Cunningham, *The Orange Journal*, 2001. Metallic thread, grommets, photos, hand-carved stamps, and metallic pens. *Photo by artist.*

SPONGE-PAINTED ACRYLICS, GOUACHE, OR WATERCOLORS

Sponge painting transfers a small amount of paint to the page and spreads it into a thin, delicate layer, leaving no brush strokes. You can also leave sponge prints or sponge through a stencil to make a regular pattern.

YOU WILL NEED

- Liquid acrylics, watercolors, or gouache (opaque watercolors)
- Water
- Mixing jar
- Mixing tray
- Flat sponge, such as a plastic dishwashing sponge
- Masking tape (optional)
- Scrap paper
- Stencil, large-holed needlepoint canvas, wire screen, lacey or openwork cloth or paper (optional)
- Hair dryer (optional)

INSTRUCTIONS

1 Mix the colors that you want to use on the mixing tray. If you're using liquid acrylics, don't dilute

them. If you're using watercolors or gouache, dilute them just enough to form paint that is about the same consistency as heavy cream. If you want a clean border, first put strips of masking tape over areas of the page that you don't want to have paint on them (see photo, bottom right, opposite page). To prevent the masking tape from tearing the surface of the paper, first stick it to your pants leg or some other piece of cloth to remove some of the tack.

2 Tap the sponge into the paint to pick up a small amount. Then tap or daub the sponge onto a piece of scrap paper until it makes the kind of marks you want. You can adjust the way the paint looks by how much pressure you place on the sponge, as well as by the amount of paint you pick up.

3 Tap and daub the sponge all over the page that you're preparing, picking up more paint and different colors as necessary. Dry the pages in the manner described on page 70.

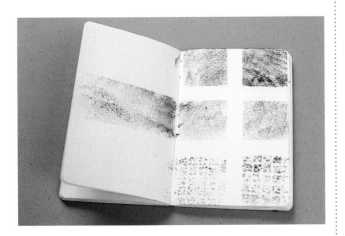

VARIATION

To sponge through a stencil, lay the piece of cloth, screen, or paper over the page to be prepared. Follow steps 1 through 3, then peel off the stencil and dry the page as usual.

Metallic pens (and metallic stamp pad ink) draw the eye to the text in spite of the strongly textured border of this page by Nina Bagley.

ACRYLIC MESH PRINT

This process results in a soft, grid-like pattern that can be an interesting underlayer for writing and drawing.

YOU WILL NEED

- Plastic needlepoint canvas, #7 or larger-holed
- Liquid acrylic paints
- Small sponge

INSTRUCTIONS

1 Use the sponge to rub a light coat of acrylic all over one side of the plastic canvas.

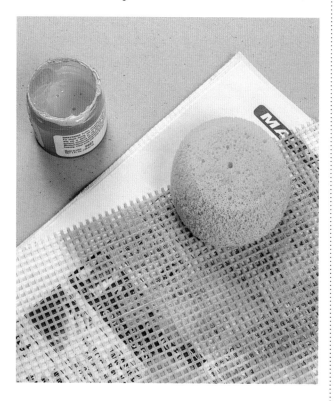

2 Carefully lay the canvas, painted side down, on top of the page to be prepared. Being careful not to shift the canvas, press firmly all over the back of the canvas to offset the paint onto the paper.

3 Peel the canvas off the paper, and dry as usual.

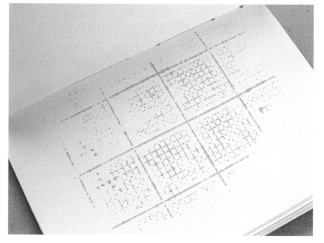

VARIATIONS

You can achieve different effects by using mesh with larger or smaller patterns. The texture of your paper will also affect the outcome of the process.

SPONGED-ON STAMP PAD INK

Pigment-type stamp pad ink can be sponged on so that graduated tones result. Cotton cosmetic removal pads or fine-grained soft sponges leave no stroke marks and give smooth coverage.

YOU WILL NEED

- Masking tape
- Cotton cosmetic removal pads or smooth sponge
- Pigment-dyed stamp pad or pads
- Scrap paper
- Wax paper (optional)

INSTRUCTIONS

1 First, mask off a border or sections of the page that will not have color, unless you want the entire page to be filled with color. To remove some of the tack from the tape, first stick it to your pants leg or another piece of cloth.

2 Daub a cotton pad onto the stamp pad, then tap it a few times on a piece of scrap paper to remove any dark blotches of ink. Then begin gently tapping and wiping the ink onto the page. You can rub in circles with considerable pressure to get smooth coverage. Increasing pressure results in darker tones.

3 When the page is sufficiently covered, peel off any tape. Place a clean sheet of wax paper or scrap paper between the sheets of paper prepared in this way until the ink is completely dry. Drying may take from a few hours to a few days, depending on the kind of paper you use.

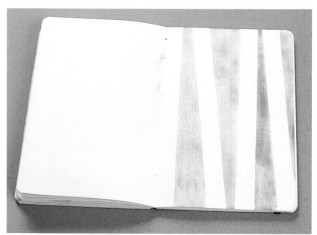

VARIATION

Try taping the page in different patterns (diagonal, grid, column) or mixing colors for a clouded effect (see photo, below).

COPIER TRANSFERS

An easy way to get an image onto a page is to make a color or black and white photocopy of it and then transfer the image into your journal. Once the copy is transferred, you can draw or paint right on top of it, adding color, simplifying forms, and otherwise altering the image to suit your purposes.

YOU WILL NEED

- A fresh photocopy
- Citrus-based gel-style paint stripper*
- Paintbrush
- Wooden spoon for burnishing
- Drafting tape (optional)

*This product is safe to use indoors without a lot of ventilation, but read all product cautions before using.

INSTRUCTIONS

1 Begin by laying the copy face down on the journal page. You might tape it lightly to the page with drafting tape to keep it from moving. Generously brush the back of the copy with citrus-based, gel-style paint stripper.

2 Rub or burnish the back of the copy with the rounded bowl of a wooden or metal spoon. Be very careful not to shift the copy at all. You can check the progress of the transfer by holding the copy in place and carefully lifting one corner at a time to see how well the image is transferring.

3 If the transfer isn't dark enough, either burnish some more, or add more gel. Fresh, new copies work better than old copies. A successful copy transfer will be dark enough to show some details.

STAMP PATTERN

Small rubber stamps can be used to make individual marks, almost like brush strokes, in an overall pattern.

YOU WILL NEED

- Commercial or homemade rubber stamp in a simple design
- Dye-type ink stamp pad*
- Scrap paper or wax paper (optional)

*Note: Dye-based inks dry faster than pigment inks; it's okay to use pigment inks for this, but be aware that they will take longer to dry.

INSTRUCTIONS

Ink the stamp, and stamp it all over the page in a regular or irregular pattern. If you are using pigment ink, interleaf the page with wax paper or clean scrap paper until it is dry.

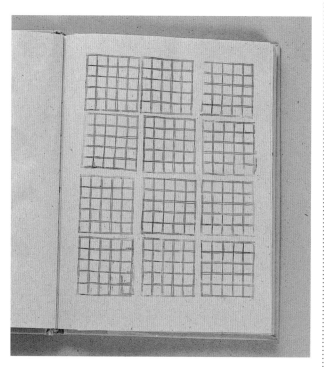

VARIATIONS

Give your page more dimension with a stamp border that extends well into the page.

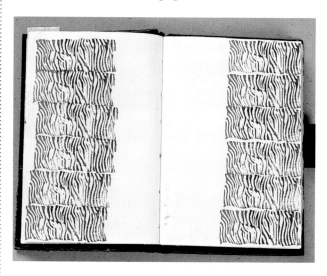

You can also stamp page stubs to turn them into design elements.

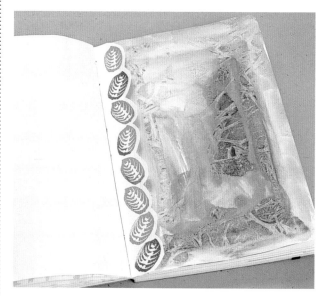

Stitching

A sometimes-overlooked way of making marks is stitching. Stitched lines lend not only color but also texture to the page. A stitched border is a tactile as well as a visual element. Depending on the expressive content of the page, you might consider using brightly colored silk threads, glittering metallics, or stark, crisp black. Stitching can also be used very effectively to attach collage elements to a page and also to attach foldouts, small booklets, and envelopes to page stubs.

CHALLENGE YOURSELF

Another type of starter comes from setting up a challenge or assignment. My friend Dana gave herself the assignment of doing a small visual journal entry every day for a year. She didn't want to do a whole page a day; rather, she drew a series of boxes on the pages of a large sketchbook. She drew small boxes, less daunting than an entire page. Each page held around 14 boxes—two weeks worth of entries. Dana began at the top lefthand corner of the first page, filling in a box a day. The challenge was to summarize the day in one succinct drawing or painting, with or without text. Dana noticed that six months into the project her entries were sometimes spilling out of their boxes. Then the boxes themselves broke ranks, as it were, and she found herself penciling in various sizes and proportions of rectangles, and the pages really began to take off!

Recently while traveling in Ireland, I decided to keep track of the dark and daylight while I was there. It would be a record of the midsummer season in this relatively northern place. I made a small journal with a 3 x 3-inch (7.6 x 7.6 cm) cover and 21 pages, one for each day that I was to be there. Using a piece of rubber-stamp material, I carved a stamp that printed a scale of small lines and numbers showing midnight, 6 a.m., noon, and 6 p.m. I printed the scale at the bottom of each page. On each page I then recorded the dark and daylight hours by coloring in the scale to correspond to the light and dark. I also recorded sunrise and sunset, the phase of the moon, the weather, and, eventually, events from each day. The finished journal shows graphically the gradual shrinking of darkness and expanding of light as we drew close to the summer solstice. The assignment worked because I had made the exact number of scaled pages to encompass the vacation. I didn't want to end up with blank pages, so I felt compelled to work away at my journal every single day. It also worked because once I had recorded sunrise and sunset I wanted to keep going, and I ended up drawing, painting, and writing many details that summarized each day.

Dana Fox Jenkins, *End of the Alphabet, the Annual Clique Weekend, and A Meeting in Boston*, 2004. 11 x 14 inches (27.9 x 35.6 cm). Acid-free and 100% cotton paper, watercolor, quick ink, stamps. *Photo by Val Dunne.*

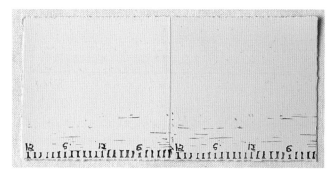

I began by stamping the scale of hours at the bottom of each page of the little journal.

While outside, I painted small watercolors.

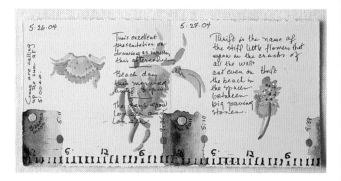

Later I wrote notes around and on top of the watercolors.

ALTERED BOOKS AND PAGES

An excellent starter is to use an old book for your journal. Alternately, you can add printed pages from an old book to a blank book or to a journal that you've made. The printed page, with its illustrations and type, sets the tone for the journal page. It might be a completely random selection or one from a book that means something to you. In either case, it will provide many points of entry and will give you a variety of images and words to build on or react against. When you're choosing a book to

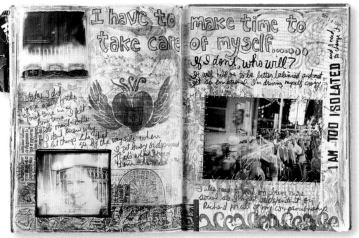

Traci Bunkers, *I Have to Make Time to Take Care of Myself*, 2004. 11 x 17 inches (27.9 x 43.2 cm). Printed book altered with gesso, marker, crayon, ink, photographs, thread, acrylic paint, transparency, copper tape; painted, glued, stitched, stamped with hand-carved rubber stamps. *Photo by Image Works, Inc.*

alter, consider the characteristics of the paper just as you would in buying a blank book (see page 22. If you're using a page that's extremely thin or fragile, it would be good to laminate it to a heavier page (see page 213).

Sometimes a base page from another book may need a little modifying. For example, if you've chosen to use a map with lines of about the same weight as the pen you'll be using, your writing is going to be hard to read. This might be the effect you're after, but if it's not, you can paint over the page (or parts of the page) with white or light-colored gouache. At first the gouache will seem to block out the underlayer completely. But as it dries, the print of the map will reappear in a lighter form than the original. When you write on it, your writing will come forward like a separate layer because it will be darker and sharper than the gouached-over map.

Gouache is good for pushing back or softening any layer or element that creates too much visual noise. The gouached-over element can still be deciphered to some extent, but it becomes a softer background message that no longer competes with what is put on top of it. Gouache is also useful for partially erasing or blotting out writing or drawing that you decide you want to erase or downplay. By applying several coats you can more completely obliterate the underneath layer. However, a ghost will always remain to create a nice palimpsest that hints at other, deeper layers of information just beyond reach (see Gouache on page 32).

Patterns Found and Lost

Sarah Midda is a British graphic designer who, in the early 1990s, spent a year in the south of France and kept a lovely illustrated diary about her experience. Midda's watercolors and pen and pencil sketches report on every aspect of life in the French countryside. She seems drawn to collections and patterns, and takes a particular delight in revealing easily overlooked details. It feels perfectly right that Midda picked up the orderliness and patterned nature of this place in her drawings and writing. Her small, flawlessly designed pages are a reflection of a place of gardens and fields with well-disciplined rows of lavender and sunflowers.[1]

Midda arranges her sketches on the page like chocolates in a box. Some pages are grids with each tiny box filled with a painting of an object. She impos pages are grids with each tiny box filled with a painting of an object. She imposes these patterns by first looking for them in an individual object or a grouping of objects. Typically, she draws and paints them, and then encloses the images in boxes. When she paints varieties of lettuce, for example, she arranges the drawings in a column five leaves high, puts text above and below the leaves, surrounds all the leaves with a red-ruled box, and paints what looks like the back of a seed packet as a frame for the whole arrangement.

Midda even turns colors into patterns. On several pages she paints a column of color boxes in the margin, and writes below where the colors are from:

a stationery store, various table linens, a field of flowers. Her book is a great example of finding beauty and order, yet not pinning it down like a trapped butterfly. Rather, all of her pages sparkle with light, and exuberance seems to spill and burst from the boxes in which the drawings are placed.

An Englishwoman named Muriel Foster kept a very different kind of journal. Foster created a diary that, from the beginning, disregarded the printed lines and columns on its pages and managed to lose and subvert most, if not all, sense of the pre-imposed pattern. The diary was never intended for publication, but was Foster's private record of her lifelong pleasure—fly-fishing. The first entry in her diary is September 16, 1913, and the last dated

DATE	WHERE CAUGHT	WATER	RODS	FLY	SALMON	GRILSE	TROUT	SEA TROUT	VARIOUS	WEIGHT LBS.	WEIGHT OZS.
1923											
June 15	Eastbourne, Sussex		1 line.						2 Dabs		
July 5	Loch Broom Glebe	Loch an Tiompain	1				1				12
" 6	" " "	Loch a charn		Silver Phantom			1			1	4
" 9	" " "	" " "	2	sunk flies			6		4		
" "	" " "	Loch an Fhiona	1	" "			2				8
" 10	" " "	Loch an Tiompain	1	Olive Dun			1				
" 11	" "	" "	1	" "							
" 12	" " "	" " "	1	" "			1				
" 16	" " "	Loch a charn	2	10 on double fly			12			5	4

From *Muriel Foster's Fishing Diary* by Muriel Foster, © 1980 by Patricia King. Used by permission of Viking Penguin, a division of Penguin Group (USA) Inc.

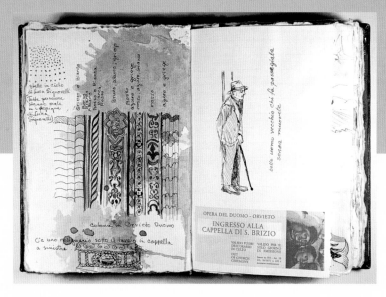

Gwen Diehn. 6 x 9 inches (15.2 x 22.9 cm). Pen, watercolor wash, and collage on handmade paper. *Photo by Aleia Woolsey.*

entry is June 1, 1949, around the time she was forced to give up fishing due to arthritis.

The book itself is a standard early 20th-century English fishing diary. It has ruled lines demarking columns for the date, where the fish was caught, the kind of water, the rods and flies used, the number of trout, salmon, grilse, sea trout, and various other fish caught, and the weight in pounds and ounces of each fish. The facing page is titled "remarks" and has a red line ruled the width of the page under the title.

Foster neatly records the date and usually fills in the "where caught" column, as well as frequently filling in other columns. But beginning with the first page, she adds sketches of subjects, such as swimming ducks, fish, or the flies she uses. Sometimes her drawings overlap several columns, as on one page near the front of the diary where a sea otter swims in a pond that encompasses four columns, and another peeks over the red line on the facing page. Foster routinely uses the "remarks" page to do more

developed paintings and drawings as well as integrate textual comments. She disregards lines sometimes and at other times makes the red line become part of the design.

On one page, meticulously painted flies seem to be threaded on the red line separating salmon and grilse. On the facing page the horizontal red line bisects a pen drawing of Leckmelm Lodge, which she was visiting. Occasionally she paints a two-page spread, completely subverting the preprinted lines and text. On other pages she draws her own charts and superimposes them on the red lines, then finishes off the page with, for example, a few seagulls sitting on a barrel that bobs about in the bottom of the "where caught" and "water" columns.

If we can learn from Sara Midda the ways of seeing pattern and variety within everyday objects and how to assemble things into collections, we can learn from Muriel Foster how to make a preformatted book our own, how to bend it to our purposes. Foster also teaches us how to notice the many

prosaic and mundane things that make up the tapestry of a long practice, how to express the flavor of a favorite pastime. Her text notes are occasionally more revealing of her emotions than are her drawings, which tend to remove them from the objects drawn.

One day in May, 1929, she writes, "Lost the fish of my life! Saw him jump out of the water thought it was a grilse—trolled over him & hooked him. He ran out a tremendous line, came up and lashed on the surface & broke me & took my minnow! Jimmy thought him an 8-pounder!"[2] The next two pages are completely without notes. A watercolor painting of a lake and hills fills both pages. The red lines hover over the hilltops. Maybe she took a day off from fishing after the 8-pounder got away!

[1]Sarah Midda. *South of France*. NY: Workman Publishing, 1990.

[2] Patricia King. *Muriel Foster's Fishing Diary*. NY: The Viking Press, 1980.

Scavenger Hunting from Life

by Jill K. Berry

Water Journal Pages. 5 x 16½ inches (12.7 x 41.9 cm). Pen, watercolor.

Fall Journal Pages. 7½ x 21 inches (19 x 53.3 cm). Gold pen, white pen, crayons, pink pen, green pen.

> *"This act of recording my daily experiences allows me to see my surroundings in a heightened way."*

I use my journals to take notice of the present, record my dreams, and note the visions and prose that inspire me. This act of recording my daily experiences allows me to see my surroundings in a heightened way. It makes me take notice of my life and acts as a kind of scavenger hunt, since I am always looking for scenes, textures, stories, and colors to record on the page.

Journaling helps me retain the journey of motherhood. When my kids were small, I loved sketching them and recording their bits of wisdom and conversations. I still do this, even though they're nearly teens. I also let them draw in my journals, which makes me profoundly happy, since they're so inventive and joyful.

In September of 2001, I journaled nearly every day. During that emotional time of national crisis, I was also serving on a jury for a trial of a horrible crime. I felt so dark inside. On our lunch breaks, I would write and draw in my journal. It was better than talking, and gave me an outlet for how profoundly disturbed I felt—way more effective than therapy.

I also journal during all my travels. I combine drawing, wax rubbings, and writings in what I call a "spontaneous deconstructed journal." I work on flat pages and bind them later because it's easier to get rubbings, do debossing, and capture other textures while working flat. When I'm ready, I only bind the pages that I select for the journal.

Travel Journal Pages. 7½ x 21 inches (19 x 53.3 cm). Gold pen, white pen, crayons, pink pen, green pen.

Just Dive In

by Kelcey Loomer

"When I look back at my journals, the descriptions and images of the mundane are what I find most magnificent now."

Kelcey Loomer, 6 x9 ½ inches (15.2 x 24.1 cm). Brown pen, colored pencil, white pen, crayon; collage.

Kelcey Loomer. 6 x9½ inches (15.2 x 24.1 cm). Acrylic, pen, colored pencil.

My best journaling comes from the heart. When I sit down to journal, I often feel intimidated by the blank page staring at me. For some reason, even though my journal is mostly private, I still feel an internal pressure to create something meaningful and good. In these moments, when I find myself being too analytical, I know the best thing to do is simply dive in.

I like to get out a few art supplies and a nice pen and just start to doodle on the blank page. Invariably, the initial doodle seems to free my head from the experience, allowing what is relevant and important to emerge. Sometimes I paint over those awkward first lines, but usually I work them into whatever my page becomes.

When I look back at my journals, the descriptions and images of the mundane are what I find most magnificent now. Once I wrote out the bedtime routine I followed with my eight-month-old baby. When I see that journal page now, I'm brought back in a visceral way to those moments. If I hadn't written it down, I would never remember the details of such a sweet time.

Jane Dalton, *Manipura*, 2003.
8½ x 6 inches (21.6 x 15.2 cm).
Acid-free paper, colored pencils, gel pen.
Photo by Aleia Woolsey.

Middles

There are a number of good ways to proceed after you've begun a page. Often you'll begin the page when you're on site and then do a middle layer later on, either at home that night or even on the plane flying back from a vacation. Sometimes middles become reflections on or responses to the starter that you've done.

WRITING

In a visual journal, writing is often done on a page that is already headed in a particular direction, making the writing a part of the image-making process. In this sense, writing becomes a visual element as well as an encoded message.

By writing, we can name and extend our drawings, tell their significance, raise questions about them, add information, and also slow down the looking process, which makes the reader dwell longer on the page. Even if the writing is in a foreign language or is in some other way indecipherable, the presence of writing always suggests that a message exists, that some meaning could be constructed beyond the more obvious message or meaning of the visual.

Consider what happens when we write: we draw certain conventional shapes that, in combination, become signs that signal the reader to create meaning. Notice that it's the reader who creates the meaning. What the writer does is provide clues and signs that point the reader in a particular direction and toward a certain meaning. The reader brings his or her entire background to the event of making meaning out of the symbols on the page, just as the writer has brought a lifetime of experience to the writing.

SUBTRACTING TEXT

Writing can also be done as a process of elimination. If you begin with a piece of printed text, either from a book that you're altering or from a piece of ephemera that contains text, you can use a pen or brush to gradually eliminate words until all that is left is the message you want to convey. These remaining words will form a piece of found poetry, and you'll be surprised at the results.

The process of eliminating words allows you to sneak up on expression. Instead of laboring to find the perfect way to say something, you simply float along on a sea of words, grabbing those that appeal to you or that seem to advance the meaning you've set out to communicate. You can rewrite the poem as you play around with spacing, letter shapes, and color, working on the poem or short passage until it feels right.

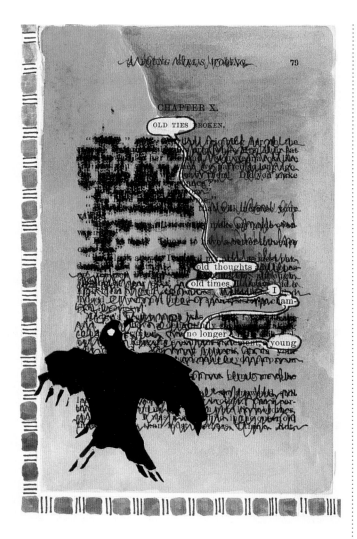

Charlotte Hedlund, 2003. 8 x 6 inches (20.3 x 15.2 cm). Bound journal, book page on bristol board, PVA glue, micro beads, acrylic paint, ink; collaged, glued, and painted. *Photo by artist.*

In the example shown above to the right, I started with a page from an advertisement flyer. I was attracted to it because it was so much a part of the community I was visiting. The oddness of some of the objects for sale especially intrigued me. Using a glue stick, I laminated the flyer to my journal page. Later, after I had selected certain words and phrases, I felt that my abridgment of the page took on a more universal meaning and became a comment about wanting and seeking. I would never have thought of writing this poem had I started with a blank piece of paper.

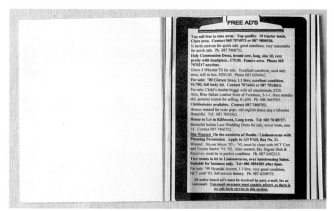

I began by laminating a found sheet of text to the journal page.

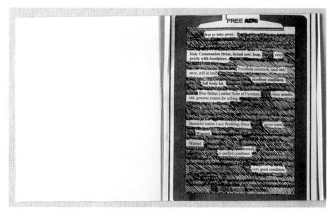

I then selectively marked out words with a black pen.

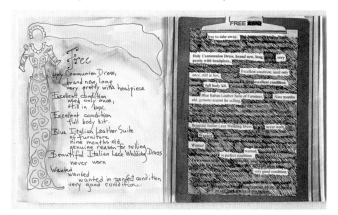

Finally, I copied the resulting poem onto the facing page, added a drawing, and washed on some light watercolors.

Becca Johnson, *The Sad People Parade*, 2004. 11½ x 12 inches (29.2 x 30.5 cm).
Handmade journal, watercolor, photographs, beeswax.

EXTENDING COLLAGE

A low-risk way to start drawing, as well as a way to bring your journal page along, is to start with a small collage and then extend it with your own drawing or painting. Here's how it works: Gather your ephemera. When you're ready to work in your journal, attach one of these gleanings to a page. Now take a pen or colored pencil, or whatever seems good to you at the moment, and extend the object or what's printed on the object. For example, you might start out by tearing a photograph in half and drawing in the other half. You may get wild and invent the second half to better express what you're really thinking or feeling. In the example shown at the top of page 86, I glued pressed flowers to a page with a glue stick and then extended them so that they became actually rather monstrous, a good expression of my overgrown garden after a month away from home during a rainy season. After the drawing was finished, I painted over the pressed flowers with matte-finish polymer varnish to seal them to the page. I did this after and not before drawing because polymer varnish isn't a good surface for watercolors.

Then I used a pen to sketch the wild profusion of pumpkin plants.

I went down to my garden after being away from home for a month during which it had rained every day. The pumpkins had taken over, but deep under the foliage forest I found a few brave pea blossoms. I started by using a glue stick to attach a pressed pea blossom to the page.

Later I added watercolor and made a written entry using a pen. Finally I trimmed the edges of the page to follow the curving shapes of the plants.

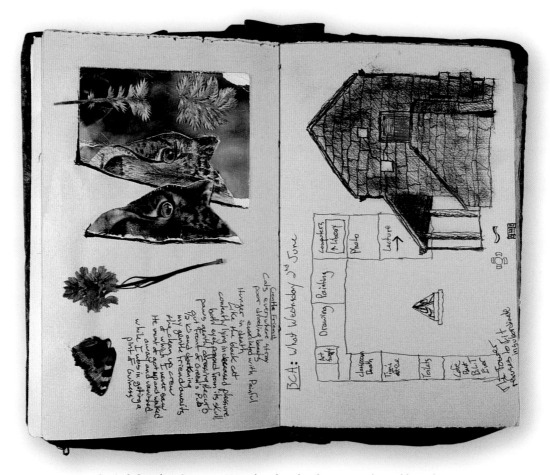

Justin S. Cantalini, *Creatures*, 2004. 8½ x 5½ inches (21.6 x 14 cm). Hand-bound journal, handmade paper, found postcard, ebony pencil, butterfly wings, pressed orchid (Ireland), white craft glue, ink; written, drawn, glued, cut and pasted postcard, and collaged. *Photo by Aleia Woolsey.*

Ivy Smith, *My Irish Bedroom*, 2004. 11¼ x 9 inches (28.6 x 22.9 cm).
Bound journal, liquid acrylics, ink, watercolor. *Photo by Aleia Woolsey.*

DRAWING

Drawing is another obvious way to work at the middle stage. If you don't consider yourself an artist, you may balk at this suggestion. But before deciding to skip this section, consider how we teach drawing in our culture. We don't teach many people how to draw because, too often, we equate drawing with artistic talent rather than seeing it as a basic human skill that is truly within everyone's reach.

If you've ever watched a young child draw, you know that drawing is as much a drive in children as speaking, reading, and writing. However, the reason most children go on to learn how to speak, read, and write fluently is that we teach these skills and expect everyone to learn them. But we don't expect everyone to learn how to draw. As soon as children begin to struggle to draw what they see, we decide they aren't "talented," and we point them in other directions instead of giving them the few instructions needed to get them over the hurdle. The rare children who happen to be precocious in drawing we

brand "artistic" and provide them and only them with instruction. (If we taught only precocious writers how to write, calling them poets or writers from the start, and told everyone else to forget about writing, most adults would be as unable to write as they are to draw.)

The more you draw, the better your drawings will be. To draw accurately you must learn how to see accurately. If you consider drawing to be an exploration, a kind of visual note taking, and if you're more interested in the process than in producing works of art, you will become a very accurate drawer. If you want to speed up the process of learning, check out *Drawing on the Right Side of the Brain* by Betty Edwards. This book, first published many years ago, has become a classic in the field of drawing instruction. I can think of no better tool to help you draw on your own.

Drawing will connect you to what you draw in a way that snapping a photograph never can. For one thing, drawing requires time and focus. It requires that you slow

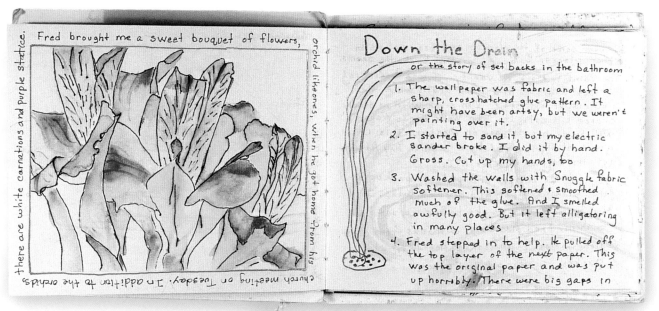

Fred brought me a sweet bouquet of flowers,

orchid like ones, when he got home from his

church meeting on Tuesday. In addition to the orchids

there are white carnations and purple statice.

Down the Drain

or the story of set backs in the bathroom

1. The wallpaper was fabric and left a sharp, cross hatched glue pattern. It might have been artsy, but we weren't painting over it.

2. I started to sand it, but my electric sander broke. I did it by hand. Gross. Cut up my hands, too

3. Washed the walls with Snuggle fabric softener. This softened & smoothed much of the glue. And I smelled awfully good. But it left alligatoring in many places

4. Fred stepped in to help. He pulled off the top layer of the next paper. This was the original paper and was put up horribly. There were big gaps in

Edie Greene, 2003. 4¾ x 11 inches (12 x 27.9 cm). Hand-bound journal, computer paper, pen and ink drawing on sketch paper, watercolor wash, gel pen; glued and illustrated. *Photo by Aleia Woolsey.*

down and spend time with the object— that you analyze the way the parts fit together. In the process, you become aware of the grace and beauty of the most common object and place. You enter into a kind of unmediated communication with the subject of your drawing, and when you look back at your drawings months or years later, the events at the time of the drawing will rush back—you'll remember the weather, the conversation at the next table, how tight your new shoes were, and how good the breeze smelled. When you draw, nothing comes between you and what you are seeing—no camera lens, no interpretive guide book, no docent or tour guide telling you what to look at, no video selecting the aspects of a place for you to focus on. (See Drawing Accurately on page 141.)

Draw in your journal. Draw small things at first— parts of bigger things, patterns on things, outlines of interesting shapes. Start with the general, large form and work to the particular, the details. Take a few measurements—length versus width for example—and sketch in the general proportions. Then fill in smaller and smaller parts. Draw whatever interests you. Draw what confuses you or who confuses you. Draw the same thing every day for a week and see what happens. Draw the same changing thing, such as a plant, every day for a month and see what happens, both to

the plant and to your drawing skills. Draw with a pencil, a pen, a marker, or a crayon. See the effect of different drawing tools on your drawings. Check out artist Danny Gregory's website (www.everydaymatters.net) and study his book, *Everyday Matters* (NY: Princeton Architectural Press, 2003), to find inspiration from someone who has inspired hundreds of people to take up drawing.

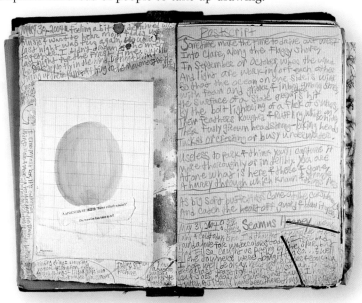

Clare Duplace, 2004. Splattered painted paper with writing and painted sun. *Photo by Aleia Woolsey.*

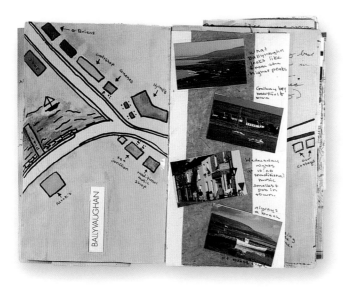

Megan Gulledge, 2004. Watercolor, pen, collage.
Photo by Aleia Woolsey.

MAPPING

We've talked about using maps as a background to set a particular context for whatever else happens on the page. Mapping is also a good process to use to record information during the middle stages. Drawing your own map lets you experience a place in a profoundly different way than looking at someone else's. Once you've mapped a place, whether it's as small as the top of your desk or as large as your neighborhood, you know many things about it that you didn't know before.

Since it's impossible to put everything in a map, the act of mapping is an act of selection, and that implies choices based on your point of view or area of interest. You will have to be selective. What do you want your map to show? Maps can be drawn for the purpose of recording a place. They can also be made to show directions. They can be projections or plans, a way of recording ideas for a new building or a rearranged room, a garden, or a city center.

The maps in your journal don't have to be accurate or to scale unless you want them to be. They might be maps that you make while you're walking somewhere, such as little records of which flowers are blooming this week in the woods near your house. They might be

drawn to scale if they are going to be used as plan drawings to help you decide how much paint or tile to buy for the addition to your house that you're planning.

In the example shown below, two students on a college field course had encountered a small deserted village in rural Ireland. They were interested in discovering the layout of the village—not an easy task, as it was overgrown with trees, bushes, ferns, mosses, and vines. In order to map it, they walked around the perimeter of the village several times, pacing off the various areas. Once they had a rough outline, they were able to begin to make sense of the low stone walls, which were all that were left of the houses and stables. They discovered what seemed to be a central green or square, the remains of a surrounding wall, and a number of small structures. They also discovered the remains of trees and plantings that gave clues as to how the land was perhaps once used. When they compared the maps they had made separately, they were pleased to note many concurrences and points of agreement. They learned much more about the village than they would have had they simply snapped a few photographs and moved on to something else.

Matt Rogers, *Ireland Journal Page*, 2004. 5 x 5½ inches (12.7 x 14 cm). Hand-bound journal, ink. *Photo by Aleia Woolsey*.

Figure 1   *Figure 2*   *Figure 3*

PAINTING

Sketchbook or journal painting can be thought of as drawing in color. If you're a little insecure about getting the proportions right, start out by using a pencil to measure (see Drawing Accurately on page 141) and then lightly sketch the overall dimensions of the object or scene you want to paint. Next, put away the pencil. Then follow these two easily mastered practices to get you on the road to being comfortable with drawing in watercolor. First, know that if you paint over wet paint, your outlines will be fuzzy and diffused. If you want crisp definition, you must wait for the paint to dry completely before painting over it. Secondly, always start with the general shape and the lightest color and move to the particular details and the darkest shade.

Let's see what this looks like in action. Let's say I want to paint a small building that I can see across a field. Quickly I measure to find the relationship of its height to its width. I use a pencil to lightly sketch in a rectangle to reflect that relationship. I might also make a few other marks to indicate where the door is in relation to the chimney, how high the roof is relative to the height of the wall from ground to roof bottom, etc. Next, I mix up a light color that seems to underlie all the colors of the building, here a pale yellow. I brush a diluted coat of this watercolor all over the rectangles and roofs (see figure 1),

and let it dry until the paper is no longer cool or damp to the touch. This will take a few minutes. While I'm waiting for the paint to dry, I analyze the colors to determine the next darkest color that is on the building. I mix up that color and paint it all over the building except in those places where I need the pale yellow to show (see figure 2). While that coat is drying, I determine the next darkest color, and so on until I have painted the smallest, darkest details and the building is complete (see figure 3).

Layered painting such as this can be done with any subject matter. Over time you'll grow more and more skillful in mixing colors and in deciding exactly where to place colors and where to leave the underlying color showing through. Note that you won't use your darkest colors until the very end, and then only in the few places where the subject is truly that dark.

There are many books to help you learn watercolor painting on your own. Most important, however, is practice. As with drawing, painting puts you in direct contact with the subject. The process slows you down and makes you pause, reflect, focus, truly look, and reconsider the mental stories you tell about what you think you see. (See Watercolors on page 27 to 28 to learn more about paint mixing and handling.)

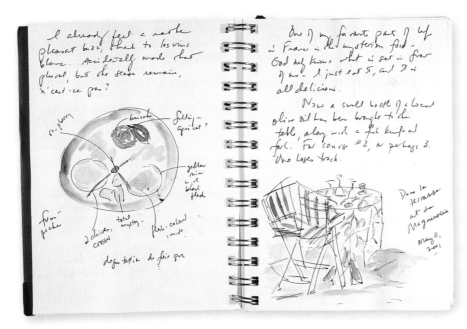

Faith McLellan,
In Provence, 2000.
7½ x 5½ inches
(19 x 14 cm). Bound journal,
ink, watercolor; painted and
written. *Photo by artist.*

RELIEF PRINTS AND RUBBINGS

Relief prints and rubbings both make use of the same principle: a relief or design that's raised above a flat surface prints, whereas the recessed background doesn't. In making relief prints, you apply paint or ink to the relief areas of the printing block only, and then transfer that to a piece of paper by means of pressure. In a rubbing, the relief areas provide resistance when you rub the whole area with a crayon or pencil, yielding a print of the relief area.

The world is filled with relief textures, and it's easy to do rubbings, even in a bound journal. Keep your eyes open for textures, beginning with the ever-popular tombstones and moving onto water main and sewer covers, embossed plaques and labels, tree bark, textured wallpaper, pressed plant parts, seashells, pottery shards, coins, etc. To do a rubbing, press the page or piece of paper flat against the surface,

attaching it with small pieces of masking or drafting tape to keep it from moving around. Then use the broad side of a piece of crayon, graphite stick, or even the side of a pencil point, and gently stroke over all the area. Gradually the relief areas begin to show up and the recessed areas remain either uncolored or become only lightly colored. If your journal paper is too thick to do a good rubbing, or if the binding makes it too awkward to carry out the process, do your rubbings on separate, thinner paper and laminate or tip them into the journal afterwards.

A relief print is made from a piece of wood, linoleum, or eraser-like material on which the design area stands up from the rest of the surface. A fingerprint is a simple example of a relief print because it's the ink attaching itself to the ridges of our fingers that makes the print possible. You can make your own small

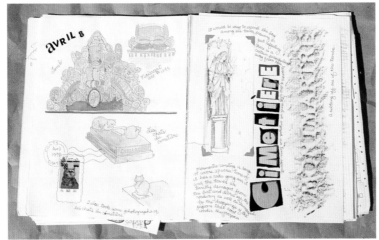

Judy Rinks, *Paris Travel Journal*, 1998. 8½ x 11 inches (21.6 x 27.9 cm).
Bound journal, graphite stick, watercolor, ink, paper scraps, postage stamp,
pencils; drawn, painted, rubbed, and glued. *Photo by artist.*

Gwen Diehn, *Untitled*, 2004.
6 x 7 inches (15.2 x 17.8 cm). Journal
made with an old book cover, handmade paper,
gouache, eraser print, watercolor, pen.

relief printing blocks, or stamps, using rubber or plastic erasers, corks, or even foam earplugs. You might try carving an alphabet or numerals or make stamps of motifs or designs from the environment about which you are writing and drawing.

To make a stamp, use a black pen to draw the shape onto a cork or eraser or piece of rubber stamp-carving material. Remember that the print will be a reverse of the stamp, so be sure to draw letters and numerals in reverse. Then use linoleum carving tools or a razor knife to cut away the background, leaving the design area raised, or "in relief." Corks may need to be lightly sanded before carving or have a thin slice removed if they have bumpy ends. You can carve the rounded sides of a cork as well as its flat ends. If you don't generate sufficient used corks from your own bottles, you can buy corks from hardware stores.

Buy stamp pads from craft supply stores—keep in mind that while dye-based inks dry faster than pigment-based inks, they will bleed through some papers. The pigment inks tend to be more opaque and more intense in color. The people in the craft supply store will usually be happy to explain the differences among all the myriad kinds of stamp pads they sell.

Stamped prints can be used alone, in borders, and even to design entire backgrounds or page surfaces. Relief prints are a low-tech process and often seem to have a somewhat old-fashioned look. They're frequently used to evoke nostalgia, and, conversely, they are often used ironically. They are often very effective when juxtaposed with more high-tech materials, such as crisp black pen lettering. They are also very useful for carrying a recurring motif throughout a book.

A collection of homemade stamps carved from test-tube stoppers.

Emblem Books

Those of us who enjoy drawing in our journals (and writing in our sketchbooks) are part of a very long tradition. From early in the history of Western art, people have been trying to combine writing and pictures on the same sheet of parchment or paper, and the two systems of meaning-filled marks have existed in uneasy relationship to one another. Either the meaning of the page is conveyed mainly by the text, with the illustrations providing some enjoyable but nonessential embellishment, or the illustration is the most important element, with the text merely labeling or identifying it. Rarely have text and visuals formed a seamless and balanced whole. In fact, some contemporary linguists tell us that the mental processes needed to decode text are different from those that we use to make sense of images, which perhaps accounts for the sense of shifting gears that we often experience as we move between reading text and looking at images.

An early example of an attempt to combine text and image in an equal relationship is the 16th-and 17th-century emblem book. Emblems were combinations of a picture (either a woodcut or an engraving) and a motto, which served as a title and a short verse or prose passage. By reading the verse and viewing the image, the reader was able to interpret a moral meaning or lesson. Emblem books, which were collections of emblems, were a popular means of education throughout Europe at that time.

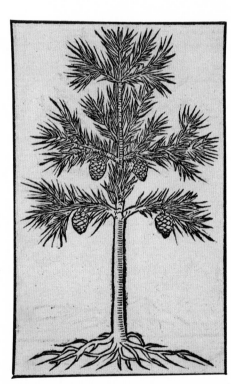

From left: "Le Pin" and "L'Orengier" from *Alciato/Aneau Les Emblems*, 1549. *Courtesy of Glasgow University Library.*

"The pine has no shoots from its roots; it is the sign of a man who dies without children."

"Oranges are of Venus, a sign of love, for the fruit of love is bittersweet."

Emblem 25, "Envy Accompanies Love", from Philip Ayer's *Emblemata Amatoria, Emblemes d'amour en quatre langue (Latin, Italian, French and Dutch).* Courtesy of Penn State University Libraries, Special Collections.

What sets the emblem book apart from other illustrated books is the density of symbolism in the images. Some scholars consider them to be in part an attempt to create and define a pictographic language, something like ancient Egyptian hieroglyphics. In the world of medieval Europe, every plant, animal, insect, celestial body, and human figure was endowed with meaning that was beyond the literal meaning of the object. The secondary meanings were usually derived from the teachings and beliefs of the Christian church. A lily, for example, was not simply a sweet-smelling white flower, but was universally recognized as the embodiment of the attribute of purity. If a person appeared in a scene with a lily in her arms, the viewer understood the intention of the scene. The crescent moon in the sky, a scallop shell underfoot, or a lion and a lamb reclining on a distant rock promontory, all held symbolic meaning beyond the literal.

The reader of the emblem book read all of the symbols embedded in the picture as well as the literal meaning of the picture. So rich and many-layered were these images that the textual elements on the pages simply added another dimension, rather than provided a definition or explanation of the images. Many people couldn't read the text and depended completely on their knowledge of iconography or the meaning of the symbols to "read" the images. For them, the text was actually more decorative than meaning-filled.

The combination of deeply symbolic images and text in emblem books was inspired indirectly by Egyptian hieroglyphics. Since hieroglyphics were not decoded until the 19th century, they remained mysterious and indecipherable images to people during the Medieval and Renaissance periods.

No Inward Griefe, *nor outward* Smart,
Can overcome a Patient-Heart.

28

A DVRIA VICTRIX PATIENTIA

ILLVSTR. XXVIII. Book. I.

Some *Trees*, when Men oppreſſe their Aged Heads,
(With waighty Stones) they fructifie the more;
And, when upon ſome *Herbs*, the *Gard'ner* treads,
They thrive and proſper, better then before:
  So, when the Kings of *Ægypt* did oppreſſe
The Sonnes of *Iacob*, through their Tyrannies;
Their Numbers, every day, did more encreaſe,
Till they grew greater then their Enemies.
So, when the *Iewes* and *Gentiles*, joyn'd their Powre
The *Lord*, and his *Annoynted*, to withſtand;
(With raging *Furie*, lab'ring to devoure
And roote the *Goſpel*, out of ev'ry Land)
The more they rag'd, conſpired, and envy'd,
The more they ſlander'd, ſcorn'd, and murthered;
The more, the *Faithfull*, ſtill, were multiply'd:
And, ſtill, the further, their *Profeſſion* ſpred.
Yea, ſo it ſpred, that quite it overthrew
Ev'n *Tyranny* it ſelfe; that, at the laſt,
The *Patience of the Saints*, moſt pow'rfull grew,
And *Perſecutions* force, to ground was caſt.
  The ſelfe-ſame Pow'r, true *Patience*, yet retaines,
And (though a thouſand *Sufferings* wound the ſame)
She ſtill hath *Hope* enough to eaſe her paynes;
That *Hope*, which keepeth off, all *Feare* and *Shame*:
For, 'tis not *Hunger*, *Cold*, nor *Fire*, nor *Steele*,
Nor all the *Scornes* or *Slanders*, we can heare,
Nor any *Torment*, which our *Fleſh* can feele,
That conquers us; but, our owne *Trayt'rous Feare*.
  Where, *Honeſt Mindes*, and *Patient* Hearts, are Mates;
They grow victorious, in their *Hardeſt-Fates*.

By

In 1419, a monk discovered a manuscript from the fifth century. This manuscript was known as the "Hieroglyphica" of Horus Apollo and was found on the Greek island of Andros. When it was first discovered, it was believed to be a Greek translation of an Egyptian work that explained the secret meanings of Egyptian hieroglyphics. Although the manuscript later proved to be false, at the time of its discovery it was enormously influential and was one of the factors that led to the Renaissance idea that densely symbolic images could carry complex and subtle meanings.

Emblem books were printed throughout Europe in at least a dozen different languages from 1531 until around 1700. Many of them exist today in museums and rare book collections. They provide us with an unparalleled view of the daily life, ideas, morals, and art of the 16th and 17th centuries in Europe.

Illustration XXVIII, "No inward Griefe, Nor Outward Smart Can Overcome a Patient Heart," from George Wither's *A Collection of Emblemes, Ancient and Moderne, Quickened with Metricall Illustrations, Both Morall and Divine: And Disposed into Lotteries, that Instruction, and Good Counsell, May Bee Furthered By an Honest and Pleasant Recreation*, 1635. Courtesy of Penn State University Libraries, Special Collections.

Toppings

Going back to edit and rework your journal allows you the opportunity to mine a repository of ideas. Even a journal that was originally intended to be a private record of daily happenings and emotions can provide information and images that become the seeds of future artwork and writing. You'll also want to go back sometimes and finish some things that you were unable to complete on site. Look for unfinished drawings, outlines and lists that seem to need expansion, questions that you've posed, and drawings and paintings that could use written explanation.

Especially seek out pages that seem hopeless, pages that you wish you had never written, failed drawings, pathetic attempts at mapping, or boring collages. These bad pages make the best grist for your mill. It's easier to take risks and try out new processes and approaches with them because there's nothing to lose—even if you just make more of a mess. Toppings are ideas for going back—for enhancing, expanding, finishing, erasing, morphing, even completely obliterating the images and information you've gathered.

Gwen Diehn. Watercolor, gouache, fluid acrylic, and pen on handmade paper. *Photo by Aleia Woolsey.*

Nancy Pobanz, 2002. 9⅞ x 15¹¹⁄₁₆ inches (25.1 x 39.8 cm). Coptic bound journal, handmade paper, fabric, black and maroon ink, soil pigment, acrylic matte medium, magazine clipping; hand written, drawn, painted, collaged, and glued. *Photo by Lightworks Photography.*

WRITING

It's a good idea to bring your journal up to date as frequently as possible. Writing is often the first and easiest way to expand the information in a drawing or map. Even if you took notes on site while making the drawing, take time to review and add to them as soon as you get home so you don't forget important details and ideas. If you didn't leave a space for your writing when you made your painting or drawing, you can write right on top of it. Or, try making your writing part of the design by using the writing for a border around the page or by placing it in a box within the image. When using poured or pre-painted paper, the paper itself will often suggest places where you can tuck your writing.

This was a page that already had poured fluid acrylics on it.

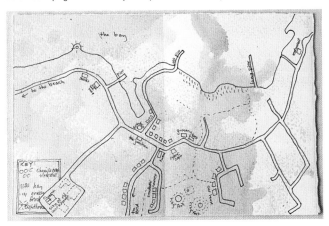

I drew a map and wrote some captions.

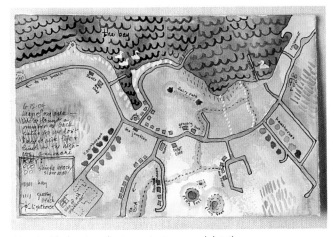

Next I added watercolor tones, textures, and details.

WATERCOLOR WASHES

Another easy and natural topping, one that will add color to your pages, is to add a watercolor wash to a drawing or a map. If you've used a waterproof pen, the wash will have no effect on the lines of your drawing. If you've used a pen that will run when it has a wash put over it, use colored pencils to add color. Or, let the running of the drawing ink be a part of the design. Use color behind writing and in the spaces behind and around small drawings. Alternatively, you might use a strip of colored boxes at the bottom or side of a pen drawing to show the colors associated with the drawing or place.

You can also use watercolor washes to organize a cluttered page. Use different colors to create columns, a grid, or abstract shapes that will put emphasis on parts of the page and lower the intensity of others.

ELIMINATING WORK

Sometimes you just want to get rid of what you've done. Gouache, depending on whether or not you dilute it, will completely or partially obliterate what you've done. Even if you paint just a light coat of gouache over some writing or drawing, the gouache will lighten your work and will reduce the contrast between the paper and the ink or paint so that you can overpaint or overwrite clearly (see Gouache on page 32).

Another way to get rid of something is to use a pen to draw fine lines of texture over the area you want to obscure. You can weave the words you don't want to see into a mesh of lines that can't be read. As a last resort you can always cut the page out and turn it into a stub to which you can attach another sheet of paper or an envelope.

SEPARATING LAYERS

Sometimes a page, especially in a layered journal, has good information but seems cluttered and full of visual noise. A remedy for this problem is to separate layers. One way to do this is to raise elements so that they seem to float above the surface of the page. You can do this easily by painting a shadow under the element. Another similar layer separator is to first box in drawings and then add shadows under the boxes. When you write, let

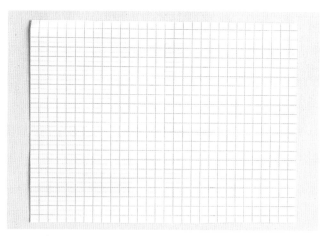

Visiting the grave of writer Flannery O'Conner, I wanted to do a journal entry about her and about that hot July day spent with my family in Milledgeville, Georgia. I started with a sheet of grid paper that was already bound into the journal.

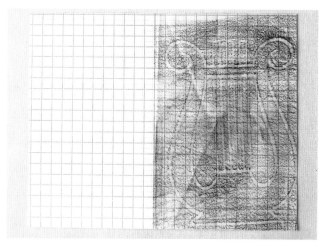

I did a gravestone rubbing using a dark blue crayon furnished by my niece, Grace.

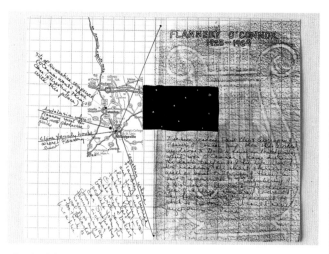

I finished the page by drawing and annotating the map, writing a journal entry around the rubbing, and painting a dark blue night sky "hole" in the page with Payne's gray acrylic.

it go right up to the edge of the box, stop, and continue on the other side. This gives the appearance of a line of text that travels beneath the box (see page 131).

Another way to separate out layers is to use metallics or warm tones to add light to a page. Metallic and warm-colored areas seem to come forward visually. If you think a collage or other visual will appear cluttered if you write over it with a black pen, consider using a gold or silver pen. Try painting a metallic or golden-yellow background behind a visual. Using a metallic pen to emphasize an initial letter or to box in a visual will draw the eye to that spot.

Besides raising layers you can also lower them. A wash of a cool color, such as a blue-gray, will make an area appear to sink a little below the level of the rest of the page. To punch a deep "hole" in a page, draw a box or other shape where you want the hole to be and fill it with a very dark color (you can overwrite with silver or white ink). Alternatively, draw a box around an element and paint a very dark background around the drawing in the box.

Of course, you can literally cut holes in the pages to link one to another. This process takes some advanced planning—you don't want to cut a hole that will remove something from the other side of the page. This technique is an interesting way to build continuity between pages. A related idea is to trim the edges of one page so that material on the next page is visible.

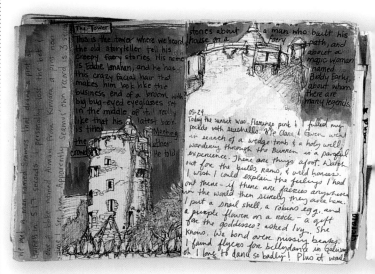

Miriam McNamara, *Journal Page*, 2004. Bound journal, ink pen, colored pencil, acrylic paint. *Photo by Aleia Woolsey.*

Journaling with Children

JULY 6, 2004

ANTS AND BABIEZ

HAVE HOME?

Jacob Diehn, *2004*. 6 x 10 inches (15.2 x 25.4 cm). Watercolor paper, watercolor, and pen. *Photo by Sarah Bourne.*

When my eldest son was in kindergarten, he came home from school one day with a well-worn little book that was made out of red construction paper, stapled along one edge, and embellished with a crayon drawing that included tentacles, many eyes, and six large circles. The book was not an object of great beauty, but it was clear from its condition that it was well used. He plopped it down on the kitchen table and asked me to tell him the date. I did, and he proceeded to slowly print "March 13" at the top of an empty page.

He explained to me that this was his journal, and that he had not finished working in it that day and needed to do it at home. He then began to draw, explaining what was going on in his picture as he worked. When he finished, he gave the book to me and asked me to write down the story he was going to tell me about his drawing. He began to dictate: "This is my truck that I lost but now I found it this morning." After I wrote the words, he took the book back and copied each word beneath the words I had written.

Because children love to draw and tell stories, making illustrated journals comes naturally to them. All it takes is an interested adult or older child. After the child draws an event of the day, have him or her tell you about it and write down the words. One or two sentences are enough. If the child is learning to write, leave space for him or her to copy the words underneath. This is a great way to help a child to read. Children are extremely motivated to read back the words they have "written," and before long they'll be able to write on their own without needing to dictate or copy the words.

Travel journals are great fun for children and their families. These can be either individual journals or group journals with entries added by everyone in the traveling group. I remember a journal that one of my sons kept during a long car trip. The first few pages consisted of lines that looked like the tracings of a seismograph. When asked about these strange lines, he explained that he had rested his pencil lightly on the page and let the motion of the car draw the line while the car was moving, and every time we hit a bump the line got wiggly. His lines were a record of the movement of the car during certain segments of the trip. Another son kept a record of out-of-state license plates during a long drive across country.

My neighbor and his 12-year-old son took a road trip from the east coast out to California. Both father and son kept illustrated journals to record the trip—the waves they surfed, the beaches visited, memorable meals, unbelievable sights. Because the son was old enough to write reflectively as well as draw and paint, the journal contained reflections about the experience as well as a narrative of events.

My five-year-old grandson and I have journals that we work in together on our regular Sunday morning outings. Our usual practice is to go to breakfast at our favorite grocery store/café, and paint and write in our journals while we sit at the table. Sometimes we draw and write our plans for the rest of the morning. Other times we record what we see going on around us in the café. Sometimes we wait and work in our journals while at the park or at the lake near his house. In the example shown, Jacob drew an ant house based on our observations of an anthill in a sidewalk crack in his front walkway. We had watched it for a while before setting off, and when we started working in our journals, he was still interested in that ant colony. He began by drawing, and then he asked me how to spell the words as he printed them on the page.

Another time, Jacob and I worked together on a page in my travel journal while we were on vacation together. I had drawn a map as the basis of the page, and he added his own map to the center of my map. We added watercolor to the page together (see page 11).

Mary Ann Moss, 2004. 8 x 6 inches (20.3 x 15.2 cm). Handmade journal, gesso, acrylic paint, ink, watercolor markers, ephemera, magazine and newspaper scraps; collage and illustrated. *Photo by artist.*

COLLAGE AS A LINK

A final idea for a topper is to use collage to link elements or to create a focal point. Collage can be used as a starter or middle for a page, and it can also be used as a final element, the one that calls attention to itself. If the collage is a pressed flower or leaf, a piece of newspaper, or any other fragile element, it's a good idea to coat it with a layer of polymer varnish in order to seal it from the air and to protect it from the friction of page turning. Any element sealed this way will last for years on a page. If you use matte-finish varnish, you will not be able to see the varnish once it is dry.

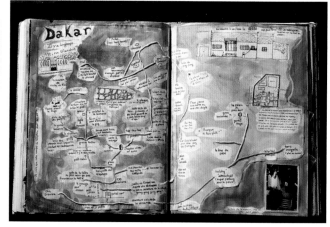

Aude Iung-Lancrey, *Memory Map*, 2004. 17 x 11 inches (43.2 x 27.9 cm). Bound journal, matte medium, acrylic paint, yarn, ink, photograph; glued and collaged. *Photo by David Swift.*

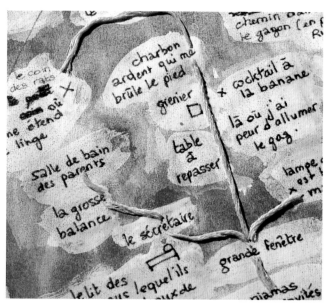

Detail, Aude Iung-Lancrey, *Memory Map.*

Pamela Lyle Westhaver, *Salt Spring 2000*, 2000. Assorted papers, memorabilia, surface decorations, watercolor pencils, pencil, and crayon. *Photo by artist.*

Collaborations and Group Journaling

Traci Bunkers, *The Scales Have Tipped to Happiness (from An Ongoing Conversation with Juliana Coles)*, 2004. 10 x 20 inches (25.4 x 50.8 cm) open. Children's book, pinhole Polaroid photos, acrylic paints, postage stamps, paper scraps, transparency, ink, masking tape, labels, brads; collaged, painted, stamped, glued. *Photo by The Image Works, Inc.*

Traci Bunkers and Julianna Coles kept this journal as a prolonged conversation, mailing it back and forth for many months.

Keeping a group journal during a family vacation can be a means of enlarging everybody's experience. When people look at and read each other's entries, they see things they may have missed on their own. Those who have never kept an illustrated journal quickly learn from those with more experience. A good idea is to keep the group journal in a place where everyone can have easy access to it—the living room of the rental cottage or on the dresser in the hotel room. If that's not practical, people can take turns carrying the journal. Each person can have the journal for a day and then pass it on to the next person. At the end of the vacation, you can make copies of the journal for everyone in the group, including some blank pages at the back for people to add individual reflections on the trip as well as photographs—a very nice memento of the trip.

Pauses

As we've seen in the section How Does Your Journal See the World?, some people like a more spare, quiet way of working. If you're the keeper of a wabi-sabi journal or a naturalist's journal, you'll probably be more interested in simplicity than in the complexity that results from working in many stages or layers. For you, uncluttered, minimalist pages are more appealing, and the kind of pages that I am calling "pauses" may form the majority of the pages in your journal.

Even if the majority of the pages in your journal are complex and many-layered, there's nothing wrong with occasional single-layer pages, pages that signify a pause or just a quiet period. All of our days are not equally frantic, so consider including simple, uncomplicated, unlayered pages when the day seems to warrant them.

Today's visual journal sometimes seems to be on the forefront of a new form: the journal as artwork. In an interview with Chris Gage (mediabistro.com, June 8, 2004), journal-keeper and illustrator Danny Gregory says, "I create my art in journals. I document what goes on around me constantly."

If you're thinking of your journal as artwork in the form of a book, an art piece that will someday be leafed through and looked at by other people, then you might want to think in terms of overall design of the journal as well as that of the individual pages. Even though the genre of the journal may be less formal and consciously

Kelcey Loomer, *First Page*, 2003. 9¼ x 6¼ inches (23.5 x 15.9 cm). Journal, cutout from a children's encyclopedia, milkweed seeds, pen. *Photo by Aleia Woolsey.*

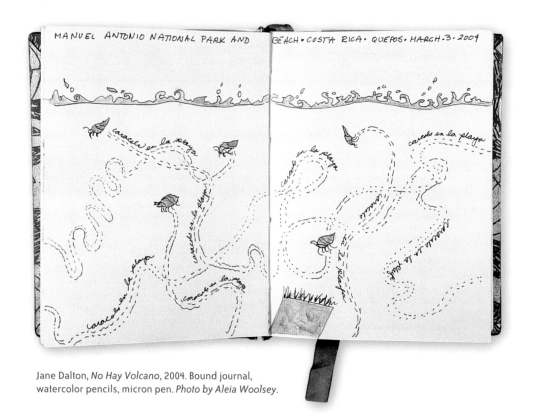

Jane Dalton, *No Hay Volcano*, 2004. Bound journal, watercolor pencils, micron pen. *Photo by Aleia Woolsey.*

designed than that of other artists' books, it's still good to provide some rhythm to the overall work by putting in some occasional pauses in the form of minimally-worked pages. Such pauses are the equivalent of rests in music.

Simple pages can slow down the rhythm of the book, invite introspection, and provide a rest. Even if you don't think of your journal as book art and never plan to show it to anyone else, as the writer/artist you need some rest, too. Instead of skipping those days when you're too busy to spend much time on the journal, make a plain page. A particular day might need only a few lines scrawled across a light blue ground or a small drawing perfectly centered and unembellished. Also consider blanks, pure pattern pages, text-only pages, single small images, and other uncomplicated pause pages.

Remember, the object isn't to turn your journal into something as bulky as a roofing-tile sample book. Paper is a relatively light and fragile support. A book is generally a handheld object, and as such it's improved by being comfortable to hold and pleasant to manipulate. Journals are handled much more than most other books, so these principles especially hold true for them.

My Journal: The Story of Me

by Ann Turkle

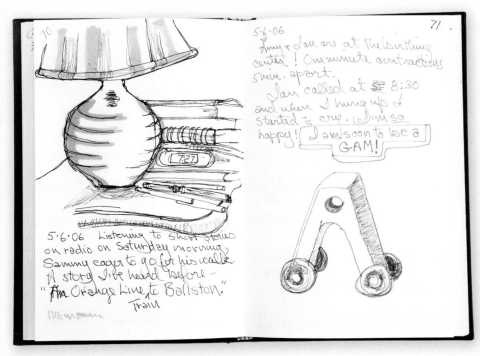

8 x 11 inches (20.3 x 27.9 cm). Colored pens, markers.

"They're my intellectual compost heap, my seedbed, a delight and a wonder."

My journals are imperfect, messy, fragmented. They're also absolutely lived-in, for when I look back through them, I find my life—which, in retrospect, is pretty cool. If I didn't keep my journals, I couldn't see my story.

I tell my students that their journals can be lifesavers. Meaning, that if their journals become a record of generous attention paid to the immediate moment, they'll preserve their lives on paper, and those lives will be available to them as long as they hang on to the journal.

When I draw in my journal, I blow it wide open. When I look back through a journal, I first browse for the drawings, and my appetite for image is satisfied no matter how shabby the drawing may be.

One of my favorite journal pages is the sketch of the two skinny bookcases that sit in the corner of my bedroom and hold my past journals. These journals—the story of me, occasionally illustrated—are juicy reading. They're my intellectual compost heap, my seedbed, a delight and a wonder. If I hold on tight to a journal, I can almost feel the breath in it, the heartbeat.

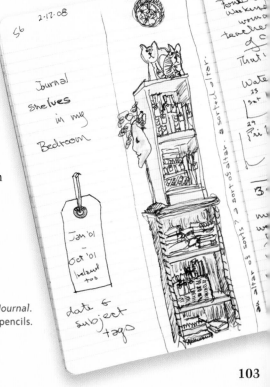

Thailand and Cambodia Journal.
8¼ x 10¼ inches (21 x 26 cm). Pen, colored pencils.

Wallowing in the World

by Linda Chaves

"*Through journaling, I've found an inner balance and rediscovered the world.*"

Page from Algarve, Portugal Travel Journal. Spiral-bound journal, 10¾ x 6¾ inches (27.3 x 17.2 cm). Spray paints, fluid acrylics, gesso, charcoal, pastels, glue stick, white pen, pen 0.5. *Photo by artist.*

Page from India Travel Journal. 8 x 5 inches (20.3 x 12.7 cm). Pigment pens 0.1, 0.5, watercolor pencils. *Photo by artist.*

A couple of years ago, I would have described myself as purely practical, not artistic at all. However, two events changed everything—the death of my dear partner and retirement after 30 years of teaching. Living in sunny Portugal, the inspiration was already in place, so I read an article, bought a large journal, and life was transformed.

Through journaling, I've found an inner balance and rediscovered the world. I've traveled round the globe, journal in hand, and drawn and photographed elephants, temples, mountains, and skyscrapers. Now I have the means to observe, synthesize, and wallow in the world, plus a way to remember these experiences for life.

My favorite pages incorporate color and quirky comments. I'm still no artist. But the process is such fun! Journaling has lifted me out of my sadness and given me a new slant on how to appreciate every moment of every day.

Layouts

Now that you've gathered materials, customized your blank book, and prepared the pages, you can begin to focus on filling the pages with your thoughts and reflections, drawings, photographs, mementos, scraps, and whatever else you wish. But where do you start, and how do you arrange everything? Planning the layout of your page in advance will help you to make the most of the space you have available, and help you to achieve an effective and appealing visual presentation. You may even find that it helps you to organize your thoughts and express yourself in ways you hadn't even considered.

In this section of the book, we'll review different layout alternatives and discuss the characteristics of each. You'll learn how using one layout over another can help give a page a different feel—make it seem bigger, provide a sense of order, or complement the emotional nature of a written entry. You'll see examples of each kind of layout so you can review how different journalers have applied a variety of layouts to their own material.

The layout of a page is the foundation of its design. More specifically, layout refers to the proportioning and balancing of elements (text, illustrations, headlines, or titles, etc.), that give a page a certain unity and help it to achieve its purpose. Graphic designers work very intentionally with layout; journalers rarely consider it. Most often, layout is done intuitively, or the journaler or scrapbook maker falls into a habit of repeating the same layout on many pages in a book. But attention to layout can help you express an idea or emotion just as it helps graphic designers sell products or tell stories. Even though a prepared page is not as intimidating as a completely blank one, you still have to decide how to take the next step. Awareness of layout possibilities can make the first steps of page building easier. Sometimes you can unstick a debilitating creative block simply by experimenting with a different layout.

The materials used in a book must have certain characteristics in order to yield good and lasting results. When it comes to page layout, the only limitation is your imagination. Let the following ideas get you started; then combine and customize these ideas as you go along. Before you know it, you will be returning each day to a rich, many-layered book that will continue to grow and inspire you each time you open it.

Kelcey Loomer, 2000. Collage, pen and ink.
Photo by Elyse Weingarten.

Full-Page Designs

Using a solid block of text or a drawing or painting that fills a page is a popular strategy used by journalers and sketchbook artists. But also consider some variations within the full-page design, such as creating borders.

Andrea Peterson, *Albania Sketchbook*, 1992. Tempera, chalk, and pencil. *Photo by artist.*

BLEEDS

A design that comes to the edges of a page is called a *bleed*. A bleed can make text, as well as visual material, seem to be part of a bigger whole, a bigger scene. It can give a sense of openness to the content and make it seem to grow beyond the page.

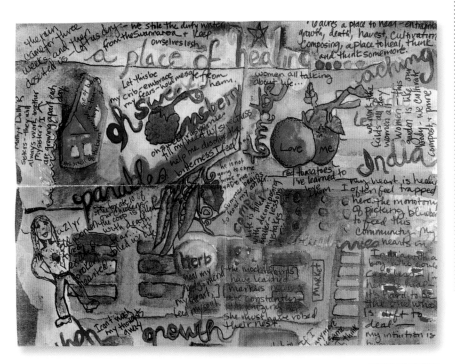

Christine Toriello, 2000. Collage, pen and ink. *Photo by Elyse Weingarten.*

Colleen Stanton, 2000.
Pen over watercolor.
Photo by Elyse Weingarten.

BORDERS

An edge, either plain or decorated, frames a page of text or illustration and in some ways confines the material on the page. It can make each page seem like a separate entity. A decorated border is especially good at highlighting or emphasizing the material within it. A plain border can invite editorial comments and later additions.

Blair Gulledge, 2000. Watercolor and pen. *Photo by Elyse Weingarten.*

Kelcey Loomer, 2000. Collage, pen, watercolor.
Photo by Elyse Weingarten.

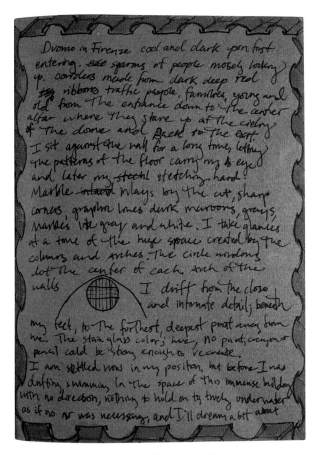

Laura Carter, 2000. Pen, colored pencil on blue paper.
Photo by Elyse Weingarten.

Kelcey Loomer, 2000. Watercolor, pen. *Photo by Elyse Weingarten.*

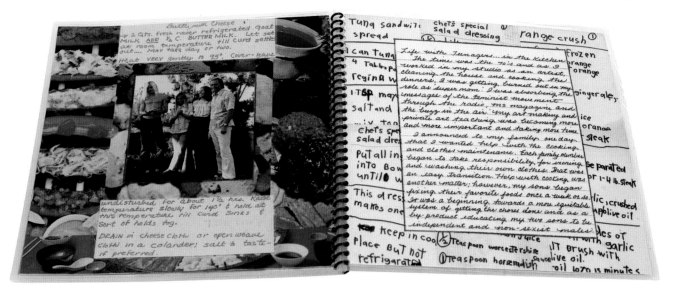

Mary Ellen Long, *In the Kitchen*, 2000. Collage and pen. *Photo by artist.*

Escaping from Flatland

Edward Tufte has spent much of his life studying and teaching the art and science of information design, the visual presentation of information. He has written, designed, and published several award-winning books on the subject, two of which are of particular interest to visual-verbal journal keepers: *Visual Explanations* (1997, Graphics Press) and *Envisioning Information* (1990, Graphics Press).

According to Tufte, the main challenge of information design is to represent the multidimensional visual world of experience and measurement on the two-dimensional, flat surface of a piece of paper, which he calls "Flatland." His books are elegant examples of how to do just that, and in them he includes many analyses of various attempts to present information in visual form. After years of analyzing visuals that clarify and those that obscure, he has developed several strategies for information design that can help us escape from Flatland. Three of these seem particularly appropriate for journalers.

One of Tufte's basic principles of good information design is based on an old maxim known as Occam's Razor: "What can be done with fewer is done in vain with more." Tufte's application of Occam's Razor is what he calls *the strategy of the smallest effective difference*: Make all visual distinctions as subtle as possible, but still clear and effective. This strategy is easy to understand in the case of grids. Let's imagine that you want to use a grid to present some information you've gathered about several different kinds of birds that you've seen at your bird feeder over several months. You could draw a heavy, dark grid and place the information in the boxes using bright red pen. The result would be filled with what Tufte calls visual static. The jarring grid lines would compete loudly with the information contained within them, resulting in an unpleasant, overly bright display.

The strategy of smallest effective difference suggests that when you prepare pages, you use the lightest and subtlest tones (unless in a particular case you know that you want the page to be brighter and more forceful than usual). Light underlayers are easier to distinguish from whatever is placed on top of them, leaving the possibility of more range in the kinds of marks that you make on each prepared page.

Edward Tufte, *Colored T-Shirts*, from his book *Envisioning Information* (Graphics Press, 1990).

Following the strategy of smallest effective difference, you would draw the grid with pale lines, just dark enough to be distinguished from the paper tone. Information could be added to this subtle grid in fine, crisp, black print that would be easily distinguished from the grid lines. The result would be easier to read and more elegant and pleasing to look at. In the example shown here (see photo, opposite page), the white space between the elements functions perfectly as an implied grid.

A second Tufte strategy is to use what he calls *small multiples*. In a design using small multiples, the same design structure is repeated for all the images. Small multiples can be arranged side by side and one on top of the other on the same page, allowing the viewer to see all at once and make comparisons more easily than if the designs were on separate pages. In Tufte's *T-Shirts* (see photo, opposite page), the t-shirts and vests are all identical in size and shape. The constancy in design allows the viewer to focus easily on the changing element, in this case the color combinations.

You might use the strategy of small multiples if you are comparing the colors of olives in a marketplace or if you are showing the variation in butterflies that have visited your garden this week. Tufte says that the strategy of small multiples gets to the heart of visual reasoning in that it helps us see, distinguish, and choose.

A third strategy that Tufte discusses is what he calls *visual confections*. A visual confection is an arrangement, a gathering of many different visual events. Whereas an illustration is similar in content to a snapshot (it shows what is happening at a particular time in a single narrative or story), a confection brings together elements from several different story lines, narratives, or times and puts them in one place at the same time, even though these elements (or people or events) have not been and couldn't logically be together in one place at the same time. A confection differs from a chart, diagram, or map in that it does not place the people, events, or objects into conventional formats.

There are two strategies for assembling confections: One is the imaginary scene, often filled with symbolic objects or people. The other is compartments, in which boxes or bubbles or sometimes just space separate the elements. Many confections use both strategies simultaneously, with compartments holding elements in a scene that unifies the various compartments.

Tufte's books are filled with wonderful reflections on the visual representation of information. You can find out more about them from Graphics Press, PO Box 430, Cheshire, CT 06410.

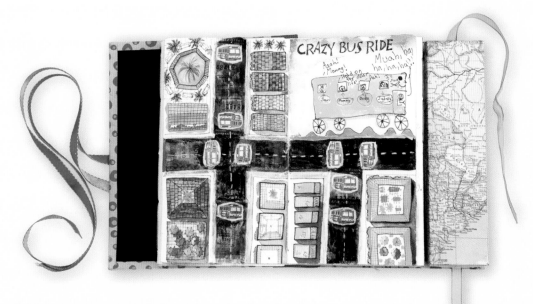

Jill K. Berry, *Mexico 2009 Journal Pages*. 8¼ x 16 inches (21 x 40.6 cm). Watercolor, white pencil; collage.

GRIDS

Grids are basic organizing systems that consist of the repetition of a certain unit. They project a sense of order and control. When used with strongly emotional material, they can introduce an edgy contrast that heightens the impact of the design. You can create grids in an infinite variety of sizes and shapes, depending on what you want to express.

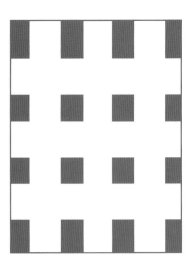

Gwen Diehn, 2000. Watercolor, cork stamps, pen.
Photo by Elyse Weingarten.

Kerstin Vogdes, 2001. Watercolor, pen.

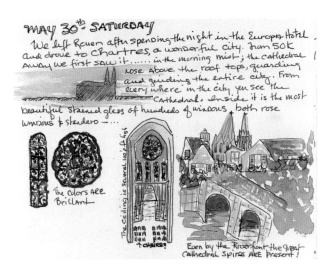

Dorothy Herbert, 2000. Watercolor, pen.
Photo by Elyse Weingarten.

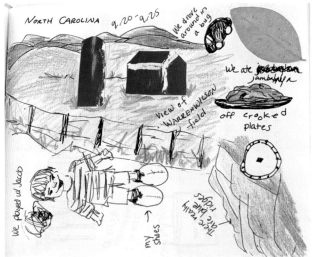

Susan Saling, *Untitled Journal Page*, 2000. Collage, watercolor, pen.

MANDALAS

A mandala is a symmetrical design based on a circle, with a central focal point; it can cover one page or be a two-page spread. A mandala is a good way to highlight a main point as well as show supporting ideas, images, or context. It's also a very calm layout and lends itself well to content with a meditative focus.

Gwen Diehn, 2000. Watercolor, stamps made from foam rubber earplugs and corks. *Photo by Elyse Weingarten.*

Laurie Adams, 2000. Colored pencil, pastel, pen and ink. *Photo by Elyse Weingarten.*

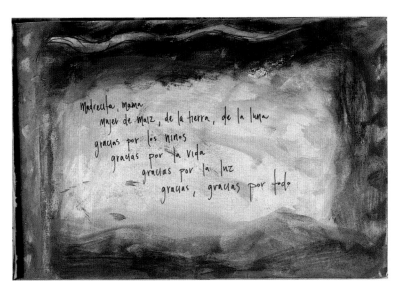

Colleen Stanton, 2000. Watercolor, pen. *Photo by Elyse Weingarten.*

COLUMNS

Columns can be of any width. They can be made of text, image, or a combination of the two. Columns and grids can be combined on the same page. Like grids, columns connote a certain orderliness. They also make long text passages easier to read because they shorten the length of each line. Columns are a good layout to use when many small visuals illustrate the same block of text or when you want to make comparisons among many ideas or units.

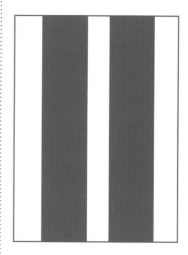

Colleen Stanton, 2000. Watercolor, pen.
Photo by Elyse Weingarten.

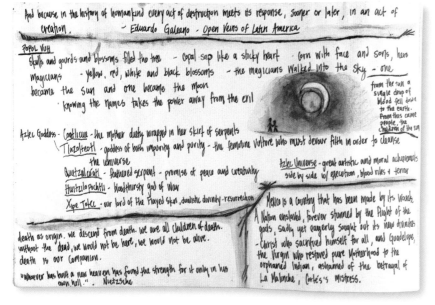

Colleen Stanton, 2000. Watercolor pencil, pen.
Photo by Elyse Weingarten.

Coranna Beene, 2000. Collage of cut train tickets written over with pen, on colored vellum pages. *Photo by Elyse Weingarten.*

Gwen Diehn, 2000. Watercolor pencil, pen. *Photo by Elyse Weingarten.*

DIAGONALS

Diagonals are always more emotional and attract more attention than the horizontals and verticals of grids and columns. Their inherent motion and instability communicate action and emotion. Diagonals need not be simple straight lines. Jagged and curved diagonals can be even more powerful and evocative.

Gwen Diehn, 2000. Watercolor, pen, gold foil and sugar wrapper. *Photo by Elyse Weingarten.*

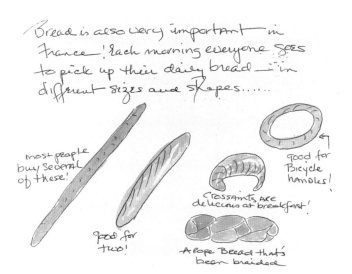

Dorothy Herbert, 2000. Watercolor, pen. *Photo by Elyse Weingarten.*

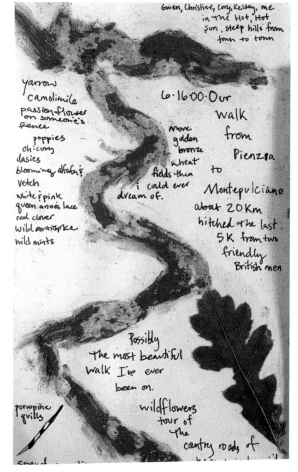

Laura Carter, 2000. Soil mixed with PVA; pressed leaf, pens. *Photo by Elyse Weingarten.*

ORGANIC SHAPES

These are curved shapes that feel more natural than the abstract forms of columns, grids, and even diagonals. Organic shapes flow and melt, grow, evolve, and meander.

Dorothy Herbert, 2000. Watercolor, pen. *Photo by Elyse Weingarten.*

Christine Toriello, 2000. Collage, pen. *Photo by Elyse Weingarten.*

Bruce Kremer, 2001. Pen and ink, collage. *Photo by artist.*

CUTOUTS AND ADD-ONS

Although not strictly considered layout elements, cutouts and add-ons introduce complexity and surprises. Cutouts can link pages and the ideas on them and thereby create the effect of a third and even fourth dimension in a book. They can highlight certain text and visuals. Consider cutting windows through from one page to the next, or cutting the corners and edges of pages, so the page corners and edges behind it can be seen. You might also glue or stitch on foldout pages or elements that extend from the page. You can attach small booklets or pockets to pages for a hypertext effect.

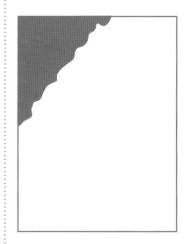

Laura Carter, 2000. Watercolor and cutout vellum page. *Photo by Elyse Weingarten*.

Coranna Beene, *Untitled Journal Pages*, 2000. Watercolor painted on white vellum over pen and watercolor; collage and pen on front of colored paper pocket. *Photo by Elyse Weingarten.*

Laurie Adams, *Costa Rica Journal Page*, 2000. Colored paper cut into leaf forms over colored pen, colored pencils. *Photo by Elyse Weingarten.*

Nina Bagley, *Untitled Journal Page*, 2000. Collage, metallic pens, rubber stamps, metallic ink. *Photo by artist.*

Writing Small

by Ann Turkle

Writing in a journal when you are considering page design may present some challenges, but it also introduces many opportunities. The decorated or visually defined page may invite words the way the stark white of an untouched page never would. If you aren't sure where to begin or what to write in your journal, start small. One of the most common complaints about journal-keeping of any kind is that it takes too much time. The verbal collecting you may do for a journal can fit so neatly into moments of available time that this objection will fall away, and, as it does, the value of the writing may become so apparent that making time for it is easier. Here are a few suggestions for approaching the written aspect of your journal.

WORK SMALL

There is no denying we have many small openings of time in our day. We wait at the stoplight, in the checkout line at the supermarket, for our e-mail connection to come online, or for a return phone call. These "in between" moments can leave us tapping our toes in impatience, but they can also allow us to turn with pen in hand to a small notebook or 3 x 5-inch (7.6 x 12.7 cm) card kept close at hand. It may seem a little tedious or obsessive to get into the habit of making observations or brief reflections throughout your day, but gradually this practice can yield great results: you'll learn to pay attention and be aware of what is going on around you, not just what is going on in your head.

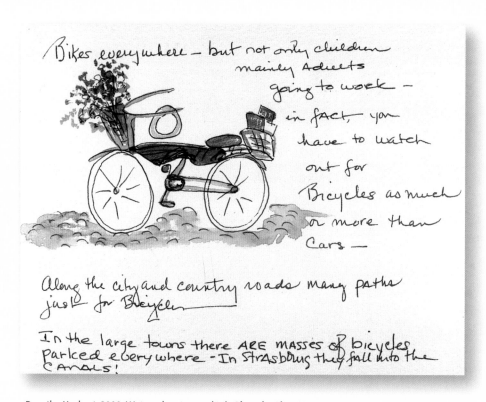

Dorothy Herbert, 2000. Watercolor, pen and ink. *Photo by Elyse Weingarten.*

Kelcey Loomer, 2000. Watercolor, pen and ink. *Photo by Elyse Weingarten.*

Choose a convenient method for collecting your observations. Plain-paper notepads come as small as business cards, and range in size from 2 x 3¹/₂ inches (5.1 x 8.9 cm) to 6 x 4 inches (15.2 x 10.2 cm) to 7 x 5¹/₂ inches (17.8 x 14 cm), the same size as a daily planner. You can easily carry a few 3 x 5-inch (7.6 x 12.7 cm) cards or a tiny notebook with many pages. Since any of these options are small and easy to buy or make, you may want several so they are available in the places those openings of time happen—in the car, at the telephone or the computer, in your handbag or briefcase, or, best of all, in your pocket. Your collector notebook may go many places your larger journal would not easily fit, so you don't need to be quite so obvious about using it if you are at first a little shy about working on your journal in public. If someone asks what you are doing, you can always respond by saying "Oh, just making a list," because you may be doing precisely that.

STARTING A COLLECTION OF THOUGHTS

Writing exercises can bear a close resemblance to drawing exercises. The goal is to focus and to record the object of your attention. Although part of your aim may be to be more present or more aware in your surroundings, you don't want to ignore what you are thinking. In a sense, you may be opening a door to allow flashes of connection to come to you.

"Nonwriters" may perceive "writerly" creativity as something that happens in a writer's studio, or at least at the keyboard, but the beginnings of works (poems, verbal sketches, memoirs) are the quick apprehensions you will lose if you do not write them down: the perfect pattern of the cups and glasses stacked on the waiter's tray as he sets the café tables for dinner; the almost conversational tone of the crows' exchange outside your window at daybreak; or the delighted smile of a six-year-old picking out a box of crayons as part of her back-to-school shopping. Tiny things may provide images and associations to build upon.

121

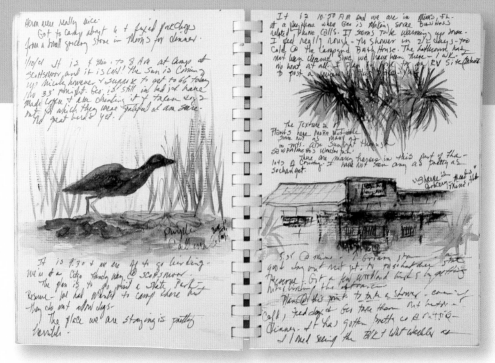

Elizabeth Ellison, 2000. Watercolor, pen and ink.

MAKE LISTS

Lists are liberating. They are much easier to generate than carefully constructed sentences, and they give us an opportunity to discover patterns, similarities, and differences. List every flower you have seen blooming today. Record the names of the tree species in your yard. Look over your lists and try to determine patterns which may evolve from similar sounds or a visual memory of color.

DESCRIBE

Try using very descriptive language to record your observations. For example: One morning I came upon a pretty box turtle about the size of a large coffee cup, as she sat between the broccoli and the tomato plants in my garden. She looked up at me with gold eyes, perfectly coordinated with the gold and greenish brown of her shell.

WITNESS

As you people-watch, try to record the actions of those you observe. Sitting on a park bench, I observed four children running through a puddle left by a recent rainstorm. First, they ran keeping their feet low to create a wake, then took huge steps, stomping up the biggest splash possible, and finally they ran and slid. They took turns initiating the action, almost the way members of a jazz ensemble take turns improvising.

LISTEN

Eavesdrop, record dialogue, and listen to what your surroundings tell you. I lived for two years on a corner in a residential neighborhood in Tallahassee, Florida. Gradually, I realized that I could describe that neighborhood, the time of day, the season, and the weather just by listening. The bus service to my corner started at about 7:00 a.m. and ended in the early evening, each pass punctuated by the distinctive squeal of brakes.

The magnolia tree outside my bedroom window dropped its leaves with a sound almost as decisive as smashing plates. And as the direction of the wind changed, so did the approach that planes took toward the local airport, adding the rush of jet engines overhead. How would you describe the distinctive qualities of your neighborhood by sound? Can those sounds be made visible?

Once, sitting in a booth in a restaurant waiting for my meal to be served, I overheard a conversation between two couples, retirees. Without turning to look, I visualized them, making notes and a small sketch on a notecard, entirely on the strength of their voices and their way of speaking.

COLLECTING AND PLEASURE

An unintended payoff of paying attention is that we simply begin to take pleasure in our noticing, and suddenly, the collecting notebook becomes a "pleasure journal," the repository for unexpected moments of delight. Whereas you once fumed over the moments wasted on the price check for the patron in front of you in line, there is now the opportunity to quickly observe the precarious efforts of the five-year-old unloading the shopping cart, one item at a time, into the hands of the checker who is dutifully saying "thank you" at each handoff.

Colleen Stanton, 2000. Collage and pen. *Photo by Elyse Weingarten.*

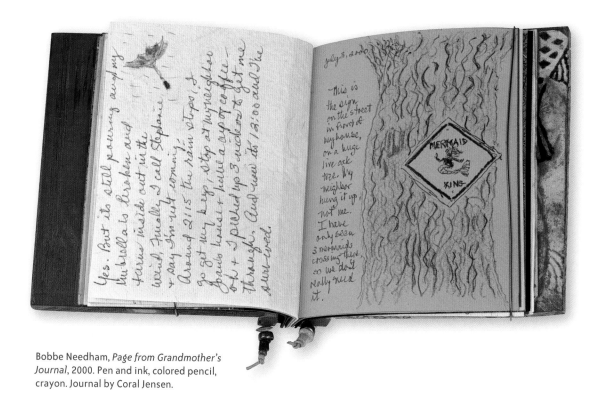

Bobbe Needham, *Page from Grandmother's Journal*, 2000. Pen and ink, colored pencil, crayon. Journal by Coral Jensen.

FROM PATTERN TO METAPHOR

Collecting material in notebooks before transferring it into your journal allows you a lot of options. You may transfer material into the journal in many different ways, adding layers not only to the physical presentation, but to your appreciation and understanding of what you have collected. You may simply paste in a page of observations, or recopy it, then elaborate, reflect, or comment on the article you've added.

The interplay between the visual and the verbal elements of a journal often provides opportunities to explore metaphors. The kinship of images and words can suggest themes or motifs. Figures of speech that you remember from English class can come alive when words and images meet and influence each other. As you pay attention to your emerging metaphors, they may define an agenda, a plan, or projects for you to develop over many journals to come.

Try a visual representation of the feeling of a journal entry. Start with a small, rich idea plopped in the middle of a page, and spiral it out to the margins in a gyre of color and text. The lists you create may suggest linear patterns of design or ornamentation. If it suits your style, record moments in the color that you associate with an experience or narrative. You can even express an experience with one large, dark word or image on each page.

Living Out Loud

by Kore Loy Wildrekinde-McWhirter

10 x 14 inches (25.4 x 35.6 cm).
Pen, pencil, postage stamps.

"When something I've read gets me to thinking, I transcribe it into my current journal and then write and draw about it; it becomes a conversation within and beyond me."

A journal allows me stream-of-consciousness commentary and contemplation I can't find anywhere else. I've always drawn and written on every available surface in an abiding obsession to try to understand what is real under the surface of consensual human realities. Because I find the "humyn whirled" difficult to live in, I pay close attention to, contemplate, and talk back to and/or defy it with line and shadow, both literal and figurative. I use drawing, writing, and poetry, which I consider drawing with words.

As we all do, I live in front of others and am subject to their perspectives, no matter how quiet and unobtrusive I try to be. In a journal, as among the living trees, I can live out loud, so to speak, without being too disruptive to the sensitivities of others as I search for understanding of the myriad disparate wonders.

In a journal, I can talk with others from present, past, and future. I read a lot about places and times other than my own. When something I've read gets me to thinking, I transcribe it into my current journal and then write and draw about it; it becomes a conversation within and beyond me.

I prefer those parts of my journals where drawing and words converge. I don't care what the drawings look like because I'm only trying to figure out and understand something through them. I draw what something feels like from the senses of the body, heart, and mind. Some of the drawings accomplish this more eloquently than others. Then the writing flows around the drawing, and the evolution of the two reveals itself over time through the journals. Through this process, another perspective comes effortlessly forth.

13½ x 16 inches (34.3 x 40.6 cm). Pencil.

Falling into the Rabbit Hole

by Melanie Testa

"I also use my journal to learn. As a birder, I love to identify the birds I see on my daily walks."

8 x 10½ inches (20.3 x 26.7 cm). Gesso, acrylic, marker; collage.

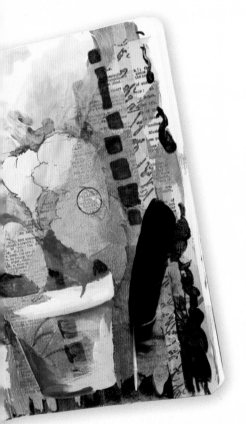

8 x 10½ inches (20.3 x 26.7 cm). Gesso, acrylic, pencil, stamps, gold paint, collage.

Journaling is both balm and boon to my daily life. I use my journal to learn about my world, my creative pursuits, and to heal my mind. Mostly I journal artistically, in the hope that I might derive inspiration for textile-driven wall art. But I don't pressure myself with that; I just know, at some point, this goal will transpire.

I don't want journaling to be a nerve-racking experience, so I make the rules. If a page is imperfect, I cover it up because bad pages tighten me up. Yet, our needs will be different from one another, as they should be. My journaling practice should suit me, just as your practice should suit you.

I also use my journal to learn. As a birder, I love to identify the birds I see on my daily walks. When my favorite birding magazine arrives, I devour the images one by one. If I find an image I am in love with, I contact the photographer and ask permission to draw it and possibly upload it to my blog with acknowledgements. I have become very good at bird identification this way.

And if drawing, painting, and falling into the creative rabbit hole aren't perfect forms of meditation, I don't know what is. My breath slows, my mind focuses, I lose track of time and forget the niggling doubts, worries, and woes of the day. Using my creative talent is the best form of personal therapy I have ever engaged in.

How Does Your Journal
See the World?

Art always tells us something about how its maker understands the world. For example, artists who lived in 16th-century Europe, at the time of the Renaissance, represented the world by carefully rendering its material details from a fixed perspective, a single vantage point. Paintings were like windows onto scenes of exquisite naturalism. Painters were reflecting a worldview in which people saw the material world as fixed and certain, and they believed their truths to be absolute. They enjoyed new-found control over the world, thanks to new discoveries by explorers and scientists, and they felt confidently placed at the center of the universe.

A few centuries earlier, during the Middle Ages, people did not consider the material world to be so important. Instead, the earthly world was seen as merely a prelude to the afterlife of the spirit. Accordingly, the figures in Byzantine church mosaics seem to float in an unearthly space of color and light, surrounded by golden halos or auras. All of the figures look like members of a large extended family who

shared genes for almond-shaped eyes, elongated bodies, dark curling hair, and tiny, insubstantial feet that seem incapable of bearing the weight of the bodies, much less moving them around. They live in an indeterminate space, and their eyes are fixed on the world beyond the senses.

It's interesting to tease apart the different strands that make up our current expression. In our artwork today, we borrow from many different traditions because we have access to so much of the past as well as the work of other cultures. When we allow ourselves to try on different ways of seeing as we work in our journals, we can enrich our practices as well as increase our appreciation of the variety that surrounds us.

Journals, those strange amalgams of image and text, utilitarian purpose and art, also reflect the interests and values—the worldview—of the people who produce them. Considering different ways of making sense of the world can help you enlarge your journal pracice. In this section we'll look at seven different ways of seeing the world and reflecting those visions in a journal.

Sarah A. Bourne, *Ireland Journal Page*, 2004. 8½ x 11 inches (21.6 x 27.9 cm). Hand-bound journal, handmade paper, watercolor, ink. *Photo by Aleia Woolsey.*

Juliana Coles, *Life Within: Untitled,*
2000-present. 35½ x 28½ x 2 inches
(90.2 x 72.4 x 5 cm). Hand-bound journal,
figure drawings from open model session, masking tape, ink, acrylic, collage,
glue stick, India ink, pen, rubber stamp
pads, German book pages, water-based
wood varnish; larger pages taped in
journal, glued, collaged, and stamped.
Photo by Pat Berrett.

The Layered World

The Layered World

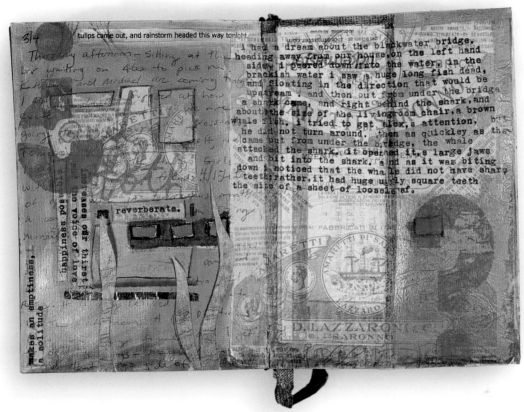

Kelcey Loomer, 2004. Journal, typewritten dream and quote on transparent cookie wrappers from Italy, pastels, ink, PVA glue, gold acrylic paint; collaged. *Photo by Aleia Woolsey.*

Why are so many of us crazy about layers these days? Is it simply because it's easy to work in layers on a computer, making the layered look fashionable in graphic design? Clearly there's more to it than layers simply looking good to many people. Maybe it's because layers are a kind of visual equivalent of talking on a cell phone, while driving in traffic, while listening to the radio and answering kids' questions, while trying to keep from spilling a cup of hot tea. It's the quintessential post-post-modern lifestyle—lots of things going on at the same time.

Artists working in layers today represent a world that they see as existing on many different levels: one that is constructed differently by individuals and diverse groups of people all at the same time. Layers can represent different levels of meaning in the world as well as in the piece of artwork. They show how one event can color the others around it, how one meaning changes as it intersects with others, how nothing is simple and nothing stays the same. They show the randomness that causes interesting things to happen when two layers generate a third set of images that no one could have predicted.

Creating the Illusion of Layers

To produce the illusion of layers in a journal you need transparency and translucency so that it's possible to see more than one layer at a time. You also need bottom layers that stay put once they're on the paper. The main characteristics of a transparent medium are the absence of fillers and opacifiers, and the presence of transparent pigments. The main characteristic of a permanent medium is that when its water evaporates, its binder is no longer water soluble. Therefore, it glues the pigment to the paper permanently and won't let it move around when another water medium is placed on top of it.

You can begin working in layers by writing, drawing, painting, printing, or pouring the bottom layer with a waterproof medium. Some waterproof mediums are graphite and wax-based colored pencils, acrylics, waterproof pens—colored gel pens as well as black ones—wax crayons, and varnish-based or other waterproof inks, copier transfers, and some stamp-pad inks. Collage items are often waterproof, especially color copies and scraps of commercially printed images and text. It's important to let the bottom layer dry thoroughly before working over it if you want to create the effect of transparency when you add the top layer.

Some transparent materials that are suitable for use in books are fluid acrylics, acrylic mediums, watercolors, water-soluble crayons and pastels, inks, and translucent or transparent papers such as vellum, some oriental papers, and thin tissues. Figure 1 shows a variety of

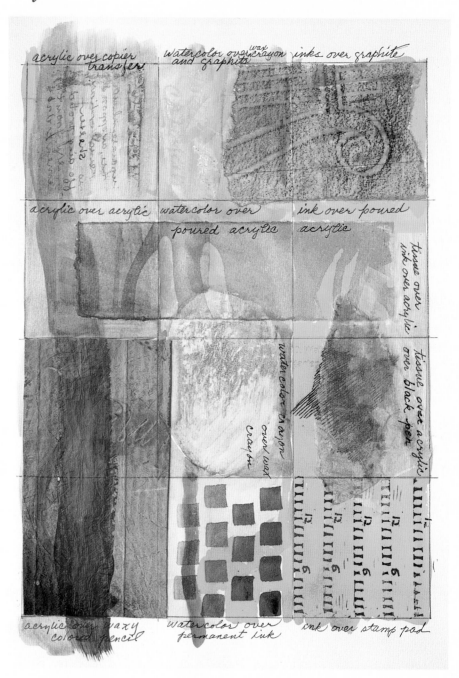

Figure 1

acrylic over copier transfer

watercolor over wax crayon and graphite

inks over graphite

acrylic over acrylic

watercolor over poured acrylic

ink over poured acrylic

tissue over ink over acrylic

tissue over acrylic over black pen

watercolor crayon over wax crayon

acrylic over waxy colored pencil

watercolor over permanent ink

ink over stamp pad

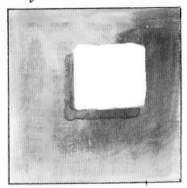

Figure 2

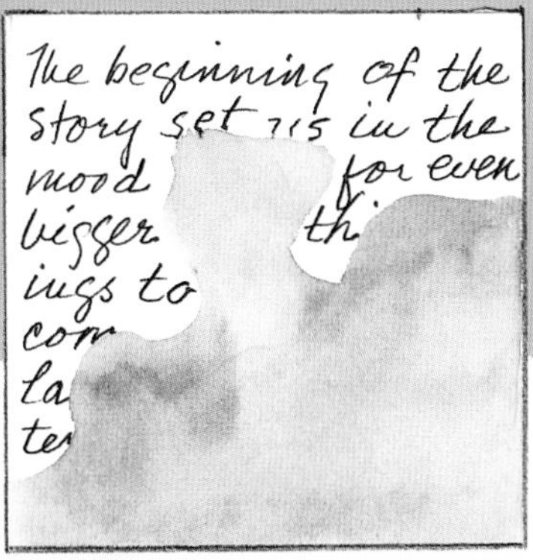

The beginning of the story set [?]is in the mood for even bigger th[?] ings to com la te[?]

Figure 3

waterproof bases with different transparent top layers applied. Experiment and you'll discover which combinations you like best. By remembering the principles outlined above, you'll also figure out other materials to use and other ways to generate the effect of layers.

In addition to actually layering art mediums, you can get the effect of layers by placing materials on a page in such as way that they appear to be in layers. One way to do this is to write or draw right up to the edge of another element on the page so that the writing or drawing appears to pass under the second element, as shown in figure 2. Another way to create the appearance of layers is to use small amounts of an opaque medium, such as gouache, to make areas seem to come forward from the bottom layer. This works especially well if you then add transparent shadows to the opaque elements, as shown in figure 3.

The Creative World

"Creative" is one of those overused words that pops up in the most banal of settings: "Be creative! Flambé those bananas!" And, "Now you too can create the environment you want using our new Kreatif Kolors to sponge paint your walls. Follow these easy directions..." The *Oxford English Dictionary* defines creation as "The action of making, forming, producing, or constituting for the first time or afresh; invention; causation; production," and it is in this sense that I use the word here.

Leonardo Da Vinci's notebooks or journals are often cited when the word creative comes up. They're well known for many reasons. For starters, we all know that he wrote in mirror writing. We also know that he described and even invented many things centuries before the rest of the world got around to thinking about them—flying machines, submarines, farm machinery, and even instruments for various surgical procedures. His journals have been appreciated as much for the beauty of his drawings, with their lovely inscrutable filigree of text, as for the ideas expressed. These are creative journals in the original sense of the term.

Because Leonardo reflected the worldview of the Italian Renaissance—a world possessing order, one capable of being perfectible—you won't find him whining about his relationships in the pages of his journals. No ecstatic travelogues either. When he does describe a natural phenomenon (e.g., a baby in utero or a river system), it's with the intention of discovery and disclosure.

Many artists and inventors use their journals in this way. Stage and costume designers, poets and writers, painters, choreographers, and musicians often keep notebooks close at hand for a daily updating of their ideas. Teachers have their plan books; inventors have their notebooks; and I once saw a carpenter's lovely handmade,

131

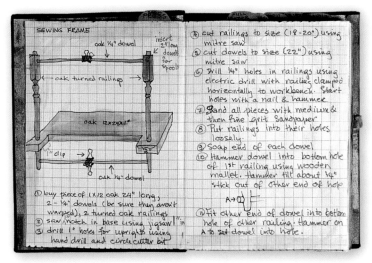

SEWING FRAME

oak ¼" dowel
insert 2" long dowels for spool?
oak turned railings
oak 12x24x1"
1" clip
oak ¼" dowel

④ cut railings to size (18-20") using mitre saw
⑤ cut dowels to size (22") using mitre saw
⑥ Drill ¼" holes in railings using electric drill with railing clamped horizontally to workbench. Start holes with a nail & hammer.
⑦ Sand all pieces with medium & then fine grit sandpaper
⑧ Put railings into their holes loosely.
⑨ Soap end of each dowel
⑩ Hammer dowel into bottom hole of 1st railing using wooden mallet. Hammer till about ¼" stick out of other end of hole

A→◻︎

⑪ Fit other end of dowel into bottom hole of other railing. Hammer on A to set dowel into hole.

① buy piece of 1x12 oak 24" long, 2 - ¼" dowels (be sure they aren't warped), 2 turned oak railings
② saw notch in base using jigsaw 1" in
③ drill 1" holes for uprights using hand drill and circle cutter bit

Gwen Diehn. 5 x 6½ inches (12.7 x 16.5 cm). Coptic journal, handbound by Sandy Webster, watercolor and pen. *Photo by Aleia Woolsey.*

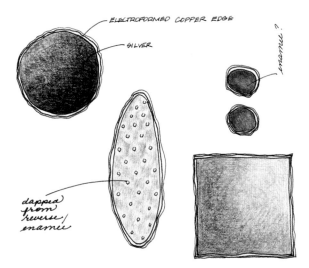

ELECTROFORMED COPPER EDGE
SILVER
enamel?
dapped from reverse/ enamel

Billy Jean Theide, *Edges*, 2004. 8½ x 11 (21.6 x 27.9 cm). Hand-bound journal, sketch paper, ink, colored pencils. *Photo by the artist.*

leather-wrapped, grid-paper notebook. In it, he kept detailed sketches of all his projects along with notes about materials, costs, construction problems, and solutions. He used a flat, wooden carpenter's pencil for his drawings and notes, and he rolled pencil and sewn-together text pages in a wrap-around cover, a well-used rectangle of leather, which he stuck in his back pocket.

A creative journal focuses on the future and how to get there. It's a tool of the imagination, but it's also a means for realizing dreams and plans. This is a journal that goes along to the hardware store, or the garden center, or the junkyard. If you work near water, it may get wet. If you work in a garage or workshop, it may get greasy.

This journal needs to be weatherproof and sturdy! Leather or heavy canvas are ideal cover materials. A waterproof pen or a graphite pencil makes sense as a medium for working in it. Quadrille or grid paper as well as a supply of tracing vellum tucked into the back pages may be handy. Colored inks can be useful in making diagrams, maps, and drawings, but these should be varnish- or acrylic-based in order to withstand hard use and occasional overnights outside on a damp work site. I've seen waterproof quadrille paper designed for surveyors who must often work in the rain.

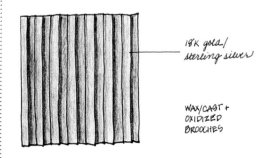

18K gold/ sterling silver

WAX/CAST + OXIDIZED BROOCHES

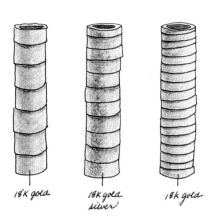

18K gold

18K gold silver

18K gold

Billie Jean Theide, *Stripes*, 2004. 11 x 8½ inches (27.9 x 21.6 cm) Hand-bound journal sketch, paper, ink, colored pencils. *Photo by artist.*

But the water-repellent surface also repels liquid ink and water media. It's okay for graphite, but that's about it. If you know you're going to be working in your journal while standing in a drizzle, and you're content to limit yourself to graphite, you might look for this paper to use in making your journal. I found it in a bookstore, but I imagine drafting supply stores would be a more likely source.

Whatever the materials, the contents of this journal will always be enormously useful. While the practical information in the journal will help you work out the details of current projects, the journal can also become a repository for ideas for future projects. You might keep a section in the back just for jotting notes and making sketches of glimmerings of ideas, thoughts that you don't want to lose but that you haven't yet figured out what to do with. Someday, when you refer back to the journal, one of those sketches may well become the seed of your next project.

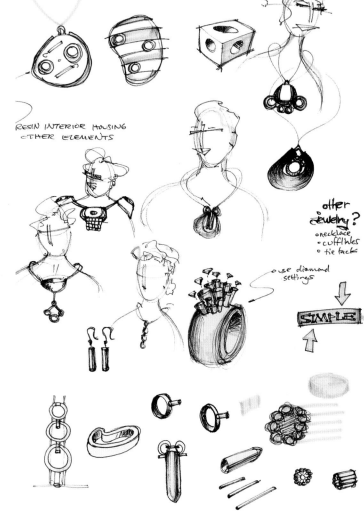

Eric Larsen, *Jewelry Sketch Studies*, 2003. 11½ x 14 inches (29.2 x 35.6 cm). Hand-bound journal, marker, ink. *Photo by artist.*

Sandy Webster, *Working Journal Series*, 2000. 6 x 4 x ¾ inches (15.2 x 10.2 x 1.9 cm) Hand-bound journal, papers, book cloth, acrylic paint, shoe polish, wrench; glued, painted, waxed, sanded, and shellacked.

133

Brains on Paper

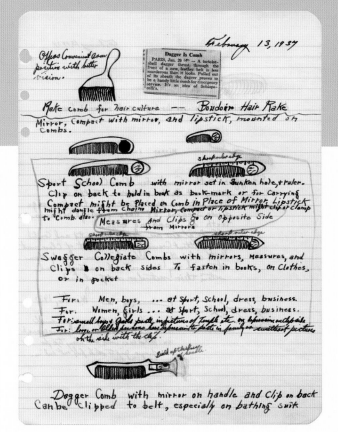

Earl Tupper's sketches for the *Dagger Comb*. *Earl S. Tupper Papers*, Archives Center, National Museum of American History, Behring Center, Smithsonian Institution.

Journals have always played a big part in inventors' lives. They're the nets that catch new ideas and hold them gently while the inventor fine-tunes, modifies, erases, adds on, and sometimes even admits to being unsure, puzzled, or at a dead end. One of Charles Darwin's notebook pages contains a tree diagram with text in which he speculates on the theory of evolution. At the top of the page Darwin has written two words: "I think."

Earl Tupper was a journal keeper who was an unlikely candidate to make a million before he was 30. Poor and uneducated beyond high school, he had grown up on a small family farm in New England. His father tinkered about to invent laborsaving devices for the farm and greenhouse, such as a frame to help in the cleaning of chicken houses. It was from watching his father design these items that Earl began to see the path that would lead him to his fortune.

When Earl graduated from high school in 1925, he worked on the farm for a couple of years, then took on a number of different jobs, including work as a mail clerk and a job on a railroad labor crew. In 1928 he studied tree surgery and set up his own business, which he and his wife ran throughout the early 1930s. The income from this business enabled Tupper to continue to play around with ideas for inventions that he had pursued from boyhood. Even after Tupper Tree Doctors failed in 1936, Tupper remained confident that he could make a living from some of his inventions.

While inventing was the thread that ran through Tupper's life, the repositories of his ideas were his invention notebooks or journals. These are wonderful examples of a brain on paper, and they span much of his lifetime. They give us a glimpse into the thought processes of the inventor, recording not only the spectacular successes—such as his work with plastics that led to the invention of the Wonderbowl with the Tupper seal and to the refinement of plastic that became Tupperware—but also all the near-misses and spectacular failures that were part of the risk-taking an inventor goes through on the road to success.

Tupper never stopped inventing. He carried little pads of paper in his shirt pocket for getting his ideas down when they came to him. These he copied into his invention notebooks, a set of loose-leaf binders filled with his drawings, explanations, and revisions. His ideas included a fish-powered boat, a no-drip cone for ice cream, a fishing pole with built-in scale for weighing the catch, a belt buckle into which a photograph could be pasted, a folding comb that he called a dagger comb (shown above), and a waterproof watch, which he called a water bracelet. Long after selling the Tupperware Company for $16,000,000 in 1968, Tupper was still hard at work, coming up with inventions and ideas for products.

One of Tupper's later notebook pages contains a design for a device (made out of two modified Tupperware rolling pins) that was to be used for washing clothes in a motel. The traveler would not only be able to wash small items of clothing, but would also get his exercise by performing a series of maneuvers for which Tupper would provide a description to accompany the product. At the end of the process, the traveler not only had clean underwear, but he had also had a good workout and would sleep soundly while his clothes dried over the back of the motel's desk chair.

The Wabi-Sabi World

The Wabi-Sabi World

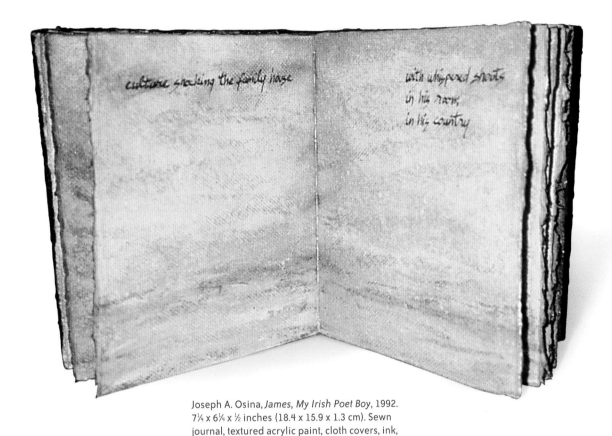

culture shocking the family house

with whispered shouts
in his room,
in his country

Joseph A. Osina, *James, My Irish Poet Boy*, 1992.
7¼ x 6¼ x ½ inches (18.4 x 15.9 x 1.3 cm). Sewn
journal, textured acrylic paint, cloth covers, ink,
Dutch linen paper. *Photo by artist.*

The Japanese aesthetic of wabi-sabi is a nature-based idea that is very much the opposite of the materialistic aesthetic of our digitized world. It's also very different from the rich complications of the layered world. While it's difficult to define wabi-sabi, Leonard Koren comes close in his book *Wabi-Sabi for Artists, Designers, Poets, and Philosophers* (1994, Stone Bridge Press, Berkeley, CA). when he says, "Wabi-sabi is a beauty of things imperfect, impermanent, and incomplete. It is a beauty of things modest and humble. It is a beauty of things unconventional."

Wabi-sabi is closely aligned with the qualities of simplicity, the transience of life, and a lack of perfection. Wabi-sabi materials are natural and often corroded in such a way as to be richer and more poignant be-cause of their degradation. In the wabi-sabi worldview one arrives at truth by observing nature, especially its inconspicuous and often overlooked details. Wabi-sabi teaches that beauty can come from ugliness and from acceptance that life is fleeting and always changing.

A wabi-sabi journal might be the focal point of a practice in which you seek to simplify your life, where you begin to find meaning and beauty in unadorned events and objects. It can be a tool that helps you come to terms with the fleeting quality of life while relaxing into an enjoyment of the passing parade. Accordingly, wabi-sabi materials are those that suggest erosion and other natural processes—the irregular, the earthy and unpretentious, the intimate.

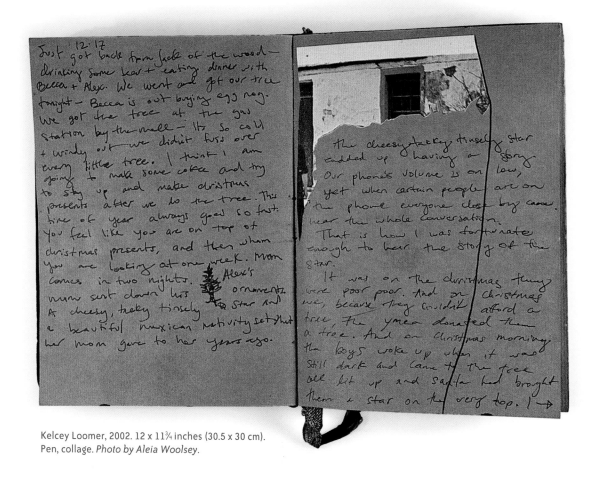

Kelcey Loomer, 2002. 12 x 11¾ inches (30.5 x 30 cm).
Pen, collage. *Photo by Aleia Woolsey.*

Wabi-sabi colors are generally warm, dark, and low in intensity. (Think of a soft, faded, apricot-colored brick wall with a few fragments of paper and a rusty staple left behind from a long-gone poster.) A slightly crooked clay pot on a rough, wooden bench is infinitely more wabi-sabi than a Ming Dynasty Chinese bowl on a gleaming mahogany end table.

The wabi-sabi journal, then, is one that's simple rather than elaborate, rough rather than smooth—and certainly never slick. It will be made of natural materials to remind us of the change that's constant in nature despite our efforts to hold onto things and to preserve the present for the future. Flour paste, handmade papers, cloth, and leather come to mind, as well as humble natural elements such as leaves or a feather. The mediums used will be minimal: a pen with black ink, a soft graphite pencil, some warm washes of grays and tans, perhaps made from local clay pigments. Some pages might be prepared by pouring strong tea or coffee on them. Collage elements will not only be simple, but will be beautifully and thoughtfully arranged. A single small spot of color might accentuate an otherwise empty page.

Opacity is a useful quality in a wabi-sabi journal. A wash of white gouache can soften elements on a page like a fine layer of clouds can soften the landscape seen from a mountaintop. A thick layer of acrylic absorbent ground can furnish a base that can be loosely engraved with words or images that need no added color. Multiple layers of absorbent ground and thin paper can create a peeling or decaying look.

Coloring the Wabi-Sabi World

Jeanne G. Germani, 2003. 9 x 8¼ x ½ inches (22.9 x 21 x 1.3 cm). Altered book, acrylic paint, PVA, vintage decorative piece; painted, glued. *Photo by artist.*

Since wabi-sabi colors tend to be low in intensity, a little knowledge of color theory can be useful when you need to dull an overly bright green or take away the bite from a particularly acid yellow. A color wheel is an easily constructed tool that you can use as a reference whenever you want to mix colors. By making your own color wheel from the paints you'll actually use, you can get an accurate picture of your available palette.

Using the most transparent watercolors or fluid acrylics that you have, begin by painting three spots of color arranged in a triangle. Put a spot of blue (ultramarine works well, or pthalo blue) at the top, then a spot of clear, lemony yellow to the right and below the blue, then a spot of magenta, or dark pinkish-purple red to the left and below the blue (see figure 1, page 138).

Next, mix a very little bit of the blue with a brush load of the yellow in order to get a clear green. Paint that between the blue and yellow spots. Mix a small bit of magenta into a brush full of yellow to get a bright orange. Paint the orange between the magenta and the yellow. Finally, mix equal amounts of magenta and blue to get a violet or purple. Paint that between the magenta and the blue (see figure 2, page 138). This is your basic color wheel showing primary and sec-ondary colors. Now the fun begins. There are two basic principles of color theory that will serve you very well:

• Complementary colors are the colors opposite each other on the color wheel: red (or magenta) and green, blue and orange, purple and yellow. When these are mixed together, they lower each other's intensity. For example, if you want to dull that grass-green, add a small amount of red (magenta) to it and watch the intensity drop. If you want to make your red a little less cherry-like, add a small bit of green, and so on.

• However, complementary colors intensify each other when they are placed side by side. If you want a blue to really stand out or "pop" for example, put a spot of orange next to it or in the middle of it and watch the intensity of both colors rise.

Another skill that color theory helps you with is the mixing of subtle grays, which is very important for working in a wabi-sabi manner. Taking the principle that complementary colors mixed together lower each other's intensity to its extreme, complementary colors can be mixed and balanced carefully so that

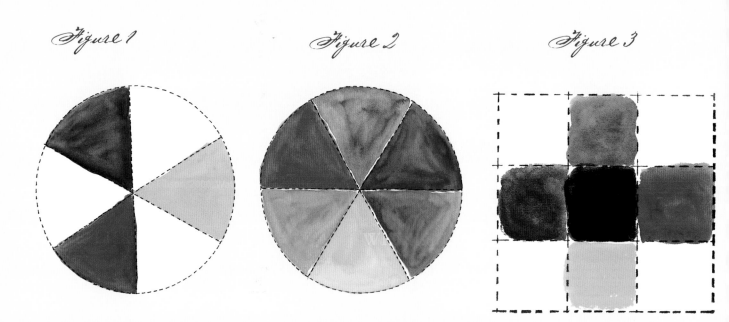

Figure 1   *Figure 2*   *Figure 3*

Figure 4

the wabi-Sabi range

the mix yields a very beautiful neutral gray. You can mix far more nuanced grays using complementary colors than you can by mixing black and white. If you want a warm gray, try mixing red and green. If you want a cooler gray, try blue and orange or purple and yellow (see figure 4).

You can use the same principle to mix the richest blacks imaginable (see figure 3). To mix black, start with ultramarine or pthalo blue and add magenta to it until you have a very dark violet. Then add a very small bit of yellow to warm up and neutralize the violet. You can cool down the black by adding more blue, or warm it up by adding more red (magenta).

A muted wabi-sabi range of colors is shown in contrast between more intense counterparts.

The Naturalist's World

The Naturalist's World

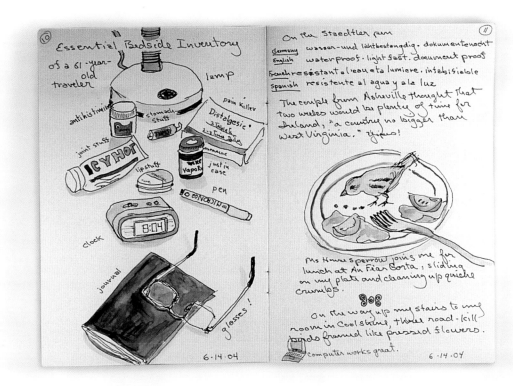

Ann Turkle, *Bedside Table*, 2004. 8 x 5 inches (20.3 x 12.7 cm). Hand-bound journal, ink, watercolor. *Photo by Aleia Woolsey.*

Naturalists write about and draw what they observe. In the days before photography, every expedition that set out to explore an unknown continent—or mountain range, or archipelago—included people whose job it was to document all the plants and animals encountered, as well as any indigenous people, structures, and other artifacts. Because the naturalist was the person who documented and communicated what the group saw. Accuracy was imperative. Amateur naturalists were no less careful as they recorded their own finds, and many of their observations also added greatly to the body of scientific information.

The naturalist sees the world as describable, catalogable, and ultimately controllable and understandable. This is very different from wabi-sabi: whereas the wabi-sabi world is always in flux, always shifting and changing, the naturalist's world is made up of creatures and objects that can be described and become, in a sense, fixed. Although typically about the natural world, a naturalist's journal can include any subject matter. If you have a naturalist's worldview, whether you're interested in unusual fungi and lichens, the ruins you encounter on a vacation in Mexico, or the intriguing variety of lawn ornaments in your neighborhood, your concern will be with getting all the details right.

This type of journal will probably be kept on plain, unadorned paper with entries done in pen or pencil with perhaps a little light watercolor wash. Rather than having extravagant embellishment, this journal will be functional, and its beauty will lie in the precision of its sketches, maps, and diagrams. A crisp descriptive text that explains and expands the entries will never overwhelm them. A naturalist takes a look around and says, "Let me describe, not judge, not get emotional about all of this. I'll put down the facts, as clearly as I can and without interpretation, and let the facts speak for themselves."

Edie Greene, 2004. 8¾ x 6¾ inches (22.2 x 17.1 cm). Hand-bound journal, computer paper, pen and ink, watercolor wash; left-handed drawing and painting. *Photo by Aleia Woolsey.*

Kerstin Vogdes, *Travel Journal: Thailand and Cambodia*, 2004. Bound journal, PVA glue, ink, shells. Photo by Aleia Woolsey.

GOLDEN ACRYLICS & (PAYNES GREY) (IRIDESCENT COPPER LIGHT)
BOOK FRAME + CLIPS
PAPER (PAINTED W. ACRYLIC PAINTS)
LEATHER
GOUACHE - WHITE
PILOT VBALL - EXTRA FINE
RAVEL KIT:
WATER BRUSH PENS
mini WATER COLOR KIT
PENS
WHITE GOUACHE
GLUE STICK

WATERCOLORS (YARKA ST. PE ARTISTS W
ARCHES TEXT
-COVER
-TEXT
-BUFF
-WHITE

Drawing Accurately

Pamela Averick, 2004. *Photo by Gwen Diehn.*

One of the main skills that you will use in your naturalist's journal is realistic drawing, which is more about learning to see than about making art. The task of this kind of drawing is to render in two dimensions that which exists in three. The first step of this process is to choose a point of view and to maintain it throughout. Neither subject nor viewer can change positions once the drawing has begun because of the simple fact that when either you or the thing you are drawing moves, everything changes.

The main obstacle to drawing accurately is your brain, which is filled with information that will not help you: "Tabletops are rectangular," your brain whispers to you, so you draw a perfect rectangle. "The table has four legs of equal length," says your brain, so you draw them; and immediately you realize that your drawing looks like your five-year-old nephew made it. To overcome your brain, you need to measure and compare—that's all there is to it.

Let's draw just a tabletop to learn this measuring method. Look around and find a tabletop. The first step will be to pick out the four lines that make up its edges, lines A-B, B-C, C-D, D-A (see figure 1 on page 142). Choose the shortest of those four, A-B in this example, and measure it using the pencil tip and your thumb like this: imagine you are looking at the table through a glass windowpane that's an arm's length in front of you. Close one eye and look at the table, as if holding a pencil flat up to the glass. Keeping your elbow straight so that your eye and your pencil remain the same distance apart at all times while measuring, and always keeping the pencil flat on the glass, rotate the pencil on the glass until the line you are measuring appears to be parallel with or covered by the pencil. Place the tip of the pencil at the start of line A-B, and mark with your thumb the end of line A-B on your pencil. This measurement, from the pencil tip to your thumb, is your "unit." You'll use it to measure the other lines so they all appear on your paper in correct proportion to one another.

Holding the position of unit A-B on your pencil, see how many of them fit along line B-C. This gives you the first proportion. To transfer it to paper, start by choosing a length for line A-B. The size of this first line will determine the size of the finished drawing, so choose the size while considering how big your page is, as well as how big the drawing needs to be. Draw line A-B, angling it as

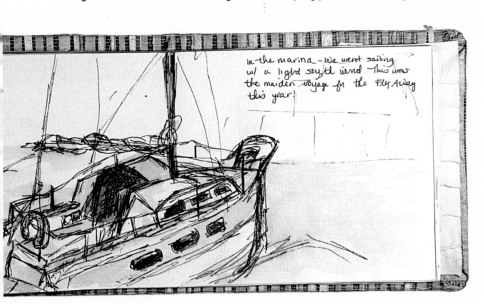

Kerstin Vogdes, *Sketches of LBI*, 2001. Bound journal, ink, watercolors. *Photo by Aleia Woolsey.*

nearly as possible to the way it's angled in real life. Now draw line B-C, making it as many units long as it was when you measured it. Continue measuring and drawing in the same way for the other two lines of the tabletop.

Besides measuring, comparing one part to another is a very helpful device. Look at point B on the back of the tabletop. If you want to be sure you have angled line A-B correctly, imagine a line dropping straight down from point B and intersecting the front of the table, line D-A, at point E (see figure 2). How does the distance between section A-E compare in length with your original unit, A-B? If you've put point B too far over in either direction, move it to the right spot so that point B relates to line D-A correctly. Now erase your original line A-B and redraw it. This time the angle formed by line A-B and line D-A should be accurate (see figure 3). Check point C in the same way.

A third useful device is that of using horizontals and verticals to check how far off the horizontal or vertical a line should be. Hold the pencil straight up and down. Notice how far off the vertical line of the pencil the side of the table, line A-B, seems to move. Hold the pencil horizontally and use it to judge the rise or fall of the back edge. Does it rise slightly, fall slightly or remain truly horizontal? It's good to check horizontals and verticals periodically while doing a drawing.

You can use these same three techniques to draw anything. Always start by lightly sketching in the general shapes. Once the general parts are drawn proportionately, apply the same three devices—

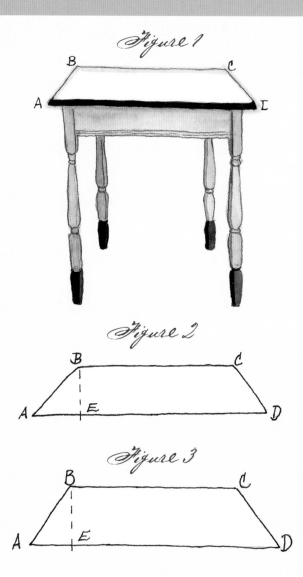

Figure 1

Figure 2

Figure 3

measuring, comparing, and judging horizontals and verticals—to smaller and smaller parts. It's very important to move from the general to the particular. If you don't have the general proportions right, no matter how perfectly you've rendered tiny details, the drawing is not going to look right. You have to earn the right to draw the details.

This is a very brief introduction to drawing, but mastering these techniques will enable you to make much progress. Take these very basic drawing instructions and use them over and over. Drawing is to art as arpeggios and scales are to composing music. A drawing teacher can jump-start you and give you some hints, but the only way to really learn how to draw is to do it. And do it. And do it.

The Spiritual World

In the Medieval period in Europe (between A.D. 500 and 1450), the visible, material world was viewed as merely a prelude to the spiritual world in which souls were believed to live after earthly life was over. The artwork of the time reflected this worldview in that, rather than focusing on the muddy details of everyday life, it abounded in colors and images that expressed and aroused emotion and helped move the viewer to a more spiritual attitude. It was not concerned with describing the natural world, but used elements of the natural world as symbols that spoke to people about the world to come.

Gothic cathedrals, such as Chartres in France, are in a sense machines that work on the body—the perceptions and senses—in order to catapult the visitor or worshipper to a higher spiritual plane. The means used to achieve this transformation include light and geometry. The light comes from the expanse of stained glass that encloses and fills the interior with pure color and luminance. The geometry comes from nature.

The builders of these cathedrals understood that certain proportions and sequences of intervals occur over and over throughout the natural world. Because this geometry seemed to be the foundation of nature, it was assumed to reflect the mind of God. One of these universals is known as the Golden Proportion. The Golden Proportion is found in the human body, in the wings of birds and

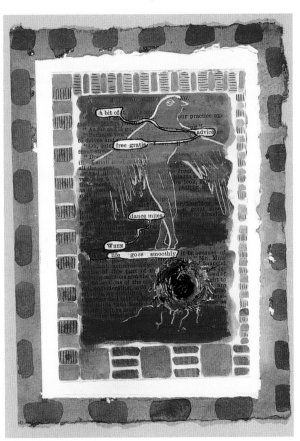

Charlotte Hedlund, 2003. 8 x 6 inches (20.3 x 15.2 cm). Bound journal, bristol board on handmade paper book page, PVA glue, acrylic paint, ink; glued and painted. *Photo by artist.*

insects, in seashells, and in many other places. In a Golden Rectangle, which is derived from the Golden Proportion, the short side is related to the long side in the same way that the long side is related to the sum of the short side and long side (see A Golden Journal on page 145). This rectangle seems to be extraordinarily pleasing to humans as it also occurs over and over, not only in nature, but also in ancient and modern buildings and in artwork from many cultures.

In a Gothic cathedral, the proportions are frequently Golden. The hoped-for result of the light, the music (whose mathematical properties echo many of the geometrical properties of the architecture of the cathedral), and the architecture is that worshippers are emotionally transported out of their everyday lives and into a state of meditation and prayer. (This is a gross simplification of a subject that warrants greater discussion. For more information, an excellent source is Robert Lawler's *Sacred Geometry*, published in 1982 by Thames and Hudson.) Well now, how on earth can a journal transport someone in such a way? Tim Ely is a book artist who considers some books to be akin to cathedrals in that they also can act on the body to attune it to a higher, more spiritual frequency. Ely uses some of the same means as the cathedral builders. He constructs his books so that the dimensions form Golden Rectangles. Many elements on the pages also display the Golden Proportion and Rectangle as well as other

Jane Dalton, *La Playa*, 2004. 8 x 5 inches (20.3 x 12.7 cm). Hand-bound journal, watercolor pencils, micron pen. *Photo by Aleia Woolsey.*

Even though the term *journal* itself refers to the everyday, this journal doesn't have to stay with the quotidian or mundane interpretation of things. The same events and objects that might lead a naturalist to make careful and intellectually satisfying drawings and descriptions will inspire the spiritual journalist to reflect on the broader meaning, beyond material appearances. The same flower that the naturalist draws with precision becomes a simplified, colorful form—perhaps a part of a border—in the spiritual journal, a symbol that points beyond itself to the sacred, to the ecstatic, to the spiritual.

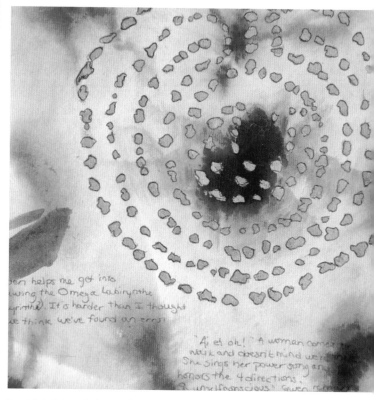

Janet Scholl, *Untitled Journal Page*, 2004. Text-weight paper, liquid acrylics, pen. *Photo by Gwen Diehn.*

proportions and geometric forms from Sacred Geometry. He lavishes enormous care and craftsmanship on the construction of his books. Often he adds a few drops of essential oil—lavender or rosemary perhaps—to the paste that he cooks to use as book adhesive. The result is a book that feels wonderful in the hand, a vibrating, auratic object that points to meanings far beyond the literal.

A spiritual-emotional journal then is one that grabs the reader by the neck and gives a tug and a shake. "Wake up!" it whispers. "Things are not what they seem to be on the surface!" This is a journal filled with rich colors and textures that invite contemplation and meditation. The book itself might be covered with velvet, soft leather, or some other material that feels good to hold. Pages may be laden with imagery, or they might consist of solid fields of colors with loose handwriting that leaps and skips and races across them. Whichever, the images and text in the journal deal with a spiritual interpretation of the world. This journal might also include reflections that draw meaning out of events and that move the journal keeper into a more spiritual realm of practice.

A Golden Journal

I f you would like to make your own spiritual journal, try using a Golden Rectangle for the overall shape. To construct this rectangle, first draw a square with its side the same length that you want the shorter dimension of the book's cover to be (see figure 1).

Now put a dot at the midpoint of sides AB and CD, and join the midpoints (see figure 2). Use a ruler to extend lines AB and CD, as in figure 3.

Now put one point of a compass (you can also use a piece of string pulled taut) at point E and the point of the compass pencil at point D (if using string, simply hold one end down at point E and, keeping it taut, hold the other end of the string with two fingers where it touches point D), as shown in figure 4. Then draw the arc to DG, which will intersect the extension of line AB at point G. (If using string, keep holding the measured length of string, one finger pressing it down at point D, and swing it to find out where it crosses the extension of AB, which is where you will make a mark, at G.)

Use a triangle to draw a straight line up from point G to a point H on the extension of line CD. The rectangle ACHG is a Golden Rectangle. Line AC is to line AG as line AG is to the sum of CA and AG.

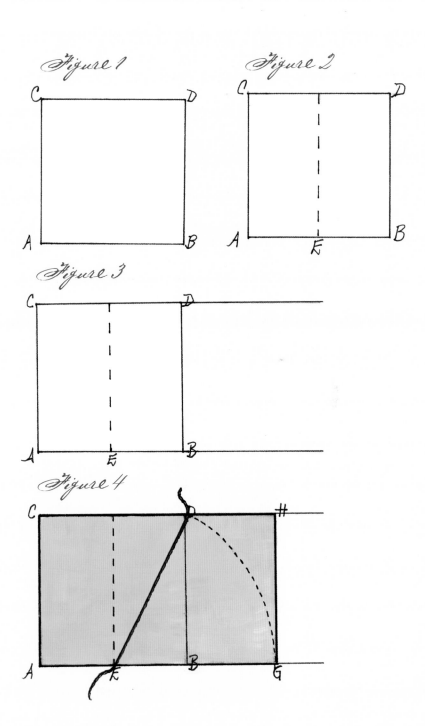

145

The Symbolic World

In Australian Aboriginal culture, the material world, and particularly the landscape, is a giant mnemonic device, a memory aid at the service of helping people remember the stories of their culture. A group of people walking across the dessert might stop at a gently sloping hill with several large boulders strewn along the ridge and there, prompted by the extremely subtle configuration of the land, sing a story about one of their ancestors. In this way the people have kept both their land and their stories alive.

In a custom completely alien to us in the west (who happily bulldoze grassy hillsides in order to flatten the land for the cheaper construction of tanning salons and gas stations, mini malls and karate parlors), Aborigines traditionally make annual walking journeys along ancient paths that they call "songlines." The stories they sing as they walk tell the history of their ancestors and of the time they call the Dreaming. For them, the material world is symbolic of a greater reality.

There are symbolic elements in our world, too. Places as well as objects that have been the scene of the events of our lives can become laden with associations. Frequently used objects sometimes seem to carry an aura of the person who used them. My grandfather's fountain pen rests on a shelf in my studio, and it never fails to remind me of the fact that he gave me my own first pen when I was in third grade—a maroon colored Esterbrook that my teacher confiscated, telling me I was too young to write with a pen!

A journal can be used to record and reflect on these symbols. Dream journals, especially, fall into the category of symbolic journals because the images in dreams are themselves symbols. Years ago I saw a beautiful, evocative dream journal in an exhibition of artwork by members of a society dedicated to the study of dreams. The little book was a journey through the nighttime landscape of the artist's dreams, and the symbols became a language that gave her a fine tool for interpretation.

The keeper of a symbolic journal will seek out patterns and motifs that summarize places, people, and ideas as well as dreams. Instead of making a realistic drawing of a landscape, this journaler is more likely to use the colors in the landscape in abstract shapes that float behind or beside text. A border of repeating abstract forms might hint at the season or the amount and kind of vegetation. When traveling, this kind of journaler might make rubbings of textures found in a place or simplify the forms of indigenous housing in the area visited.

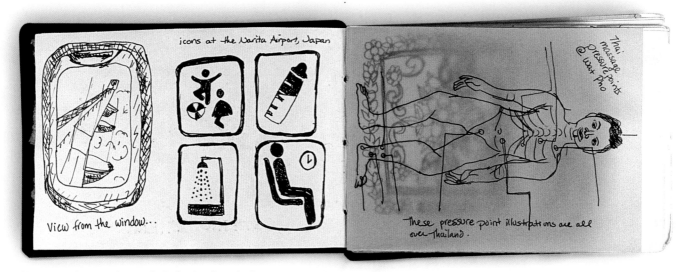

Kerstin Vogdes, *Travel Journal: Thailand and Cambodia*, 2004. 4 x 6 inches (10.2 x 15.2 cm) Hand-bound journal, PVA glue, vellum, ink, shells. *Photo by Aleia Woolsey.*

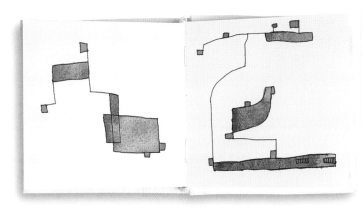

Val Lucas, 2004 journal. 4 x 4 inches, (10.2 x 10.2 cm), watercolor, pen, hand-bound journal.

Some symbolic journals have no text. The entire record is made in images, which are densely packed symbols. Let's say I have a complicated dream about driving a car that loses power slowly and can't move fast enough. Although many things happen in the dream (and many events are so fragmentary and ephemeral that I can't remember them clearly, nor put them into words), the feeling of being in a powerless car stays with me. My symbol for this dream might be my car with a large boulder tied to the back bumper, attempting to climb a hill.

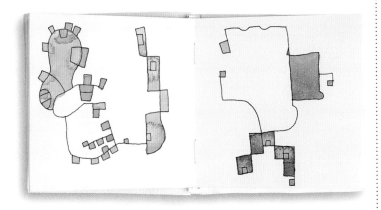

Val Lucas, 2004 journal. 4 x 4 inches, (10.2 x 10.2 cm), watercolor, pen, hand-bound journal.

Each page in Val's journal symbolically records her journey through life that day.

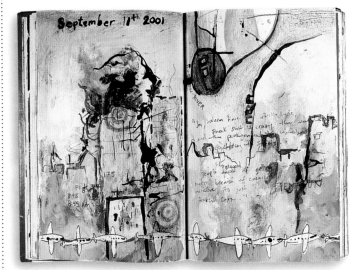

Kelcey Loomer, 2001. 11 x 8¼ inches (27.9 x 21 cm). acrylic paint, ink pen. *Photo by Aleia Woolsey.*

Other symbolic journals may be filled with text, the words themselves sketching metaphors and symbols for experiences that defy being pinned down and put into literal form. An important medium for symbolic journalers is collage of appropriated imagery. In using appropriated imagery, we harvest images as well as text from other sources and use these fragments as marks in a new, original expression. Collaged elements always carry some meaning and connotation from their former lives, and in this way they become symbolic. A piece of ephemera from everyday life—a theater ticket perhaps—will not only have the literal meaning "ticket stub," but will also carry some meaning based on its original context: "Romeo and Juliet" performed at the Folger Shakespeare Theatre or "Spiderman 2" playing at a multi-plex theater outside of Toledo, Ohio. A piece of paper with a print of a drawing or painting will obviously bring meaning, but also a scrap of patterned wrapping paper will be a reminder of a certain gift, and as such will carry connotative meaning beyond the pretty, if commonplace, pattern printed on it.

Without a Word
by Pat Gaignat

8¼ x 10¼ inches (21 x 26 cm). Gesso, acrylic pen, crayons, white pen; collage.

"I can open a volume at any page, and instantly I'm taken to the moment that prompted the image."

5½ x 7½ inches (14 x 19 cm). Gesso, acrylic, sharpie marker.

Slapping a mixture of leftover acrylic paint or gesso onto the journal pages takes the preciousness of the clean page away. It gives me permission to relax and just go with the flow, get in the zone, loosen up, and not be concerned about working consecutively. The book is for me, and I know what's going on.

I can open a volume at any page, and instantly I'm taken to the moment that prompted the image. I'm transported back in time and can experience the events without reading a single word. Yep, I still feel myself tripping on the cobblestones of Amsterdam, and I'm still embarrassed and look around to see if anyone has noticed.

Open another book and I flash back to the trepidation of the first time I went to Woodstock for a workshop—I can feel the butterflies and remember how I had to force myself to enter the studio. Still, another page will remind me of a broken lamp, even though the image was a chair. I remember how I had to interrupt the painting and go out into the cold, dark, winter evening to try to find the repair shop. No words are on that page. None are necessary.

Memories of Place and Time

by Sandy Webster

> *"Opening to a label from a southern Queensland winery brings with it the bonfire, the star-filled sky, and the laughter of friends."*

Australia 2003 Journal and Case. 6 x 19½ inches (15.2 x 49.5 cm). Pencil, watercolor.

Many of my journals are travel journals, primarily visual diaries of a place and time recorded in image with little text. I make the journals by hand in advance of traveling and format them to what seems to me to be the necessary size. I like them to be filled by the time the trip ends.

I look forward to these relived memories kept between the covers of my journals. Small drawings and paintings of scenery and collected bits of nature inevitably share space with wine labels and names of recommended books and movies. Opening to a label from a southern Queensland winery brings with it the bonfire, the star-filled sky, and the laughter of friends.

On another page in a different journal, I'm sharing a meal with a Maori woman who is telling me her life's ambitions. Other entries recall quiet times when I needed to just draw something from there, or mark the colors of that day and place.

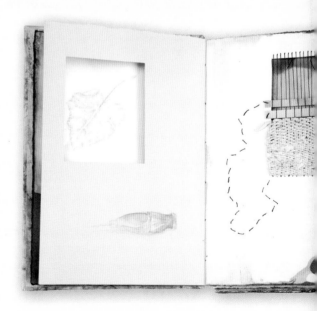

Paducah, Kentucky Artists' Retreat Journal.
7½ x 11¼ inches (19 x 28.6 cm).
Pencil, watercolor; stitched, woven.

Making the Invisible Visible

The bringing of one's past, present, emotions, hopes, fears, fleeting interests, prejudices, and any other contexts to the act of drawing enlivens it in a way that pure objective copying of nature never can. All the possible ways of seeing and of experiencing a place are crucial to the various possibilities for representing it. For this reason I love drawing the same scene over and over at different times in my life. I also love looking at 20 different people's interpretation of the same scene.

It's true that sometimes we draw to fix something in our minds or to learn more about it. (Today I drew a map of my house and yard so I could remember which bushes the tree man will remove when he comes to do some major yard work in a couple of weeks.) But it's also true that we draw to give visible form to that which can't be seen—to give form to evening breezes, creepy feelings, and unearthly coincidences. Drawing in many different ways—sometimes tight renderings, sometimes the barest minimum of fat lines, sometimes a spattering of color, sometimes a fretful hatching of lines—allows us to not only reproduce what we can see but also to make the invisible visible for ourselves as well as to anyone else who might look at our work.

Years ago, the painter Jennifer Bartlett rented a villa in the south of France for several months. Her dream of working in a beautiful place with balmy weather came crashing down around her ears when the place itself turned out to be ugly and the weather even worse. After days and days of cold rain and wind, after staring out of her windows into a mediocre little garden

Jennifer Bartlett, *In the Garden, #51. Photo ©Jennifer Bartlett.*

with its indifferent pool and trite little garden statue, its row of tedious trees, its uninspiring shrubbery—Bartlett decided to not only accept the circumstances in which she found herself, but to use them as the foundation of an experiment that would test the parameters of an artistic problem.

Bartlett went out and bought a large supply of paper and an assortment of materials: pencils, pens, charcoal, paints. She began setting up a journal-like situation in that she ruled off two rectangles on each of the first several dozen pieces of paper. The pile of neatly ruled paper was in a very real sense a blank (if unbound) journal. Her assignment to herself was to draw what she could see out of her window, and to draw it again, and again, and again, and again until she

had used up all of the paper. She began drawing on an afternoon in January and completed the project some 15 months later with nearly 200 completed drawings—all of the same patch of garden.

Bartlett did the first drawings from life, getting down as much as possible of exactly what she could see. She began with pencil, moved to colored pencil, and then back to pencil. These first drawings are similar to each other in composition and in their inclusion of details, varied surface renderings, and in Bartlett's apparent attempts to create three-dimensional space. She then moved to pen and ink, and the drawings became more simplified and veered toward the abstract. She varied the focus: in one drawing the trees are prominent, in another the pool and statue dominate and seem to stand on end, in another the entire scene is reduced to a series of dashes and dots. Periodically she returned to a more naturalistic rendering, but here also the focus and point of view changed from drawing to drawing.

By drawing number 15, the drawings, although still grounded in the pool, statue, trees, shrubbery, and grass, seem to be more about Bartlett's response to the scene than about literal rendering. Some drawings have a brooding quality. Others seem light-hearted and playful. When she begins to use watercolor, outlines melt and the drawings become even more abstract. There are drawings that focus tightly on the water in

the pool and the way light plays on the surface. There are others that take a high point of view and reduce the pool to a tiny feature in what looks like a huge expanse of space. Some drawings explode out of their borders, with the trees behind the pool shooting up like flames.

When Bartlett returns to pencil after a number of color drawings, the drawings return to a more literal, naturalistic type, but there is a new looseness to them. Portions are left unfinished in some; another is rendered as meticulously as an architect's drawing, but the trees behind the pool dissolve into squiggles and melt into the sky. Pen and wash drawings become bolder and simpler as the series

progresses; watercolor drawings dissolve into dots or pale washes with barely any reference to the scene. And always, after a number of abstract drawings, there is a coming back to the naturalistic, which seems a sort of summing up of new things experienced or learned.

About a quarter of the way through the series, the drawings get bigger, and each one takes up its own sheet of paper. Then suddenly a tiny set of two drawings appears, looking like something seen through the wrong end of a telescope, with a fat white border framing the drawings. Later, the drawings return to the original two-to-a-page format.

The enormous variety of these drawings points to the enormous variety of the garden itself when one stops imposing expectations on it and begins to experience it as a new place every day. What Bartlett has done is to bring her constantly changing emotions, memories, stories, and interests to this place, and allow her drawings to be guided by her daily varying purposes and intents. And this is where, to me, her work has great interest to any journal keeper. Her work highlights the fact that what we do in our journals is as much a part of who we are as what we see and experience. It doesn't matter if "nothing ever happens to me" or "I live in a boring place."

Bartlett's complete series has been dispersed, but a record of it still exists in book form. Search used bookstores and libraries for *In the Garden* by Jennifer Bartlett with an introduction by John Russell, published in 1982 by Harry N. Abrams, Inc., New York.

BURANO

Faith McLellan, *Lunch on Burano*, 2004. Bound journal, gluestick, watercolor, pencil, rubber stamp, pen, candy wrapper ephemera; painted, drawn, glued, stamped. *Photo by artist.*

The Inner World

The Inner World

Andrea A. Peterson, *Ox Bow*, 2003. 12 x 18 inches (30.5 x 45.7 cm). Coptic hand-bound journal, cotton rag handmade paper, tracing paper, colored pencil, charcoal, pastel; drawn and glued. *Photo by artist.*

When my friend Bette begins a new drawing, she makes random marks on a piece of paper, back and forth, up and down—soft sweeps of her pencil, marks made with no conscious intention. Inevitably, after a while, an image begins to emerge. For Bette, the image is often a face, but sometimes animals or objects appear. Only then does Bette begin to work consciously on the drawing. She believes that by restraining her conscious mind at first, she allows images to well up from her subconscious.

Bette's manner of working is related to ideas developed by a group of artists and writers in the early 20th century called the Surrealists. The Surrealists were influenced by the then-new practice of psychoanalysis, in which the patients' unconscious or subconscious minds were revealed by means of certain techniques. The intended result was to free the patients from the hold these hidden parts of the psyche had on their lives.

The Surrealists invented games and practices aimed at releasing subconscious imagery. One of their practices was what they called automatic writing—writing that was done spontaneously with no thought and with no effort at making rational sense or even recognizable meaning. Games, too, with names such as "The Exquisite Corpse," involved random acts of writing that were believed to generate true creative results. Dream imagery was very important to them because it emerged from the unconscious mind.

A recent practice designed to get around the censoring intellect (which can so easily freeze us in our efforts to come up with new ideas) is Julia Cameron's Morning Pages exercise. Cameron has designed a program to free the artist she believes to be within each person. One of the core practices of her program is to bounce out of bed in the morning and immediately write three pages in a journal. If nothing comes, it's okay to write something along the lines of, "I have nothing to write today," over and over again to fill the pages. Once the pages are complete, they are put away unread until much later. Cameron believes that morning pages tap into our unconscious minds in a way that can't be done later in the day after we're fully awake and functioning.

If a naturalist's journal is focused on the world outside of us, the inner journal is the polar opposite. An inner journal is about me: the writer and artist. The visuals in the journal may grow out of doodles and random marks, or they may be fragments of images that we've come across and that have somehow beckoned to us, like shiny objects calling to a crow. Poured paint might suggest an image that the journal keeper will coax out of the random shapes on the page. Words overheard in a restaurant might spark associations that lead to revelations. This is the journal in which to explore just what it is that your eye loves to look at, and also just why it is

Kelcey Loomer, 2004. 9¼ x 6¼ inches (23.5 x 15.9 cm).
Pen, pencil, oil pastel, watercolor, ribbon. *Photo by Aleia Woolsey.*

that your eye loves to look at that particular image. It is a place to express your thoughts and feelings about the sounds your ear loves to hear.

This is the journal to angrily fling paint at without understanding quite why, and then to come back to later and refine the shapes that seems to peek out from behind the colors. Lists of words, collections of sounds, pieces of ephemera, and patches of texture—all of these can be held safe in this journal, percolating, until someday, years later, you return to this old book and find yourself able to see patterns and ideas and images you never suspected at the time.

This is also the journal for whining about relationships, and fretting about your children, and getting excited about new discoveries, and explaining your feelings in more detail than any of your friends would have the patience to listen to. This journal is the grown-up sister of the diary I kept in high school, the one in which I carried on for 12 pages trying to decide exactly what it was that so-and-so-meant when he said thus and so, and not only that, but—12 more pages—how would I possibly live without him, and moreover, he certainly wasn't worth all this agony, so there!

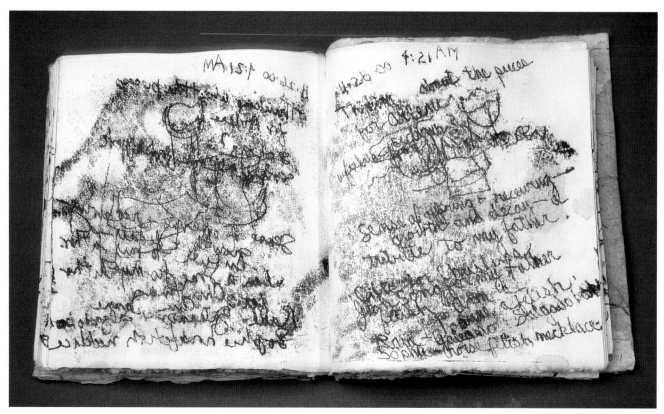

Julie Wagner, *Insomniac's Journal*, 2001. 9¼ x 8¾ x 1 inches (23.5 x 22.2 x 2.5 cm). Stab bound journal, mulberry paper, ink, oil-transfer drawing. *Photo by Dan Morse.*

Victoria Rabinowe, *Dream Journal Drawings*, 2004. 8¼ x 7 x ½ inches (21 x 17.8 x 1.3 cm). Text woven paper, hand-drawn graphite images, pen, watercolor, pastel; concertina structure, scanned, manipulated, computer printed. *Photo by artist.*

Stepping-stone to the Future

by Sarah Bourne

Seattle Journal Pages. 7¼ x 11¾ inches (18.4 x 29.8 cm). Pen, watercolor; collage.

"Journaling is critical to how I see the world, and it becomes a stepping-stone for future work."

Recently when visiting my parents, I discovered a pile of journals in the closet of my old room, maybe 15 of them, dating back to 1989 when I was in the second grade. It seems that I've been journaling since I could put sentences together. It started as a way of recording my day—with many incorrectly spelled words—and has evolved as a way to record life's happenings with words and images.

Journaling is critical to how I see the world, and it becomes a stepping-stone for future work. It provides me with a way of processing my life, understanding, collecting, and categorizing all of the tiny parts so they make sense, so I can remember and reflect.

I tend to journal more when on a trip or when doing something out of the ordinary. But my recent journals have become more about recording the seemingly insignificant details of everyday life, which makes things a little spicier and creates a way for me to appreciate day-to-day existence.

Seattle Journal Pages. 7¼ x 11¾ inches (18.4 x 29.8 cm). Pen, watercolor; collage.

Applications

In this section, we'll look step by step at 10 sample pages, each featuring a different approach to content. These approaches range from the most familiar and commonly used—information gathering and storytelling—to increasingly reflective and analytic processes, including mining your journal for materials that can be developed into other creative projects.

The choices you make about the content grow directly out of your reasons for keeping a journal or making a scrapbook. You may have chosen to record everything of interest that happens to you each day. Or you might want to focus more narrowly and create an ongoing collection of ideas and images about a particular subject that interests you: ancient music, ferns and mosses, your new baby. By keeping in mind the purpose of the book, you can create beautiful pages that express your intentions both visually and verbally.

Wendy Hale Davis, *Transformer*, 1993. Pen, ink, collage. *Photo by Bob Daemmrich.*

Information Gathering

Traditional diarists, logbook keepers, and sketch artists have always used observation and information gathering as a primary approach. Observation is also a favorite tool of researchers in fields such as anthropology and education. When you observe, you simply focus and record whatever you perceive as closely as possible, either in writing or by sketching.

For example, you might have a particular goal or question in mind: What kinds of birds are visiting the bird feeder this week? Or you might set out to record whatever happens around you as you walk through a foreign marketplace or ride a train from one city to another. Observations simply present information. They don't interpret, judge, or ask questions, or reflect. Observation is a process for gathering raw material. After you've made your initial observations, you might choose to go back and reflect on them, but while you're writing or drawing, your only interest, your focus, is on being an instrument that witnesses and records. You can do some recording and observation after an experience, but don't wait too long or you'll forget details. It's best to observe and record on the spot. Next best is to rush home to your journal and catch up before you've forgotten too much. A good compromise is to take very quick, sketchy notes, both visually and verbally, on the spot and then go over your notes, filling in the gaps, as soon as you get home.

Ann Turkle used black pen for her information-gathering entries.

SAMPLE PAGE: ANTIQUE CHAIRS

I wanted to gather information about some antique chairs I had recently purchased. They were constructed in a very clever way that wasn't at first easy to understand. Drawing the chairs helped me understand how they worked.

STEP 1

I had prepared a page by sponging on stamp pad ink (see pages 73 to 74). The sunny color of this page suited this journal entry. If the next available page in my journal had been prepared in a way that didn't seem to go with this idea, I would have skipped that page and used the next page that did. Skipped pages are useful for going back and reflecting on entries or further developing them in various ways.

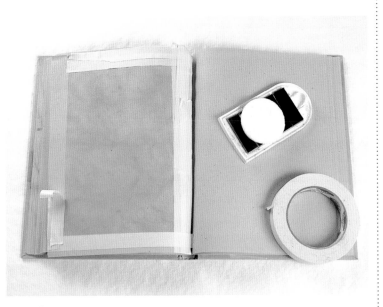

STEP 2

I chose black waterproof pen to work in because I wanted the crisp, clear detail this kind of pen can give. I decided to use a full-page layout with a border because the written entry was rather short and could fit nicely on the same page as the dawings, making a pleasing and easy-to-understand composition.

I sketched out the chairs lightly, looking very carefully at details, such as the way the legs fold together and bend when the chair is closed. To get the proportions right, I measured the length of the backs of the chairs against their widths. I was careful to draw only what I saw, not what my brain told me about chairs. For example, from where I was sitting, the seats of the chairs looked thin and flattened, rather than square. Had I drawn them as I knew they really were, that is, square, the chairs would have looked strange because from the point of view from which I was drawing I could see only the front ends plus a little of the top surfaces of the chairs. It's important in drawing representationally to maintain a uniform point of view. Keep your head still and draw only what you can

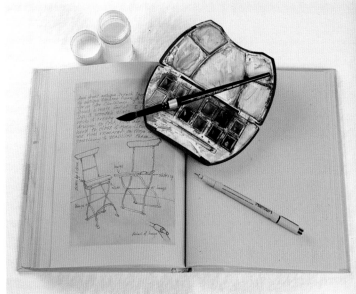

159

STEP 3

After I had drawn the chairs and the detail of the hinge, I wrote the entry and tried out a watercolor wash on the detail of the hinge.

Since all of the information was gathered in step 2, I could have done step 3 later. I simply added a watercolor wash to the chairs and printed a border using a cork stamp of the letter "H." The shape of the H reminded me of the back of one of the chairs, so I used it as the basis of the pattern that decorates the border.

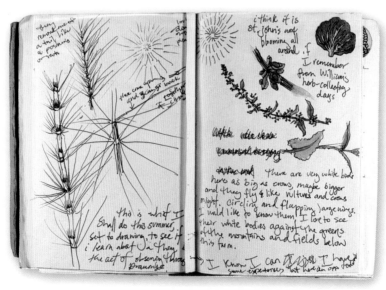

Laura Carter chose black pen highlighted by touches of watercolor to gather detailed information about plants on this page. *Photo by Elyse Weingarten.*

Storytelling

Storytelling differs from simple information gathering in that when we tell a story, we select details and events that help shape information for a certain purpose. The story can be based on fact or fiction; have a moral or lesson; have a funny or a surprising outcome; or reinforce, present, or question certain cultural ideas or history. Anne Frank's famous diary is essentially a storytelling journal in which each day's entry presents a part of the story of a Jewish family's experience in Germany during World War II.

Whatever the purpose of a story, it generally has a beginning, a climax, and an ending. The visual counterpart of the story is an illustration. An information-gathering sketch aims at accuracy and clarity. An illustration has a similar relationship to a story. It not only presents information but also evokes certain emotional responses in the viewer. When we draw illustrations, we select details, colors, and a composition that will help tell the story we want to tell. Illustrations and stories can enhance each other or stand on their own.

On these pages, Kelcey Loomer recounts the story of a moonlight swim at the summer solstice through a written entry and painted image. *Photo by Elyse Weingarten.*

In this page by the author, one side of the entry tells the story verbally, while the other illustrates the event in watercolor and handcarved cork stamp, on a page that was prepared with poured acrylic. *Photo by Elyse Weingarten.*

SAMPLE PAGE: HAYING IN ITALY

In the example shown here, the story was very simple, but it served to tell about a cultural practice in a small village in Italy where I was spending a few weeks. This story doesn't have a great moral point, an exciting development, or a surprise ending, but it does explain the sudden appearance of a curious structure made of hay.

The field behind & beyond the pozzo vecchio has been planted in hay this year. One day we awaken to a distant soft clattering sound. Mowing is going on all over the valley, and today it's happening in the prato field. Two men are doing the job with a tiny tractor.

By buono sera time the dry grass has been sheared and lies in sweet smelling waves on the ground. By lunch time the next day the stems have been raked & packed into workmanlike cubic rectangles.

And the next time we trudge past on our way to the alimentari the hay bricks have been stacked into what looks like a toy barn, & a black plastic tarp has been tied like a handkerchief over the top, mooring it to the ground, fending off the infrequent rain.

STEP 1

I began on a plain, white, unprepared page. I chose a grid layout because the hay blocks were such a prominent part of the story, and this layout echoed their shape and repetition. Also, writing and drawing in separate blocks echoed the days in the long process I was describing. The first step was to lightly rule off the page with graphite pencil.

STEP 2

Next, I wrote and sketched in the boxes using waterproof black pen because of its clarity and ability to render small details. When I finished, I carefully erased the pencil guidelines I had made in the first step.

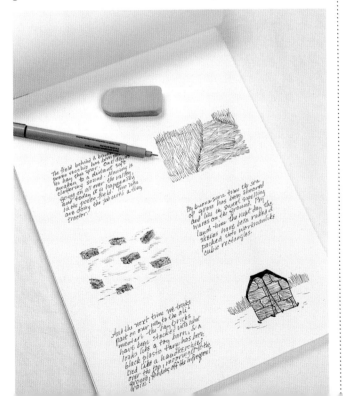

STEP 3

Finally, I used colored pencils to color in the drawings and to make a pattern of wavy, haylike lines over all the spaces that were not written or drawn on. I cut a sunlike shape from a gold foil candy wrapper and glued it to the top of the page to refer to the hot sunny weather necessary for haying.

163

Lists and Collections

Making a list or recording a collection of items that have something in common are good ways to look at a place or a situation from a slight distance. This process, besides being interesting to do in itself, can lead to longer reflections, or even, if you're so inclined, to stories and poems. The pillow book described on page 167 is an example of a journal that contains many diverse lists and collections.

Pick a category of things that interests you or that you've noticed recurring in your surroundings. Find as many examples as you can in that category. Categories can be attributes, such as "the tastes of different kinds of olives," or objects, such as "doorways," or "plants blooming during May."

Right: Bruce Kremer's lively collection of fish was done using pen and watercolor, with a line of typed text collaged at the bottom.

Left: Kremer incorporated a bird map of New Zealand into his journal to keep track of all the birds he spotted there.

SAMPLE PAGE: YOGA ASANAS

I made a collection of yoga asanas (positions) that are calming. My intention was to use the collection as a reminder. Since I knew how to do the asanas, I didn't need detailed drawings; a simple icon was sufficient. I chose wax resist, using crayons and watercolor because this medium is good for quick gesture drawings that are graceful as well as colorful. Columns were used so the list would be easy to read when I was practicing yoga, but I selected a page that had a graceful poured preparation to lend a dynamic underlayer to the design.

STEP 1

I started with a page that had liquid acrylics poured over it in a flowing design. I used a graphite pencil to lightly rule off columns for each asana and written explanation.

STEP 2

I then referred to photographs of each asana and drew them with crayons in their boxes. I outlined each figure with waterproof black pen. I wrote explanations and notes on each asana in pencil.

STEP 3

Finally, I brushed a watercolor wash over the drawings to add color and to make the drawings stand out. Then I used a stencil to do the lettering down the left-hand column.

The Pillow Book of Sei Shonagon

Sei Shonagon was a diarist and poet who lived in Japan during the Heian period, a golden age of peace and prosperity in Japanese culture. She was born in 966 and died in 1013. During her lifetime, aristocratic women enjoyed influential roles at court, even though they were excluded from political affairs.

Wit and intelligence and the ability to write letters and poems in fine calligraphy were all desirable attributes among the educated women of the court. Both men and women kept journals which were collections of their thoughts and impressions, character sketches and court gossip, and musings about such topics as the transience of life. It is thought that they kept these journals in their sleeping quarters; hence they came to be known as "pillow books."

Sei Shonagon began writing her journal in an informal notebook style that is known as makura no soshi, or pillow book style. Yet even her informal writing was done in such a pure form of prose that it is considered a model of good style. Although she began her journal in private, it was soon circulated at court because of its elegant style and witty, beautifully written contents. Once her book became well known, Shonagon began writing in a more self-conscious manner, with an awareness that her pillow book would be read by the public. She was an excellent and detached observer of her own culture. She used her sharp wit to criticize those she considered beneath her, while at the same time praising the Imperial family.

Kano Chikayasu, *Scenes from the Tale of Genji*.
Courtesy of the Saint Louis Art Museum.

The panels in this screen depict courtly life during Japan's Heian period, the era represented in Shonagon's *Pillow Book*.

Shonagon's book is a collection of anecdotes and impressions, but its most striking feature is its 164 lists. These lists, more than any other part of the pillow book, give us a detailed picture of Heian upper-class life, preoccupations, and values. The titles of the lists themselves tell us what was important and worth noticing in this ancient culture. Some of the titles are "Things That Give an Unclean Feeling," "Annoying Things," "Things Which Distract in Moments of Boredom," "Hateful Things," "Rare Things," and "Things Which Make One's Heart Beat Faster."

Shonagon's pillow book was translated into English by Arthur Waley in 1929 and by Ivan Morris in 1967. Amazingly, this very old journal has maintained its appeal, and Morris's translation is still a popular book today. Morris's original translation is in two volumes and is considered the standard complete translation. In 1991 he published an abridged translation in which some of the lists were cut. Following are lists from Morris's 1967 translation:

ELEGANT THINGS

- A white coat worn over a violet waistcoat

- Duck eggs

- Shaved ice mixed with liana syrup and put in a new silver bowl

- A rosary of rock crystal

- Wisteria blossoms

- Plum blossoms covered with snow

- A pretty child eating strawberries

THINGS THAT HAVE LOST THEIR POWER

- A large boat which is high and dry in a creek at ebbtide

- A woman who has taken off her false locks to comb the short hair that remains

- A large tree that has been blown down in a gale and lies on its side with its roots in the air

- A man of no importance reprimanding an attendant

THINGS THAT CANNOT BE COMPARED

- Summer and winter

- Night and day

- Rain and sunshine

- Youth and age

- A person's laughter and his anger

- Black and white

- Love and hatred

(from *The Pillow Book of Sei Shonagon*, translated and edited by Ivan Morris. New York: Columbia University Press, 1967).

Patterns and Motifs

Patterns and motifs refer to recurring thematic elements. A pattern usually refers to a fixed and regular repetition of shapes or of a single shape, whereas a motif refers to an element that pops up frequently in an environment. Patterns and motifs can be on a micro level, such as shapes that repeat at regular intervals on the surface of a leaf. They can also be on a macro level, such as the pattern of the seasons every year or the pattern of changes that the moon repetitively goes through every 28 days. Naturalists' journals, such as the ones described on page 20, often contain patterns and motifs.

Looking for patterns and motifs in a particular environment or in daily life can give you interesting insights. When you focus on finding them, you begin to find them everywhere. Patterns and motifs tell you something about the structures and order of places, objects, people, and events. You can become aware of visual patterns as well as patterns of speech, cultural patterns, the patterns and motifs that are found in nature, and the patterns that govern so much of your own life.

Andrea A. Peterson, NY Sketchbook, 1993. Hemp, pastels, and marker. *Photo by artist.*

SAMPLE PAGE:
DESIGNS FROM NATURE

The motifs on this page are simplified forms of things found in nature, designs I copied from ceramic artwork in a museum in Italy. Like the artist who rendered these abstracted leaves, pods, and stems, you can simplify patterns and designs from your environment.

STEP 1

In designing the page in this example, I began searching for patterns and motifs in a museum that had a collection of very old ceramics and other artifacts. I used a page that had been prepared with a stamped pattern that reminded me of the old brickwork on the walls of the museum.

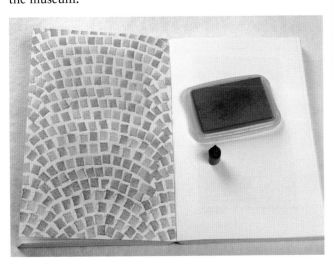

STEP 2

While in the museum, I used a black waterproof pen to sketch motifs and patterns that I found on some of the ceramics and other objects on display. I also wrote some observations about the patterns and motifs and about the pieces themselves. The pen was dark enough to show up against the pattern of the paper. I used a small grid to lay out the page because the regularity of the grid emphasized the regularity of patterns. Because I was working on site, I wasn't able to rule off the grid first, but simply scattered the drawings in a more or less gridlike arrangement.

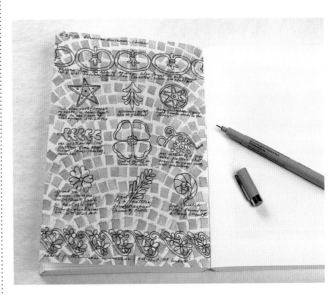

STEP 3

When I got home, I added watercolor in a cool, greenish gray color, something like the color of the ceramics and a nice contrast with the warm tones of the brick pattern.

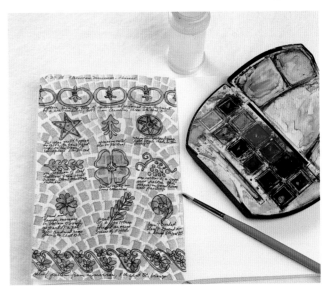

Bird's-eye View

Years ago, people used to draw a kind of map by going up to the tallest hilltop around and drawing the town in the valley as if seen by a bird flying over. These maps were called bird's-eye maps. During the 19th century, bird's-eye maps were made for a number of towns in the United States. You can still find examples, such as the one below, in the local history collections of some public libraries or in the Library of Congress. One interesting thing about a bird's-eye map is that it shows more than the unassisted human eye can see, both in terms of breadth of vision and also detail.

For our next approach to content, we'll view a subject as if seeing it from a great distance, but with good detail, like a bird's-eye map. There are several ways of pulling back and getting a broader perspective on your subject. One way to do this is by making a floor plan; another is by mapping. Making diagrams of systems can also accomplish this. Any of these processes can help you get a "big picture" view of a place or a whole system. When you put things together in a system, you begin to understand how the parts function together, as well as what proportion of the system or place is given over to a particular kind of object or activity. Maps and diagrams are also useful planning devices, helping you see your ideas before committing money and time to them.

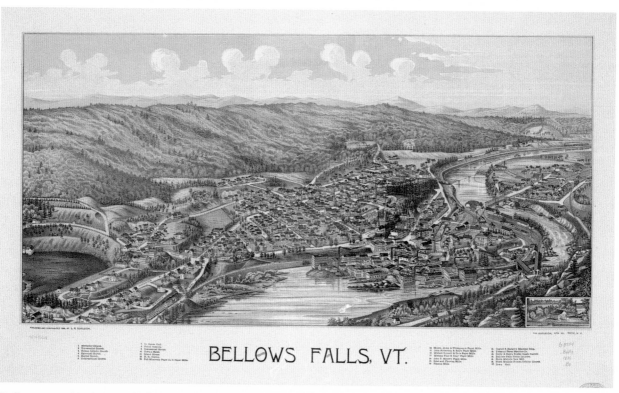

BELLOWS FALLS, VT.

Bird's-eye maps, like this one of Bellows Falls, Vermont, were common in the 19th century.
Photo courtesy of the Library of Congress, American Memory Collection.

SAMPLE PAGE: GARDEN MAP

In the example page shown here, I was interested in mapping an ideal garden. I modeled it loosely on a medieval garden plan that I found in a book and modified it to suit the space I had available. Even though I knew I couldn't build such an elaborate garden all at once, having the map was a useful guide as I went about adding elements of the plan to the space.

STEP 1

I began with a page of grid paper that I laminated into a journal. Because the grid paper was rather thin, I knew the stamps I planned to use would bleed through the paper. It made sense to laminate the grid paper to a journal page rather than tip it in because I wanted the protection of a backing page. First, I sketched the location of the different parts of the garden in pencil, including the house, ponds, walls, and all of the plantings.

STEP 2

Next, I used stamps that I had carved out of corks and erasers (see page 92) to record the garden areas on the map. The individual stamp designs became interesting patterns when I repeated them.

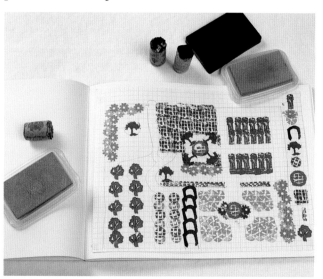

STEP 3

I colored the areas between elements with water-soluble colored pencils and brushed over the strokes with water to make washes that retained some stroke marks. Then, I used commercial rubber stamp letters to stamp on the names of the different garden elements and homemade cork alphabet stamps to add the title.

Decision Making

A journal can be a great tool in decision making. Usually when a journaler uses a journal to help decide things, she will simply write. She might make two lists, with the pros and cons of each decision written out in logical fashion. She might write an analysis of each possibility and the ramifications of each choice. These are good processes, but they have one shortcoming; they are mental or logical processes. It's important to go beyond rational and logical thoughts when making decisions. When we omit our emotions or our intuition from the decision-making process, we lose important information. We're so used to valuing the logical in our culture that we often overlook our feelings or consider them to be frivolous or indulgent. But the truth is that if we make a decision that is logical but doesn't satisfy our feelings, we will often regret that decision.

The process of using visual as well as verbal means to compare things helps us discover emotional and intuitive information. The difficult part is finding out what we really feel or sense about something. A useful way to begin is by closing your eyes and visualizing one of the possibilities. Ask yourself what colors and shapes you see. Avoid literally imagining an object, person, or a place. Stick with colors, shapes, sounds, or smells. Then open your eyes and begin to paint or draw, just putting down colors and shapes that reflect what you felt and sensed. When you're satisfied that you've represented your image for the first possibility, repeat the process for the next one.

Amy Cook, from Relocation Journal, 2000.
Pen and ink, collage. *Photo by Dan Essig.*

SAMPLE PAGE: BUYING A HOUSE

In the example shown here, I was trying to decide which house to buy. I started with unprepared paper because I didn't want to be influenced by any colors or shapes that were already on the page. I used two facing pages, one for each possibility. Watercolors were a good medium because I could work quickly and without thought.

STEP 1

I closed my eyes and visualized the first house. Immediately, I saw morning sunlight playing on a warm wooden floor. I opened my eyes and quickly painted golden yellow shapes against a warm brown background.

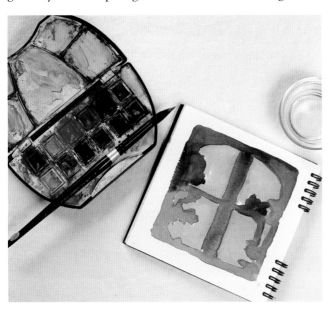

STEP 2

I then closed my eyes and imagined the second house. The colors and shapes that came to me were cool, light, and bulky shapes, a feeling of being closed in with a little cool light filtering through. I opened my eyes and painted colors and shapes to describe that image.

When both pages were dry, I made a list on each page of attributes of the paintings, such as "warm, moving, open, light, morning, flow, moving outward, shadows" and "cool, blue, crowded, looming shapes, dark, narrow, soft." I resisted making a decision or even any judgments at this point.

STEP 3

When I had finished the two lists, I began to write sentences about each painting, free-associating things about the paintings, NOT about the houses. For example, I wrote about the first painting, "Dark shapes hold light out, but the light is so penetrating that it leaks into the dark spaces. Upside down, the painting seems to be more about light flowing into a warm, dark space, a comfortable container. The edges where light and dark meet are irregular and uncertain." About the second painting I wrote, "Clunky pillows of color are piled up against a cool, blue opening. The shapes look layered and soft, like pillows, like blankets. Upside down, the shapes seem to hold up the red top part. The blue is an opening directly out into space. There is a clear openness, no barriers, but the pillow shapes look like they could fall down and smother the opening at any time."

In the border around the paintings, I wrote my logical thoughts about each house. It became clear as I wrote that the houses were equal in terms of cost, location, space, and condition. So I left the journal opened to this page on my desk for several days.

Over time I found myself gravitating to the yellow and brown image more and more. In the end, I bought the house that image represented, and lived happily there for many years. Although the other house was a good house, it didn't feel as right to me emotionally as the house I bought. Painting the image helped clarify the hard-to-describe characteristics that I recognized emotionally and intuitively but that hadn't fit into my logical thinking.

Memory Books
and More

A memory book is a journal-like book that contains carefully selected images that celebrate a specific part of one's life. One forerunner of the memory book is the family Bible, where births, baptisms, marriages, and deaths were entered in the margins and on the flyleaves. Such Bibles became a kind of family memory book. Sometimes, photographs as well as birth, marriage, baptismal, and death certificates were pasted in, resulting in true altered books that contain a history of a family. In some cases these are the only records left of a family, and altered Bibles have become legal documents.

Many early memory books centered around children and family. By the early 20th century, these had been commercialized, and people could buy already-formatted books that had drawings of idealized babies and nursery items, along with blank spaces in which the record-keeper could write the baby's weight, height, first words, first toys, and other firsts. There were pages for reflection and description, and pages devoted to photographs and other memorabilia—cards, school papers, old report cards, the little envelope of hair from the first haircut.

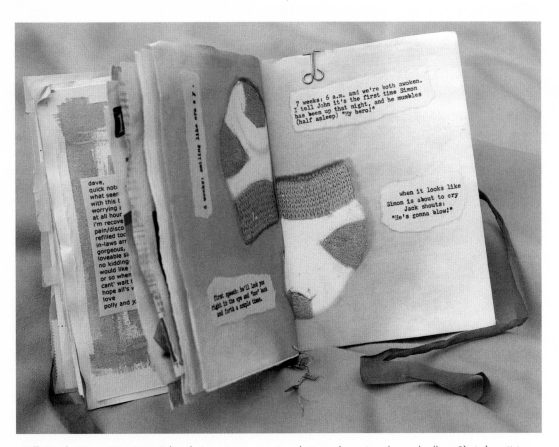

Polly Smith, *Simon*, 2000-2001. Color photocopies, mementos, photographs, watercolor, and collage. *Photo by artist.*

Beata Wehr, *My Home=My Homes*, 1997. Collage, painting, pen, and ink. *Photo by artist.*

High school memory books were soon commercialized also, and these followed the format of baby books—sentimental illustrations decorating pages with blanks left for specific information. Many of us still have these albums, bulging with dried corsages and party napkins, filled with exhortations from our friends to "Have a great life and remember ME!"

The main difference between a memory book and a journal is that a journal, whatever its focus, is inclusive of the good and the bad, the momentous and the trivial, the beautiful and the not so beautiful. Memory books, on the other hand, are focused on a particular person, event, or brief time period, and their makers tend to select certain positive aspects of the event or person to remember. In addition, memory books, because of their element of selectivity, are usually made after the fact and are designed and structured to fit their particular purposes, whereas journals are works in progress, with each day's entry simply being made on the next available page.

Journals can and often do furnish raw material for memory books. Going back into a journal to look for patterns and trends, themes and repetitions can be one of the great pleasures of journal-keeping. A memory book made to celebrate a particular event might recast images and written passages from a journal, as well as include materials that weren't included in the original journal, such as photographs.

If the makers of memory books tend to select and shape the raw material from journals and other sources, artists who make what are called *bookworks* or *artists' books* go a step further. Artists' books, or bookworks, are difficult to define, but artist Ulises Carrion gave a good definition when he said, "Bookworks are books that are conceived as an expressive unity, that is to say, where the message is the sum of all materials and formal elements." (Ulises Carrion. *Second Thoughts.* Amsterdam: Void Distributors, 1980: 25.)

Susan Kapuscinski Gaylord, *Kupuscinski Family Book*, 1990. Collage, maps, photocopies, various papers. *Photo by artist*.

Journals can be made to fit virtually any container, from a dime-store notebook to a handmade, leather-bound book. Yet the form and materials of an artists' book are integral to its expression, and the forms of artists' books are as varied, yet specific to the concept, as those of any other sculptural form. One distinguishing characteristic of an artists' book is that its folds and cuts, the way it is opened and manipulated, and the materials used in its construction all carry meaning.

Book artists use the material from journals to make books, but these books go beyond the scope of memory books in that they raise questions as well as give information about people and events. Many artists' books involve memory, but the interest of the artists is more in the subject of memory and its place in our lives than in celebrating a particular memory. Even those books devoted to a particular memory often tease apart the layers of memories and contrast different people's memories of the same person or event. Like all postmodern artwork, bookworks question assumptions and open our eyes to new possibilities.

Journals, memory books, and artists' books are distinct genres; but they all grow out of the common practices of paying close attention, of selecting parts of an experience to remember, and of transforming experiences into visual and verbal expression.

Spilling

Journals are often used for the expression of emotions, both in writing and visually. "Spilling" is a term coined by writing teachers for the process of free writing at the beginning of a class session. When students spill, they pour their emotions out onto the paper with no attention to grammar, spelling, or the niceties of composition. The purpose is to empty the emotions, to clear the mind.

Spilling can also be done visually, by painting, collaging, or drawing colors and shapes that express emotions. The person constructing this kind of visual is not concerned with appearance or with perfect composition and technique. Colors and shapes are chosen for their emotionally evocative qualities. They are laid down quickly, without giving the ever-judging mind a chance to intervene.

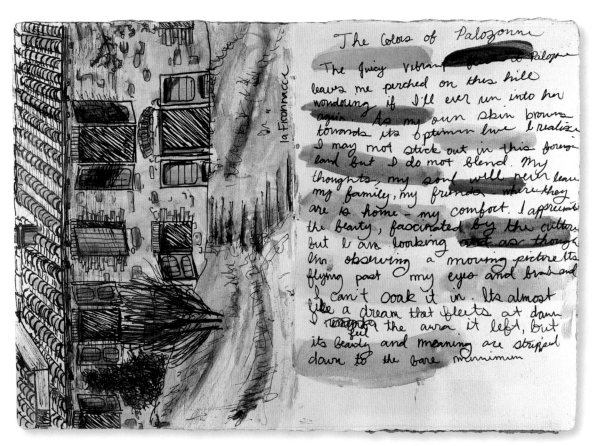

Blair Gulledge used watercolor to emphasize the emotions she wrote about. *Photo by Elyse Weingarten.*

SAMPLE PAGE:
LEARNING A NEW LANGUAGE

In this example, I was concerned with expressing the sense of bewilderment and helplessness that I felt when I was immersed in a foreign language at an intensive language learning program.

STEP 1

I began with an unprepared page to which I glued a cutout of foreign language text. I shaped the cutout and glued it in such a way as to divide the page along a diagonal, because I wanted the feeling of instability that this layout can give.

STEP 2

I wrote my feelings about the situation in wax crayon across the whole page, covering the collaged part as well as the top of the page. Then I quickly painted over the page with watercolor. Because the collage paper was glossy, I added a small amount of dishwashing detergent to the watercolor. The detergent breaks the surface tension of the water and allows it to attach itself to the glossy paper, on which it would otherwise bead. Besides helping the paint stick to the page, the detergent gave an interesting foamy texture to the paint.

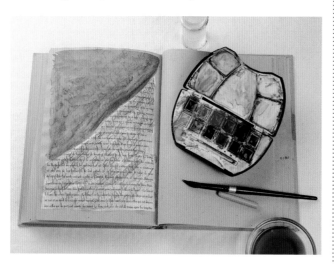

STEP 3

Finally, I cut out a small paper boat from glossy magazine paper and glued it in position. I drew over a few of the words with a dark colored pencil in order to emphasize them.

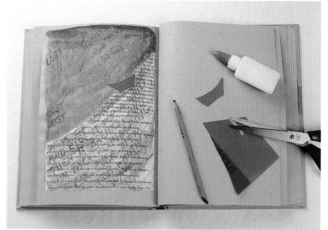

Changing Forms

Changing a form in the context of a journal means simply to record visually and in writing what you can hear, smell, taste, or touch. Changing the form of a sensation or perception deepens your experience of the original, making it fuller and richer. This visual record of a fleeting sensation or perception makes it possible to remember an experience that might otherwise be lost.

To change the form of a sensation, you need to focus intently, so you not only hear a particular distant soft clattering sound, but you associate a color and shape with it, thereby fleshing out the sound and implanting it more fully in your memory. The nostalgic odor of a lilac bush takes on a shape as well as color. The myriad tastes of young vegetables fresh from a garden become a pattern of colors moving in a shape that awakens your senses to the original every time you look at it.

This collection of sounds by the author was rendered visually using crayon resist. *Photo by Elyse Weingarten.*

SAMPLE PAGE: BIRD SOUNDS

For this page, I took my naturalist's journal for a walk at
a bird sanctuary on a warm day in July. I represented the
sounds I heard with colors, shapes, and patterns.

STEP 1

I began with a page that had been prepared by sponging on stamp pad ink in a shape that reminded me of the organic form of a pond.

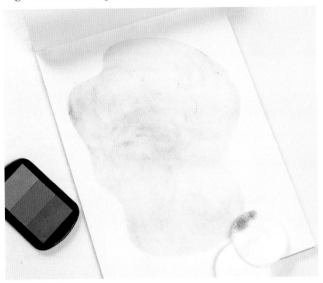

STEP 2

I stood in one place and closed my eyes and let the sounds arrive on the soft breeze. The longer I listened, the easier it became to isolate different sounds. I began to focus on one in particular, and soon I saw a particular shade of yellow every time I heard the sound. The sound was liquid and trilling, seeming to form an elongated puddle that trailed off as it faded. I recorded the sound by sketching in a puddle shape in pencil and by making written notes about the color. It would have been convenient to have a small set of colored pencils, but written color notes work well, too. I then focused on another sound and repeated the recording process. I continued focusing and recording until I was satisfied that I had gathered a good collection of the sounds of the bird sanctuary on that day.

STEP 3

When I got home, I painted in each shape using white gouache in order to overcome the background color. When the gouache dried, I colored over the shapes with colored pencils. I let the field notes that I had made stand, as they added interesting written as well as visual information.

"Songcatcher" Journal

lizabeth Ellison is an artist who lives in the mountains of western North Carolina. When the movie "Songcatcher" (Trimark Pictures, 2000) was being shot in her hometown, Elizabeth was commissioned to do some watercolor paintings for use in the film. In order to get the right feeling and look to her paintings, she needed to understand and empathize with the character, a woman named Alice, who was supposed to have painted the watercolors. Elizabeth had several conversations with the director of the movie, with the actor who played Alice, and with several other actors. She spent several days visiting the set, making some paintings, and taking some photographs of the location.

Throughout the project, Elizabeth kept a journal filled with notes and paintings as an aid to focusing and deepening her experience. She wrote her speculations about what the character's life would be like, what kinds of things she would want to paint, and what kinds of materials and techniques her life situation would make possible. She made small watercolor sketches of scenes and objects that would be in Alice's immediate environment. She also wrote about the movie-making process and her impressions of the people she worked with. Elizabeth used a journal that she made herself out of sheets of paper made partly from plants that Alice would have known.

Each page of the journal is an elegant balance of visual and verbal material. On one page, the watercolor that has been attached to the page has a small hole in the top. Elizabeth noted in her text entry that the hole was from the nail that was used to hang the painting to the wall of the cabin during the filming of scenes in Alice's home.

This journal is a very good demonstration of the power of a visual-verbal journal not only to document a project but to deepen the journaler's focus and learning during the experience. It is also a perfect example of a journal that serves as a springboard for a later creative project (see page 189).

Elizabeth Ellison, *Songcatcher Journal*, 1999. Watercolor, pen and ink.

Springboards

The material in a journal, album, or scrapbook is an invaluable stockpile of ideas and images that you can mine for future creative projects. An interesting alchemy seems to take place inside a journal over time, so that when you dip back into the book, you often see the exact image you need or the perfect phrase to jump-start a piece of writing. In this way, today's unpromising journal entry might show up transformed as tomorrow's poem, essay, painting, or artist's book. Artist Elizabeth Ellison's journal, featured in the essay on page 188, was her springboard to making paintings for the movie "Songcatcher."

Some people date the spines or covers of their journals and write titles reflecting the contents with the idea of using their journals in the future. Others go back through com-pleted journals and number the pages, then use sticky notes to write the topics that are included on certain pages. The topic labels sticking out of the journal fore edge make it easy to index the journal. The journaler need only write the number of the page on which the topic appears on the sticky note. Then she or he can gather all the sticky notes, alphabetize them, and write the topics and page numbers in the back of the journal, perhaps on the inside back cover.

Robert Johnson, *Notebook Page*, 1998. Manuel Antonio, Costa Rica, Agouti capuchin monkeys; watercolor and graphite on paper.

Robert Johnson uses his sketchbook journals to collect images for his full-scale paintings.

SAMPLE PAGE:
A SENSE OF PLACE

In the journal page seen here, I wanted to make an artists' book about the experience of being in a place where I couldn't speak the language or understand much about the culture. I wanted to convey my sense of confusion (not being able to understand or be understood, my disorientation) but also my great appreciation for the beauty of the place.

In going back through my travel journal from the place, I found some pages of maps that I had drawn, as well as some cork stamp prints of patterns and motifs. I also found pages where I had written and drawn about the language situation.

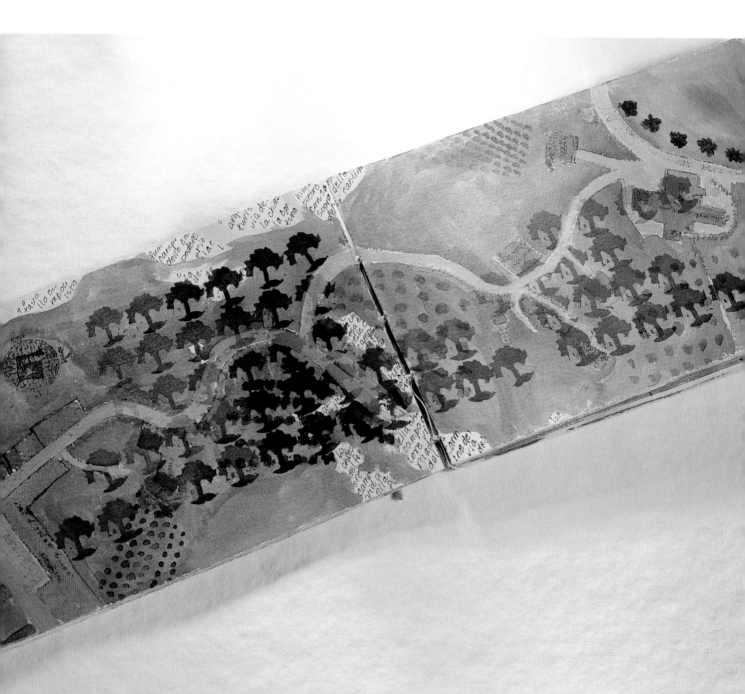

STEP 1

First, I bound the book and prepared pages with poured acrylic. I made photocopies of the map pages, then transferred them to heavy drawing paper with citrus-based paint stripper (see page 63).

STEP 2

Next, I used watercolors to paint areas around and on the map in greens, reds, and tan. I didn't strictly follow the lines of the map but painted in a more interpretive way, using the map as more of a shape than a literal map. I added some patterns that reminded me of the agricultural patterns in the landscape.

STEP 3

One of the last steps was to use a cork stamp of a tree to print tree patterns over the map and the "countryside." Finally, I copied some Italian text, using pen. I wrote the text as though it were an underlayer, allowing it to disappear in mid-word as it slid under painted edges. I followed a similar process for the other pages in the book.

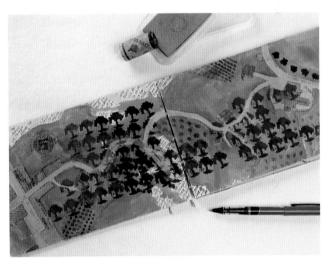

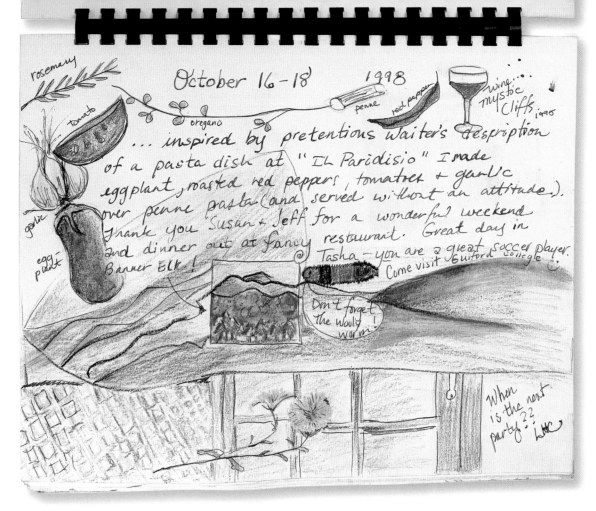

Susan and Jeff Griesmaier, page from *Dinner Party Book*, 1998.

Reflections

Another popular use for journals is to reflect on experiences, helping a journaler to make inferences and judgments about places, events, and people. Of course, reflections are often a part of other kinds of journal entries too. But sometimes reflection is the primary purpose of an entry.

My friends Susan and Jeff have kept a journal of reflections and memories of all the dinners they have given for friends during the long years of their marriage. At the end of a fine evening, they will pull out the jour-

nal and its accompanying box of colored pencils, paints, and pens. They then invite their guests to document the event by writing and drawing in the journal. Many of the pages are collaborations, as each guest draws items from the menu and writes comments about the evening. Sometimes people glue in wine labels. Some people retell jokes or write comments on the food. Susan and Jeff often write the menu and some of the recipes, and then they write ideas to make particular foods better, or to improve future picnics or holidays.

SAMPLE PAGE: A PICNIC

I wanted to create a visual record of a memorable picnic. I chose crayons and watercolor to convey the informal feel of the day, and used a mandala layout so I could include many different aspects of the event centered around the main reflection: the meal.

STEP 2

The next step was to draw the food that was served at the picnic, arranging the items in a mandala centered around the bowl of soup. I used watercolor crayons.

STEP 1

In this journal page, I began with a two-page spread that had been prepared by pouring liquid acrylics into the fold of the page, giving a more or less symmetrical underlayer—a good beginning for a mandala layout.

STEP 3

To finish the reflection, I brushed water over the crayons to turn the strokes into washes. Then I used graphite pencil to sketch the tablecloth pattern and painted it in with watercolors. I also used watercolor to darken the color of the bowl of soup since its original color looked too similar to the blue of the tablecloth. The final step was to write reflections on the picnic in pen. I slanted the writing and made it seem to go under the tablecloth in places to add to the impression of a layer.

The Reluctant Bookbinder

If you're on a quest for the perfect journal—one with the right color and texture and weight of paper, the perfect size, the perfect eccentricities of style—this section might be just what you need. Even if you have no interest in learning how to bind books, and all the fussy details of bookbinding make you cringe, you'll be pleasantly surprised to learn that you can make your own journals with a minimum of equipment, time, and skill.

I added a pocket to the back of this beach journal. It gave me a place to store the small pamphlet journal that I used for sketching when I didn't want to carry the big journal.

Basics

The most important element of a visual/verbal journal is the paper, and the choice is completely under your control when you make your own book. In fact, getting the paper you want is probably what has driven you to the extreme of learning to make your own journal, so we'll begin here. First, go to art supply, craft, stationery, office supply and wrapping paper stores, or even old map dealers to find your papers. Consider combining plain white unlined papers with old maps, sheets of brown craft paper, grid paper, or sheets of colored vellum—let your imagination be the guide. Imagine what it would be like to write on buttery yellow handmade Thai paper, crisp elegant resume paper, or even wrinkled pages torn from an old atlas.

After the text pages, the cover is the next most important element. The cover of a journal needs to be strong enough to protect and contain the text pages plus whatever ephemera—ticket stubs, small scraps of paper, photographs, postcards, etc.—that you gather and want to keep within the journal. So again, let your imagination roam freely. But realize that the cover will take something of a beating. You'll want to use paper or other material without fragile embellishments, such as embedded flower parts (unless you want to coat the cover with a varnish, which is also a possibility; see The Three-Minute Pamphlet Variations and Options on page 198). Since all the journals made in this section have soft covers, you want to find heavy, cover-weight paper, or leather that can be folded.

The Three-Minute Pamphlet

The easiest to make, and most basic of books is a single-signature pamphlet. Once you've cut or torn the pages and cover, you can sew it in three minutes. Once you know how to make this little book, you can try some options to the basic style in order to customize the journal. For simplicity's sake, directions are given for a book that is 3 inches wide x 4 inches high (7.6 x 10.2 cm), but you can make the book any size you want.

TOOLS & MATERIALS

Text paper*

Cover paper, slightly heavier than the text pages, and slightly larger than each sheet of text paper

Ruler for measuring and tearing paper

Matt knife for cutting paper

Pushpin or awl

Pencil

An old telephone directory or other thick magazine, such as an old catalog

1 yard (.9 m) of heavy sewing thread, bookbinder's thread, embroidery floss, lightweight string, or even dental floss

Straight sewing needle with an eye large enough for the thread used

4 large paper clips

*You will need a sheet big enough to cut or tear into a sheet 6 (w) x 4 (h) inches (15.2 x 10.2 cm). Each sheet will be folded in half widthwise. To make a bigger book, start with a larger sheet of paper.

INSTRUCTIONS

1 Using the ruler or matt knife, tear or cut the text papers into 6 x 4-inch (15.2 x 10.2 cm) sheets, or whatever size you need. Make sure the width measurement is always double the finished page-width measurement you desire. The number of pages is determined by the thickness of the paper. For regular computer printer paper, for example, 8 sheets will work. For heavier paper, such as watercolor paper, 3 or 4 sheets will be all you can fold together before the papers begin to stick too far out at the edge and the fold becomes too rounded. Fold each sheet in half widthwise. Use a paper clip to smooth the crease of each sheet, as shown in figure 1 on page 197. Then nest the folded papers inside each other to form a pamphlet.

2 To make the cover, cut or tear a piece of slightly heavier paper to 6½ x 4⅛ inches (16.5 x10.5 cm). To accommodate different sizes of text paper, always cut the cover ⅛ inch (3 mm) higher and ½ inch (1.3 cm) wider than the unfolded text pages. Fold the cover in half widthwise, and slip the text pages inside, as shown in figure 2.

3 Make the hole-punching pattern by first cutting a piece of scrap paper the height of the cover, here 4⅛ inches (10.5 cm), by 2 inches (5 cm) wide. Fold this strip in half lengthwise. Unfold it and then refold it in half top to bottom. Mark the center where the folds cross. Make two more marks, ½ inch (1.3 cm) down from the top and ½ inch (1.3 cm) up from the bottom, as shown in figure 3. Note: if your book is higher than 6 inches (15.2 cm), make two additional holes, each one midway between the center hole and top and bottom holes, as shown in figure 4.

4 To punch holes for sewing, open the telephone directory to a page near the middle—the telephone directory will hold the pamphlet in position while you punch the holes. Open the pamphlet, both cover and text pages, and center it on the open pages of the larger book. Place your hole-punching pattern in the crease of the pamphlet, pressing it in until it fits snugly in the crease, as shown in figure 5. Using the pattern as your guide, use a pushpin or awl to punch a hole in the fold of the pamphlet at each mark. Remove the pattern. Place a paper clip at the top and bottom of each side of the open pamphlet to prevent the pages from moving and to keep the holes lined up. Remove the pamphlet from the telephone directory.

5 Sew the pamphlet. Cut a piece of thread about 36 inches (91.5 cm) long, and thread the needle. Don't tie a knot yet. Poke the needle into the center hole from the outside of the pamphlet. Pull the thread through, being sure to pull parallel to the plane of the paper. You want to pull the thread gently, while making sure that it's tight.

Note: *Do not* pull straight up, or it will tear the paper. Leave a tail about 4 inches (10.2 cm) long (you can slip the tail under one of the paper clips to anchor it). Next, from the inside, poke the needle into either of the end holes, and gently pull the thread tight. (Heed the warning above about pulling straight up!)

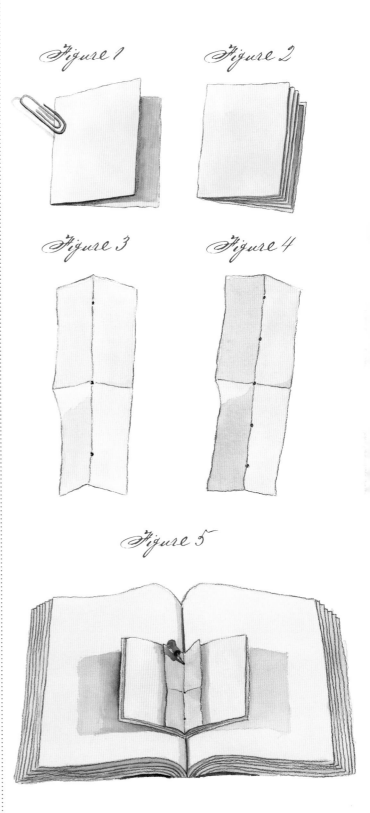

Figure 1

Figure 2

Figure 3

Figure 4

Figure 5

Next, on the outside of the book, skip over the center hole, which has the tail coming out of it, and poke the needle into the remaining hole. Gently pull the thread tight. Finally, on the inside of the book, poke the needle back into the center hole, making sure that the needle comes out on the opposite side of the long stitch from the tail.

6 Tie the tail and the thread together in a double knot close to the hole, as shown in figure 6. Cut the threads to leave ends that are at least 1 inch (2.5 cm) long. You can also leave the ends longer for threading beads, or unravel the thread ends and braid them.

Note: If your book is higher than 6 inches (15.2 cm), follow figure 7 for your sewing pattern.

Variations and Options
Once you have the basics down and can make this journal in three minutes, you can easily make a few changes to the basic model:

- Consider cutting the cover paper a few inches wider than usual so that you can make cover fold-ins. By folding in this extra width, you will make the cover sturdier.

- Stitch the top and bottom edges of the cover fold-ins to make cover pockets.

- Slip a piece of cardboard between the front cover and the first page. Use a matt knife to cut a window in the cover. Put an illustration or title on the first page that can be seen through the cover window.

- Vary the width of the pages in the pamphlet. Long pages can be folded accordion-style to make fold-out pages. Short, 1-inch-wide (2.5 cm) pages can be used as stubs for gluing single sheets of paper, such as watercolor paper, color copies, or scans of photographs, fold-out maps, etc., as shown in figure 8.

Figure 6

Figure 7

in   out

Figure 8

The Six-Minute Double Pamphlet

The only drawback to the three-minute pamphlet is that it's so small. However, once you've mastered that first reluctant foray into journal making, it's easy to simply double the number of pamphlets you fold to make a double pamphlet. There are two approaches to a double pamphlet given below. The first is called a *Dos à Dos*, meaning back to back; the second is a Pleat Book.

TOOLS & MATERIALS

2 booklets or pamphlets of folded text pages

Cover paper, ⅛ inch (3 mm) higher than the text pages and at least three times as wide

Needle and thread

Pushpin or awl

4 paper clips

Telephone directory or thick magazine

Pencil

Ruler

Matt knife

INSTRUCTIONS

1 For a *Dos à Dos*, fold the cover into a Z-shaped fold, as shown in figure 1 on page 200. For a Pleat Book, fold the cover so that it has a 1-inch (2.5 cm) pleat in the center, as shown in figure 2. Use the rounded end of the paper clip to *score* each fold. Scoring four or five times on the line of each fold makes it easier to get a precise fold. Burnish, or smooth, each fold using the rounded edge of the paper clip.

2 Make a hole-punching pattern, as described in step 3 for The Three-Minute pamphlet.

3 For either book, place an opened pamphlet into the first fold of the cover. As described in step 4 for The Three-Minute Pamphlet, place the cover and opened pamphlet in the center of the telephone directory or magazine. Press the pattern into the fold of the pamphlet, and punch the holes.

Figure 2

Figure 3

4 Stabilize the pamphlet with paper clips, and sew it as described in step 5 for The Three-Minute Pamphlet.

5 Slip the second pamphlet into its cover crease and repeat steps 3 and 4 above, as shown in figure 3 for the *Dos à Dos*, and figure 5 for the Pleat Book. If you wish to customize either of these two journals, see The Three-Minute Pamphlet Variations and Options on page 198.

Figure 1

Figure 4

Famous Reluctant Bookbinders

Paul Gauguin (1848-1903) *Album Noa Noa*. Handwritten text and Polynesian woman seated. Photo by Herve Lewandowski, Reunion des Musees Nationaux/Art Resource, NY.

Reluctant bookbinding turns up in the most unlikely places. For instance, who would have expected Vincent Van Gogh to be a bookbinder? Yet not only did Van Gogh make some of his own sketchbooks, he also made several small accordion books that he filled with his drawings for the child of one of his friends. He wrote about the process to his brother Theo:

"However, for studies and scribbles the Ingres paper is excellent. And it is much cheaper to make my own sketchbooks in different sizes than to buy them ready-made. I have some of that Ingres paper left, but when you return that study to me, please enclose some of the same kind; you would greatly oblige me by doing so. But no dead white, rather the color of unbleached linen, no cold tones."[1]

Van Gogh's bookbinding method was simplicity itself—it got the job done, but didn't take a second longer than was necessary to produce the needed object. He would take a large sheet of suitable paper and fold it twice accordion style, with the folds going the length of the paper. Then he would fold the resulting long skinny rectangle in half with the fold going crosswise. It was an easy matter to put a few stitches in the final fold and trim the folds from the tops and bottoms of the pages. Voilà! A 12-page sketchbook made of his favorite warm white Ingres paper, ready to receive his notes and drawings.

Another reluctant bookbinder was Van Gogh's friend and fellow post-Impressionist painter, Paul Gauguin. When Gauguin moved to Tahiti and the Marquesas Islands, he was aware that he was the first European artist to live in a faraway land in order to discover the culture of a people who were then considered primitive and savage by Europeans. In 1894, while spending a few months in Paris before returning to the islands, he began a journal in order to explain what his stay in Tahiti had brought to his thinking and to his art. His journal began as a text manuscript, but he left spaces in the manuscript for illustrations, which he added later. He also went back into the manuscript after adding illustrations. From 1896 on, he kept notes and jottings about his daily life. During this period he also added woodcut prints and more illustrations. He bound the book himself, but it is no down and dirty, purely functional product. In the words of Victor Segalen, who collected Gauguin's mementos and was the first person to acquire the book from Gauguin's estate after his death:

"It is a volume of [white] pages, everything written on Ingres paper folded in quartos and sewn by the author, whose hand took delight in everything that becomes decorative material—wood skins, mother-of-pearl, wax and gold. The binding is supple and opens well under a tobacco-brown cover, velvety, without joins and flat-backed...The text, whose pale brown ink is in complete harmony with the browned paper, is, here and there, interrupted by watercolours-most of them washed on paper that has been separated, cut out and pasted. There are traces of everything which, at that time, made up the everyday life of the Master as he did battle with the merciless existence of the Tropics—the splendour of the light, hard work and renunciation."[2]

[1]*The Complete Letters of Vincent Van Gogh*, vol. 1, letter 164. Greenwich, Connecticut: New York Graphic Society, 1959.

[2]Marc LeBot, *Gauguin's Noa Noa*, Assouline, 2004.

The Thirty-Minute Multiple-Pamphlet Journal

Building on the base of experience and confidence that you've gained by making single- and double-pamphlet books, you might want to venture a few steps further in complexity to make a journal that is many steps further in usefulness and beauty. A multiple-pamphlet journal uses the same skills you've gained in folding and sewing pamphlets, cutting, scoring, and folding covers, and in customizing journals; but it opens up the possibility of making the book as big and fat as you really want. It also introduces the possibility of making a hard cover for your journal.

TOOLS & MATERIALS

As many pamphlets as you want, with text pages cut and folded but not sewn.*

A piece of cover paper about five times the width of the text pages

Needle and thread

Pushpin or awl

Telephone directory or thick magazine

Ruler

Matt knife

Pencil

*Ten pamphlets are a likely limit when using most papers. More pamphlets than this will place undue stress on the spine of the book. (If you really want a bigger book, consider reinforcing the spine with a strip of cloth and a few more strips of paper.)

INSTRUCTIONS

1 Cut or tear, fold, and assemble as many pamphlets as you want.

2 Determine the thickness of the spine by piling up the pamphlets and *lightly* compressing them. Hold a ruler next to the stack. Write down the height of the stack of lightly compressed pamphlets. This will be the width of the spine of the book.

3 Follow figure 1 to determine the width of the cover paper. Make sure that the paper is ⅛ inch (3 mm) higher than the text pages. Cut or tear the paper to size. Score and fold all cover creases, as shown in figure 2.

4 Make a hole-punching pattern. Open the telephone directory or magazine. **Note:** For this book, place the pamphlet and cover flat on a page rather than into the center crease. Place the first pamphlet, or signature, opened out flat with its crease centered into the exact center of the spine section of the cover, as shown in figure 3. Lay the hole-punching pattern over the crease of the signature and punch the holes. Secure the signature to the cover with paper clips, and sew the first signature to the spine using the usual pamphlet stitch, as shown in figure 4.

| spine | text page + ¼" | text page + ¼" | spine | text page + ¼" | text page + ¼" | spine |

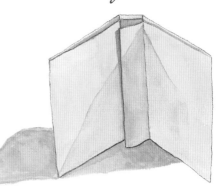

5 Close the first, sewn signature. Slide the second, closed signature either to the left or to the right of the first signature. From now on you will be sewing an equal number of signatures to the right and to the left of the center signature. Be sure to place them close enough so that they will all fit within the spine piece, as shown in figure 15. You might try placing the signatures before sewing to give you an idea of how close you can place them. Open the pamphlet, secure the pages with paper clips, punch holes, and sew each signature in turn. Trim the threads on the outside of the spine to ½ inch (1.3 cm).

Variations and Options

- To make a "hardback" book, use PVA to glue a piece of lightweight cardboard to the inside of each of the cover papers before folding the cover of the Thirty-Minute journal.

- To reinforce the spine of a very large book: Slip a piece of thin leather or heavy paper into the spine section between two of the layers of the cover paper that form the spine before sewing the signatures into the spine. Lightly glue the strip with PVA to one section of spine paper.

- For a sturdier spine and more formal, finished look, make a "new" cover out of an old hardback book cover. First remove the text pages (text block) from the old book. Using PVA and a glue brush, glue the outside covers of your Thirty-Minute Pamphlet (but *not* the spine) to the insides of the old cover, as shown in Figure 6. (For more directions see pages 222 to 223.)

You can also apply any of the options given for The Three-Minute Pamphlet Variations and Options on page 198.

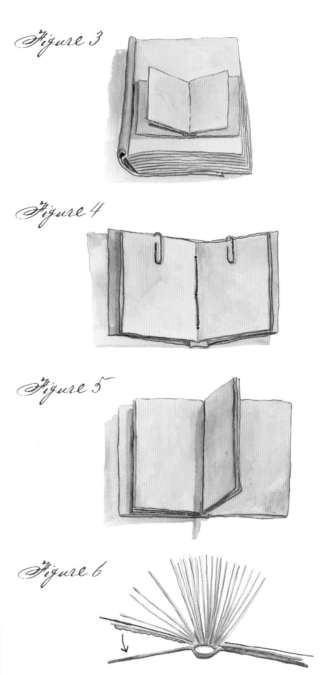

Figure 3

Figure 4

Figure 5

Figure 6

The Art of Travel

By following the instructions in Francis Galton's book, I made a model of a sloppy-but-serviceable journal binding.

Poking around in a used book-store one day, I came across a copy of a strange little guide-book for travelers. It had information ranging from how to thatch the roof of a temporary shelter, to what to pack when going trekking in the desert for six months, to how to repair a battered metal canteen using dried seeds. I stood there for nearly an hour learning how many pounds of gear a camel could carry versus a donkey, and what to do if my donkey brayed and I wanted to make him stop. (For those of you who must know: tie a stone to his tail because donkeys always lift their tails before braying, and if the tail is too heavy to lift, the donkey simply loses heart and won't bray.)

I had to have this book! I loved the odd title—*The Art of Travel* (1872): Or, *Shifts and Contrivances Available in Wild Countries*.[1] The author, Francis Galton, was writing for explorers and expeditionists primarily—although I learned that ordinary travelers had also bought his book in great numbers. There was information on every subject that I could imagine and many more. But what clinched the sale for me was the fact that the author devoted an entire chapter to the importance of and pro-cess of keeping a good journal during an expedition.

Galton suggested that the best journal notes were copious as well as accurate, and that these notes should be kept in a small but distinct handwriting. Hard pencils (HHH) on common paper were recommended. Not only should notes and observations and sketches be made on the spot, "in the exact order in which they occur," but these notes were then to be extended, expanded upon, and filled in each evening without fail—lest you forget important details and ideas. He tells about a famous explorer, Captain Burton, (short on candles, I assume) who managed to write in complete darkness. Burton would crawl into his sleeping bag, and then place a grooved piece of wood under his journal page so he could feel the grooves with his pen in order to stay on the lines.

Galton suggests the traveler keep three sets of books:

- Pocket memorandum measuring $3\frac{1}{2}$ x 5 inches (8.9 x 12.7 cm) and made of strong paper with 150 pages in each. These are to be used for on-the-spot recording, and he expects the reader will need one of these every month.

- A logbook, which should be $5\frac{1}{2}$ x 9 inches (14 x 22.9 cm) and filled with the printed forms of which Galton provides samples. He says the log-book is useful for organizing infor-mation that might be scattered about in the pocket memo book, and the use of the printed forms simplifies things. There are two printed forms to be filled out each day and then two blank sheets for the compiling of the information that doesn't fit on the forms. One form is a grid, intended to be used for mapping and making

Susan Saling's page communicates facts as well as the feeling of the Pere Lachaise cemetery in Paris. She combines her train ticket, parts of a cemetery brochure, her own sketch and painting, and a few written notes to summarize a day spent at this Paris attraction.

diagrams. The other has spaces for informaion regarding the weather, com-pass readings, altitude, the nature of the country, and latitude and longitude.

- A calculation book, the same size as the logbook, is used for recording measurements from which cal-culations must be made—latitude and longitude, star positions rela-tive to the moon, the length of the journey measured in time and converted to miles, etc.

Galton also gives instructions on what to do at the end of the journey. He tells the traveler to make drawings of everything that may not have yet been sketched— the equipment, the retinue, the encampment, and "whatever else you may in indolence have omitted to sketch." All loose items must then be pasted into the journals. Books must be stitched where they are torn. The notebooks should then be given to a bookbinder as soon as possible to rebind them and paginate them. The bookbinder should add plenty of extra pages to each book so that the traveler can write an index to the whole of the manuscript, including plenty of cross-references. The traveler should add explanations where neces-

sary and correct imperfect descriptions. It is imperative to do this immediately after the journey, Galton insists, because memories quickly fade once the traveler has returned home.

Because no stone is left unturned in this book, Galton also includes detailed directions for making ink out of charred sticks and milk, and carbon paper out of a mixture of soap, charcoal, and clean paper. He also included directions for binding books. He no doubt believed that some travelers would not have the means to have their journals professionally bound and did not want them returning home with unprotected notes.

A relative of Galton's developed a bookbinding form that Galton claims is not tidy looking but opens flat and never falls to pieces. After reading the instructions, I was compelled to make this book to see what a traveler's journal of this era, as interpreted by Galton, might actually look like. The results are pictured above. Following are Galton's instructions if you wish to attempt your own: "Take a cup of paste; a piece of calico or other cloth, large enough to cover the back and sides of the book; a strip of strong linen—if you can get it, if not, of calico—to cover the back; and abundance of stout cotton or thread. 1st.

paste the strip of linen down the back and leave the book in the sun or near a fire—but not too near it—to dry, which it will do in half a day. 2ndly. Open the book and look for the place where the stitching is to be seen down the middle of the pages, or, in other words, for the middle of the sheets; if it be an 8vo. book it will be at every 16th page, if a 12mo. at every 24th page, and so on; it is a mere matter of semi-mechanical reckoning to know where each succeeding stitching is to be found . . . Next take the cotton and wind it between the pages where the stitching is, and over the back round and round, beginning with the first sheet until you have reached the last one. 3rdly. Lay the book on the table back upwards, daub it thoroughly with paste, put on the calico cover as neatly as you can, and set it to dry as before; when dry it is complete."[2]

[1]Francis Galton, *The Art of Travel* (1872): Or, *Shifts and Contrivances Available in Wild Countries* (Mechanicsburg, PA, Stackpole books, 1971)

[2]Ibid. p 329-30

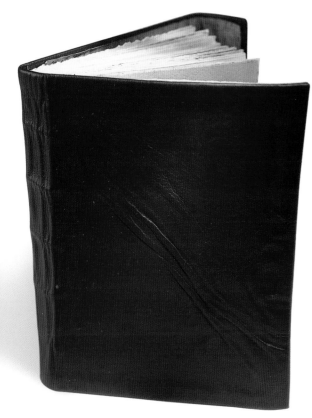

The Two-Hour leather-covered journal, sewn on cords.

The Two-Hour Extremely Beautiful, Useful, and Sturdy Journal

For those of you who have actually enjoyed making your own journals by following the patterns above, this next—and final—journal is a modification of a traditional book form called a round-back book sewn on cords. It takes more time to make, but once you master it, it's possibly all the journal you will ever need or want. It's elegant, yet sturdy and rugged, and it feels good when you hold it in your hand. You can vary the size, shape, and materials to suit any needs you may have.

In order to sew a book on cords, you will need a piece of equipment called a sewing frame. While sewing frames are expensive and hard to find, you can make a very serviceable sewing frame from an old book in about 15 minutes for almost no cost (see the sidebar called Easy Sewing Frame on page 211).

TOOLS & MATERIALS

Text pages, whatever color, texture, weight, and size desired*

Cover material, preferably leather or canvas**

Sheet of paper to use for the end paper—it should be about the same weight as the text paper, and can actually be the same paper, or you can use decorative paper

Straight sewing needle with a large eye

Heavy cotton or linen thread, preferably bookbinders' thread—you can also use heavy sewing thread, embroidery floss, or dental floss

Metal ruler

Matt knife

Pushpin or awl

Piece of corrugated cardboard

Old telephone directory or thick magazine

PVA and a glue brush

Paste and a paste brush

Pencil

Black marker with a fine tip

Headband material or 1-inch-wide (2.5 cm) grosgrain ribbon (optional)***

Sewing frame (See page 211)

*First decide the size for your pages—and remember, not all pages need to be the same size. Buy enough paper to cut or tear into sheets that will be as high and twice as wide as the individual pages. For example, if you want the largest pages to be 6 x 9 inches (15.2 x 22.9 cm), cut the paper 12 x 9 inches (30.5 x 22.9 cm). Buy enough paper to make as many sheets as you want in the journal, realizing that you will be folding each sheet in half. Using at least 20 folded sheets of medium to heavyweight paper will make the spine fat enough to round nicely.

**The cover material needs to be about 1 inch (2.5 cm) higher than the text pages and around three times as wide. For a 6 x 9 (15.2 x 22.9 cm) page, you will need a piece of cover material approximately 18 x 10¼ inches (45.7 x 26 cm). The material can be a little less wide, but it's good to have enough to make a flap to protect the pages.

***Headband material is available through bookbinders' supply outlets or at some art supply stores.

Materials for making The Two-Hour Journal.

INSTRUCTIONS

PREPARING THE PAGES

1 Cut or tear as much paper as needed for the text pages, then fold each piece of paper in half widthwise to form a folio. Nest the folios inside each other to form groups of folded pages known as *signatures*. The number of folios in a signature is determined by the weight of the paper you use. If the paper is relatively light, you can fit 6 or 7 sheets comfortably into one signature. For heavier paper, 3 or 4 may be the limit before the middle folios begin to protrude too far out from the front edge of the signature. Remember that pages don't all have to be the same size.

2 Cut or tear a piece of scrap paper that is 2 inches (5 cm) wide and the exact height of the signatures. This piece will become your pattern for punching the holes. Fold the pattern piece in half lengthwise, then unfold it, and fold it in half widthwise. Use a pencil to mark the center where the folds cross. Make another pencil mark in the vertical fold ½ inch (1.3 cm) up from the

bottom and ½ inch down from the top. Make two more marks, each ½ inch from the two end marks. Finally, make two marks midway between the center mark and the two marks in from the end marks, as shown in figure 1.

Figure 1

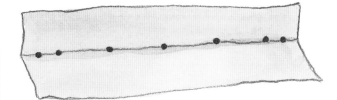

3 Open the telephone directory or magazine to a page near the middle. Follow the directions for hole punching in step 4 on page 197.

Note: After punching, there is no need to secure these signatures with paper clips.

SEWING THE TEXT BLOCK

4 To sew the text block, thread the needle with approximately 36 inches (91.5 cm) of thread. Use a single strand of thread for sewing, and do not tie a knot at the end. Lay the first signature on the sewing frame with its fold touching the strings, as shown in figure 2. Arrange each string to be next to one of the five central holes in the signature.

Note: The end holes are not associated with any strings. The horizontal string will hold the signature open while you sew. Tuck the pages of the signature that are closest to the strings *under* the horizontal string.

Figure 2

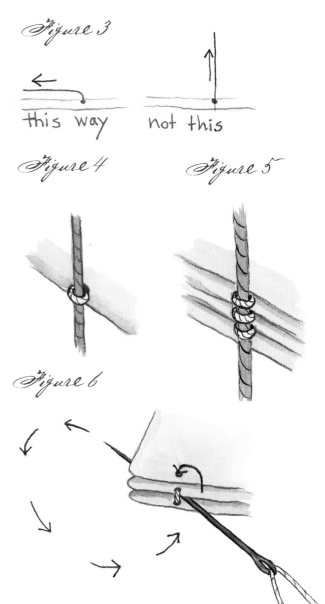

5 From the outside, insert the needle in either one of the end holes. Pull the thread, leaving a 3 or 4-inch (7.6 or 10.2 cm) tail. Next, from the inside, enter the next hole. The needle will come out of a hole near the first string, or cord. Pull the thread all the way until taut. Be careful to always tighten the thread by pulling parallel to the plane of the paper to avoid tearing, as shown in figure 3. Pass the needle over the cord and re-enter the same hole, pulling the thread so that it snugly covers the cord, as shown in figure 4.

6 Continue sewing this way until you have sewn around all five cords. Enter the last hole from the inside, and pull the thread taut. There is no cord next to the last hole.

7 Release the pages from the horizontal string by folding the signature, then lay the next signature on top of the first sewn signature. As you did for the first signature, open the second signature to its centerfold and tuck the pages under the horizontal string. Enter the end hole (the one that is nearest the needle) from the outside of the signature, and pull the thread taut to the inside. Sew this signature exactly as you did the first one. Bring the threads close together on the cords by using your fingers to gently press the signatures together, as shown in figure 5.

8 When you get to the end of the second signature, pull everything taut, and then tie the tail to the thread with a double knot. Do not cut the thread.

9 Close the second signature. Place the third one on top of it, open it, tuck the pages under the string, and sew this signature as you did the others. You should have three loops of thread over each cord when you finish sewing this signature. When you get to the end, you will need to join signature 3 to signature 2. To do this, make a loop stitch by slipping the needle behind the end stitch that is between the first and second signatures. Then enter the first hole of signature 3, as shown in figure 6.

10 Sew all the other signatures the same way, making a loop stitch at the end before joining the new signature.

Note: The loop stitch is done on the stitch between the two adjacent signatures (i.e., for signature 3, loop between signatures 2 and 1; for signature 4, loop between signatures 3 and 2; etc.). When you're finished sewing, tie a knot by slipping the needle under a stitch, making a few loops. Then cut the cords about 3 inches (7.6 cm) above and below the spine of the text block to remove the book from the frame.

MAKING THE COVER

11 To make the cover, cut the leather or canvas according to figure 7. If the leather is thin enough, allow for a ½-inch (1.3 cm) folded hem all the way around by adding the ½ inch to all edges. If the leather is too thick to fold, don't add the extra ½ inch to make a hem. You can do the same for canvas by either making a folded hem or leaving it unhemmed.

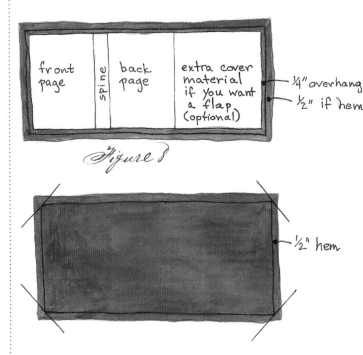

Figure 7

front page | spine | back page | extra cover material if you want a flap (optional)

— ¼" overhang
— ½" if hem

Figure 8

½" hem

12 If you're going to hem the leather or canvas, draw a fine line with a marker on the wrong side of the material ½ inch (1.3 cm) all around, and then cut a triangle from each corner, as shown in figure 8. Use PVA to adhere the hem. Be careful to wipe any drips or spills immediately. PVA stains leather and can't be removed once it dries.

ATTACHING THE COVER

13 To prepare the text block for gluing to the cover, first trim the cord ends to ½ inch (1.3 cm). Then hold the spine in one hand and grab the middle one-third of the pages, as shown in figure 9, and push in as indicated. This will slightly round the back or spine of the text block. When the spine is nicely rounded, close the text block, holding it as you do so as to maintain the rounding.

Figure 9

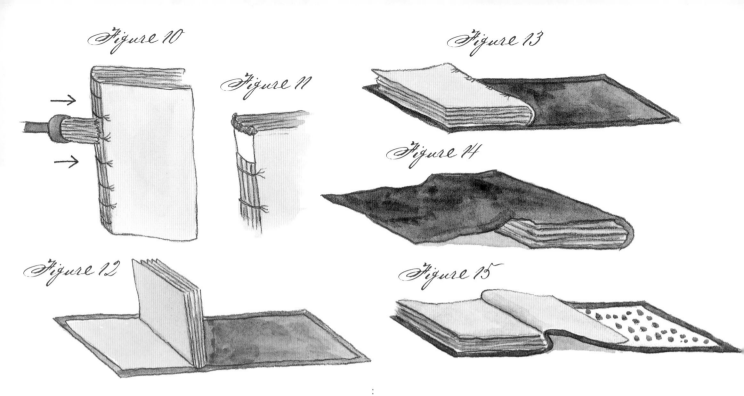

Figure 10

Figure 11

Figure 12

Figure 13

Figure 14

Figure 15

14 Apply PVA to the rounded spine to strengthen it. Using short pouncing motions, lightly push the glue brush repeatedly into the spine, as shown in figure 10. This allows you to apply the right amount of PVA—you want to get enough PVA between the signatures but don't want to apply too much or you will glue the pages together.

15 Carefully lay the glued text block on the edge of a table. Put a piece of scrap paper on top of the text block and then lay the closed telephone directory on top. This will gently compress the text block until it's dry.

16 If you're using a headband or ribbon, cut two pieces, each the width of the spine. Use PVA to glue them to the spine, as shown in figure 11.

17 To glue the text block to the cover, first put scrap paper between the first page and the rest of the text block to protect the pages. Then use a brush to apply paste over the entire page. Paste, unlike PVA that grabs more quickly and dries faster, will be easier to handle for this step since it allows you to reposition. However, you can use PVA if desired.

18 Remove the scrap paper. Lay the page with the pasted side down on the inside of the cover material, as shown in figure 12. Use your hands to rub and burnish the paper to adhere it to the cover material.

19 Put a clean piece of scrap paper on top of the page you've just pasted. Carefully close the text block, as shown in figure 13. Brush paste on the spine. Then place a piece of scrap paper under the top page as before to protect the other pages, and brush paste all over the top page. Remove the scrap paper. Wrap the cover material snugly around the text block. Be sure to pull the material tightly across the spine, as shown in figure 14.

20 Use your fingers to work the leather tight against the spine and the raised cords—you want the cords to show as bands across the back of the spine. Open the book slightly to check the position of the second piece of paper you've pasted in. If it's crooked—and only if you've used paste—peel back the cover and try again. Use your hands to rub and burnish both covers and the spine repeatedly until the leather adheres completely. Put the book aside to dry for several hours. If it's humid and you've used paste, drying can take as long as 24 hours. Note: Please be patient. If you open the book before it's completely dry, the spine will pull away from the cover and you must re-paste it.

21 If your cover has a flap and folded seams, you can give your journal a more finished look by applying an extra end paper. First, measure the length and width of the area on the inside covers where you will paste the end paper. Then cut or tear the end papers, coat the back of the paper with paste or PVA, and press it to the leather, as shown in figure 15.

Easy Sewing Frame

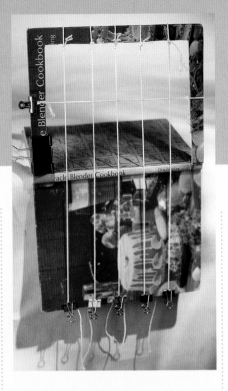

Y ou won't have to worry about a big piece of equipment cluttering up your house with this sewing frame. It's made out of an old hardcover book—the pages are the platform of the sewing frame, and the covers hold the cords taut so you can sew on it. When you're not using this frame, you can just close it up and slide it back onto your bookshelf.

TOOLS & MATERIALS

Old hardcover book, at least 9 x 13 inches (22.9 x 33 cm)—bigger is better; old encyclopedias work well

Matt knife

7 small binder clips

1 very large binder clip

Ball of hemp, jute, or seine twine

INSTRUCTIONS

1 Using the matt knife, cut a window out of the front cover of the book. Leave about 1 inch (2.5 cm) at the top, bottom, and fore edge, and cut right along the crease at the spine. Open both covers and place the book on the edge of a table, as shown in figure 1.

2 To keep the top from slamming shut, attach the large binder and one small clip to bottom of the frame, as shown in figure 2.

3 Tie 5 strings to the top part of the frame. Use the small binder clips to attach them taut to the bottom of the back cover of the book, as shown in figure 3.

4 Tie a horizontal string about 3 inches (7.6 cm) from the large clip used for keeping the book open. Use a small clip to hold the string, making sure it's on the inside of the vertical cords and faces the pages of the book, as shown in figure 4.

Figure 2

Figure 3

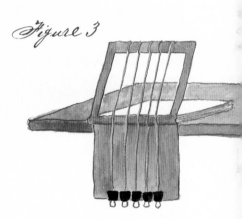

Figure 1

Figure 4

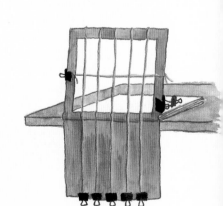

Customizing a Blank Book

If you're not really interested in making your own journal, but the blank books you see for sale lack something, consider customizing a blank book. You can modify the pages to change the book form, as well as the cover. Following are some easy-to-make changes.

MODIFYING THE BOOK FORM

REMOVING PAGES

The secret to keeping a book from bulging open when you add elements to the pages is to equalize the fatness of the spine with the fatness of the fore edge of the book. There's nothing you can do to increase the fatness of the spine of a sewn or glued book. However, you can reduce the fatness of the fore edge so that any added elements would simply plump it back to its original size.

To do this, you will need to remove some pages. A rule of thumb is to remove one or two pages, depending on the thickness of the paper, for every page on which you intend

to glue a collage element or photograph or any other added item. Keep in mind that this rule assumes that the added items are flat and are the approximate thickness of the removed page or pages.

To remove a page, first place a small, thin cutting mat under the page. Push the mat in toward the spine as far as it will easily go. Then use a ruler and matt knife to cut the page approximately ½ inch (1.3 cm) away from the spine edge. For a particular expressive reason, you might prefer to cut a wavy line or some irregular line instead of using a ruler. The resulting page stub can also become a design element. You can color it, draw on it, write on it, paint on it, etc.

ADDING AND CHANGING ELEMENTS

You might decide that you would like to add an envelope for collecting seeds, or some sheets of watercolor paper, grid paper, colored paper, tracing paper, or extremely

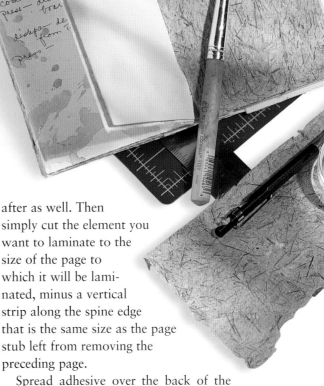

beautiful wrapping paper from that small shop in the village you visited last weekend. To do this, begin by removing a page or two, depending on the thickness of the paper you will add, as directed in Removing Pages on page 212. Then, if you've removed one sheet, simply run a bead of PVA or roll a glue stick along the spine edge of the sheet you want to add, and press it to the front of the page stub. If you've cut off two pages, put adhesive on the front of the second stub, and lay the additional element onto it. Then run another bead of adhesive along the back of the first page stub and press it on top of the spine edge of the add-on element.

LAMINATING PAGES

You can laminate, or completely adhere, one page on top of another page in the book. If the paper that you want to laminate is on the heavy or moderately heavy side, you'll need to remove the page that comes before the page you wish to laminate to accommodate the different weight paper. Depending on the thickness, you may need to remove the page

after as well. Then simply cut the element you want to laminate to the size of the page to which it will be laminated, minus a vertical strip along the spine edge that is the same size as the page stub left from removing the preceding page.

Spread adhesive over the back of the element to be laminated (see Adhesives on pages 40 and 41 to determine the best adhesive for the job). Line up the element with the fore edge of the base page, and press the pages together. Slip pieces of wax paper into the book on top and below the laminated page, and close the book to press the pages while they dry.

If the book is going to have different sections that you'll want to locate quickly, consider laminating a tabbed divider page at the beginning of each section. Follow the directions for laminating a page, but cut the page to add a tab at the top or fore edge side, making the tab extend ¼ inch (6 mm) or so beyond the pages of the book.

Nina Bagley uses old file folder tabs as dividers in this journal.

Right: Sandy Webster, *Working Journal Series*, 2000. This detail shows tabbed dividers.

A piggyback journal.

PIGGYBACKS

A piggyback is a small journal that rides along inside the main journal and can be taken out on its own when you don't feel like carrying the big journal. First, you can make a pocket for the piggyback to ride in. You can do this by trimming a page to become the front of the envelope. Then glue or stitch along the top and bottom edges of two pages, as shown in figure 1. You'll need to remove two or three pages to accommodate the thickness of the piggyback. Make a single-signature pamphlet as described on page 196, slip it into the pocket, and away you go.

Another kind of piggyback is an accordion. Make a pocket as described above. Fold a long, narrow sheet of paper back and forth several times to form a small accordion book. Remove the next few pages to accommodate the thickness of the accordion, and slip the accordion into the pocket. This is a particularly useful piggyback for a map.

Figure 1

Modifying the Cover

ENCRUSTATION

A hard-cover book can be completely transformed by a process called encrustation that was developed by book artist Timothy Ely. The effects that you can achieve by means of this process are limited only by your imagination.

TOOLS & MATERIALS

Acrylic matte medium

Quart (.95 L) jar

Thickener or texturizing material such as whiting powder or talc for a smooth texture, sand for a rougher texture, and small seashells, pebbles, or seeds for a coarse texture

Spoon

Masking tape

Small squares of cardboard, mat board, or old credit cards

Dinner knife, palette knife, or putty knife

Materials for embedding, such as small scraps of cardboard and leather, twigs, mica, shells, cloth

Liquid acrylic paints

INSTRUCTIONS

1 Pour about 1 inch (2.5 cm) of matte medium into the jar. Add whiting, talc, sand, or other thickener to make a thick paste. Stir until completely mixed.

2 If the book has a spine that you don't want to encrust, cover it with masking tape before proceeding. If you want a design that is raised above the surface of the book, glue on pieces of cardboard, mat board, or old credit cards to form these relief areas.

3 Trowel the encrusting material onto one cover of the book, spreading it as you go. Cover the entire surface except for any areas that are masked off.

Gwen Diehn, *South Haven Journal*, 2003. 6 x 9 inches (15.2 x 22.9 cm). Leather-covered spine, book board encrusted with sand and beach glass.

If you want a particularly thick encrustation and you don't want it to crack, it's better to do it in several layers, letting each layer dry completely before going on to each subsequent one.

4 Embed pieces of mica, cloth, rocks, beads, etc. by pushing or pressing them into the encrustation.

5 Let the encrustation dry. This may take several hours, depending on the humidity and the thickness of the encrustation.

6 Once the surface is completely dry, it can be sanded, carved into with carving tools, or scored with nails or a knife. Paint the encrustation with liquid acrylics and polish it with shoe polish. Carefully peel off any masking tape.

7 A finish coat of paste wax can protect as well as add luster.

An encrusted cover in process.

Materials and tools for encrusting a cover.

215

Collage

Either hard or softcovers can be changed by collage.

TOOLS AND MATERIALS

Old newspapers to put under work

PVA

Glue brush

Heavyweight acrylic mediums, such as gel medium, garnet gel, and absorbent ground

Polymer varnish—satin, flat, or gloss finish

1-inch (2.5 cm) soft, flat paintbrush

Materials to collage, such as paper, cloth, thin leather, etc.

INSTRUCTIONS

1 Brush PVA over the backs of the items to be collaged. Press collage items into place on the hard or soft-cover. You can use gel mediums and absorbent ground to build up areas that you can carve, paint, and collage over.

2 After the collage is dry, add any drawing or writing as desired.

3 Repeat for the other cover.

4 When the entire book is dry, varnish with two coats of polymer varnish.

Gwen Diehn. 6 x 9 inches (15.2 x 22.9 cm). Journal covered with collage of pieces of old drawings and monotypes, then covered with glossy polymer varnish.

Bruce Kremer laid out this page in a grid form and used a variety of media, including pen, watercolor, and collage, as he supplies directions for what he calls his "textured diary."

Juliana Coles, *In Transition: Hold Fast*, 2000-2001. 10 x 8¾ x 1½ inches (25.4 x 22.2 x 3.8 cm). Hardbound journal, watercolor paper, watercolor crayon, china marker, craft acrylics, pen and ink, rubber stamp letters; collaged. *Photo by Pat Berrett.*

EDGE TRIMMING

Another way to change the appearance of a book is to modify the edges of the pages.

YOU WILL NEED
- Sharp-edged metal ruler
- Cutting mat
- Decorative edge scissors

INSTRUCTIONS

1 Slip a cutting mat under two or three pages at a time, then use a sharp-edged metal ruler to hold the pages down while you tear a narrow (about $1/4$ inch {6 mm}) strip from the edges of each page. Depending on the thickness of the paper, you may be able to tear two or even three pages at once.

2 For a crisper look, use decorative edge scissors to cut the edges of the pages. If your book has a soft cover, you can even cut the edges of the covers this way (see photos, right and below).

Above: Coral Jensen used decorative edge scissors to give a richly textured look to the text block of this journal.

Altered Books

One of the strongest presences in the film "The English Patient" is not a person but the journal that the leading character carries everywhere. The journal is first seen before the story even begins, when one of its pages is used as the backdrop against which the beginning credits roll. The paper is slightly textured and warm terra-cotta in tone, and a paintbrush held by an unseen person is painting abstract swimming or dancing figures on it. Later in the film, there is a scene that explains this initial image: one of the characters sits in a cave and paints figures that have been discovered on the cave walls onto a piece of paper. She later gives the sketches to the journal-keeper, who pastes them into his journal.

The journal appears in so many scenes throughout the movie that it becomes a thread that holds together the many shifting locations and flashbacks of the story. In the novel on which the film is based, author Michael Ondjaanti introduces the journal in this way:

> She picks up the notebook that lies on the small table beside his bed. It is the book he brought with him through the fire—a copy of the *Histories* by Herodotus that he has added to, cutting and gluing in pages from other books or writing in his own observations—so that all are cradled within the text of Herodotus.

(*The English Patient,* Knopf, 1992, page 16)

The leading character, who is named Almasy, calls the journal his "commonplace book," and it is his constant companion. It's no ordinary journal, but rather a journal grafted onto his favorite book. Almasy's journal entries are a mixture of text and visuals—sketches, maps, a few old photographs, and memorabilia, most of which have been written on and then glued in. In some scenes in the movie, Almasy pastes sketches into his journal, while in other scenes he writes around the margins of the pages and on the empty pages at the front and back of the text. In a number of scenes, he reads (or is read to) from Herodotus's text. In a few close up shots, it's possible to see that the journal is rich and many-layered. Almasy values it above all his other possessions.

Almasy's journal is what book artists call an *altered book*. Using a found book and then altering it adds a dimension to journaling that can greatly enrich the experience. If the original book is one that has strong meaning for the journaler, the book becomes a foil against which the journal entries are played. The journaler might expand, contrast, question, endorse, or argue with the original text. The marginal entries can become a gloss,

Nina Bagley, inside cover of altered book, 2000.

or commentary, on the text, in the manner of comments written in the margins of medieval manuscripts (see pages 53 to 55). Another approach to altered books is to indirectly respond to the original book by using it simply as a mood-setting background. A travel journal might be made out of an old atlas, for example.

One way to proceed with a found book is to paint out much of the text with white gouache before writing in it. It could be interesting to leave selected words or phrases and incorporate them into journal entries. Another idea is to cut away parts of pages to expose selected passages further back in the book and incorporate these passages into multiple new entries. It's always possible to paste different paper over whole or partial pages, and write and draw on the pasted-on paper. Some journalers use only the original covers, carefully rebinding blank pages inside them.

Whichever approach you use, converting a found structure into a journal can change your journal-keeping significantly.

Jenny Taliadoros, *Evolution*, altered book made from *The World and Man*, © University of Chicago, 1937. Collage and painting. *Photo by artist.*

It can be a way of incorporating a beloved book from childhood into your daily life; or of keeping the words of another writer before you as you go about recording and interweaving your own thoughts and experiences. It can allow you to carry on a kind of conversation with another writer or furnish delicious opportunities for irony and playful commentary.

Of course, using an existing book nicely solves the problem of facing a blank page. Preparing pages in such a book involves choosing what to keep, what to modify, and what to obliterate from the original. Another benefit of using such a book is that many old bindings are elegant as well as durable. An afternoon spent in a used bookstore can yield leather-bound books with marbled endpapers and gilded fore edges, all for a fraction of the cost of a new blank book of comparable quality. Old photo albums, atlases, anatomy textbooks, encyclopedias, children's books, dictionaries, and books in foreign languages are just a sampling of the many possibilities that await the found book journal-keeper.

Above: Jenny Taliadoros, *The Wine and the Music*, altered book made from The Wine and the Music. ©Doubleday and Co, 1968. *Photo by artist.*

Karen Michel, *Art Journal 2001* (Inside spread), 2001. Gesso, acrylic medium, collage. *Photo by artist.*

Stenciling letters onto a cover.

LETTERING

Add a title to any book by carefully lettering with a stencil and ink or paint that is compatible with the surface. If the surface is very shiny or rough, follow the directions below for making a label.

TOOLS & MATERIALS

Matt knife

Ruler

PVA

Glue brush

Paper label with lettering printed on it

INSTRUCTIONS

1 With the ruler and matt knife, carefully trace a shallow cut around the outside of the label into the cover, just deep enough to penetrate the outer layers of the cover material.

2 Peel the outer layers of cover material up from inside the cut lines.

3 Paint the paper label with PVA and press it into place in the peeled-off area.

4 Varnish the paper label with matt finish polymer varnish.

DRAWING

If the book has a smooth cover, draw and paint directly on it with acrylics.

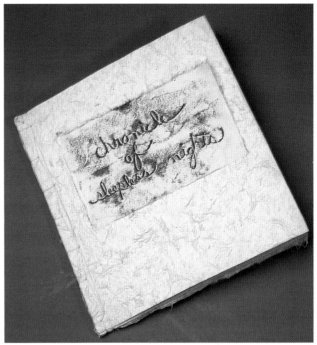

Julie Wagner, *Chronicle of Sleepless Nights*, 2002. 9⅛ x 8⅞ x ¾ inches (23.2 x 22.5 x 1.9 cm). Stab-bound journal, handmade Japanese paper, handmade Nepalese paper, ink, oil transfer drawings. *Photo by Dan Morse.*

ALTERING A BOOK

An alternative to using a new blank book or to making a book yourself is to use an existing book as the basis of your journal. Much has been written on the subject of altering books, and this will be only a brief introduction. Begin by finding a book that means something to you. It might be a book from your childhood, or a book on a subject that continues to interest you. It might be a book that you simply like for its size, shape, weight of paper, and cover.

The first step in reclaiming this book is to prepare the pages to receive your work. If the paper is old and somewhat fragile, a coat of wheat paste sizing will help to stabilize them a little. Make a batch of wheat paste following directions on page 43. Place a piece of blotter paper under the page, and brush the paste onto the page. You'll need to allow each page to dry before working on it or turning to the next page. A hair dryer can speed up the process.

Another way to prepare a page is to brush it with slightly thinned absorbent ground or with acrylic gesso (see Grounds, page 48). Yet another way to block out the parts of the page that you want to write or draw on is to paint over it with gouache (see Gouache, page 32).

Using an
Old Book Cover

Remember that if the pages are made of thin paper, they will wrinkle and cockle when you apply wet media to them. You can prepare very thin pages by using light colored or white water-soluble crayons, but not wetting them. And of course pages can be covered at least partially with collage. Use a glue stick if the paper is on the thin side.

If you're mainly interested in putting new pages or a text block into an altered book, a trip to a used bookstore can provide a fine journal cover. After making The Thirty-Minute Multi-Pamphlet Journal on page 202, you can slip the pages into a cover of your choice for a unique and interesting journal.

TOOLS & MATERIALS

Text block made by following instructions for the Thirty-Minute Pamphlet*

Old book

*The page size of the new text block should be the same as the pages you are removing from the old book.

INSTRUCTIONS

1 Using a matte knife, carefully cut the old text block from its cover by cutting the end papers in the joint or fold of the inside covers. Take care to cut through the paper only and not the book's covering material.

2 Place scrap paper between the first and second sheet of the new text block to protect them. Brush paste all over the outside sheet of the text block. Lay the pasted page over the inside of the front cover, as shown in figure 1 and burnish thoroughly.

3 Lay a sheet of scrap paper between the newly pasted end paper and the text block. Close the book with the newly pasted side down.

4 Repeat steps 2 and 3 on the other side. Note: that the spine of the text block is not glued to the spine board of the cover. If you want to further pursue making your own journal you'll find a bibliography for "not-so-reluctant" bookbinders on page 127.

Figure 1

Kelcey Loomer, 2001. 11 x 8¼ inches (27.9 x 21 cm). Bound journal, acrylic paint, ink, pen, excerpt from a phone message. *Photo by Aleia Woolsey.*

Butter-Box Book

This little book was made from a small rectangular butter box. If you don't have a butter box, or if you want to make this book a different size, you can use any box, such as a cookie box or a frozen pizza box. Score and cut the butter box as shown, or use proportional measurements to suit the box you're using.

Figure 1

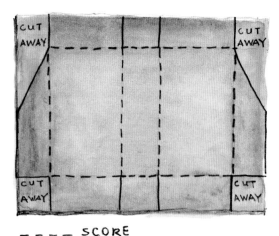

- - - - SCORE

———— CUT

Figure 2

INSTRUCTIONS

1 Carefully open all flaps of the box, unfolding it until it's one rectangular piece, as shown in figure 1.

2 Place the unfolded box, right side down, on your work surface. Score the lines on the box, as shown in figure 1. If you're using a butter box, the fold lines that are already there will act as the score lines. Use the matt knife to cut out the squares at all the corners, then cut the top left and top right of the two side flaps on a slant, as shown in figure 1.

3 Use the glue stick to glue down the three flaps along the top: the left side, the top of the spine, and the right side. On the bottom, *glue only the bottom spine flap.*

4 Fold up the remaining two bottom flaps. Glue *only the bottom fourth* of the two side flaps to the bottom left and right flaps, as shown in figure 2. You should now have two pockets, one each on the inside front and back covers.

5 Mark and cut rectangles from the spine of the cover, as shown in figure 3. Start by using a pencil to make the marks. Begin at the top of the bottom flap, marking across the spine from one score line to the other. Do the same beginning at the bottom of the top flap. Next, measure approximately ¹/₂ inch (1.3 cm) down from the top line and up from the bottom line, and then draw the lines across the spine. In the same way, mark two more lines at the center. When you're finished, you should have six lines, each approximately ¹/₂ inch (1.3 cm) apart. If you're making a larger book, use proportional spacing.

Figure 3

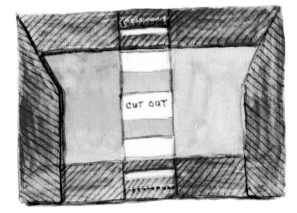

6 Use a matt knife and the metal ruler to cut the rectangles. Cut along the lines you've drawn, and along the already-scored lines of the box that delineate the spine. When you're finished, you'll have cut three rectangles, evenly spaced, along the spine.

7 Now mark and cut a thin, $1/8$-inch-wide (3 mm) strip through the two glued layers of the top and bottom spine flaps. Draw these lines approximately midway in each flap, as shown in figure 3. Use the matt knife and ruler to cut them out. Set the cover aside.

8 Make the signatures by nesting 4 or 5 small sheets of folded paper. Start with sheets measuring $4^1/_2$ x $4^1/_2$ inches (11.4 x 11.4 cm), and then fold them in half. The folded pages are called folios. When you nest the folios together, the little booklet is called a signature. After folding the signatures, press them under a pile of books for about half an hour to get any air out of the creases. **Note:** Depending on the thickness of the paper you use, you'll need four or five folios for each signature. If you use watercolor or other heavy paper, make the signatures by nesting only one or two folios. Remember that it's fine to mix up different kinds of paper in the signatures.

Figure 4

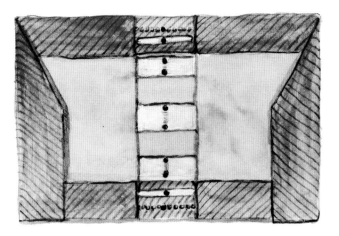

9 Make enough signatures to fit comfortably within the covers. Check this by first stacking the signatures and then slipping them into the cover—they should fit snugly in the spine, but you shouldn't have to compress them to fit. You will probably have 12 or 13 signatures.

10 When you have the right number of signatures, punch a hole for each one across the spine at the top and bottom of the cover. You can see the row of holes across the top and bottom of the spine in figure 4. Use the awl for making the holes, placing a piece of cardboard or the telephone directory under the cover to protect your work surface. Each row of holes, top and bottom, should be at least $1/4$ inch (6 mm) in from the edge. Space the holes at least $1/8$ inch (3 mm) apart to avoid tearing the cover. If you happen to make a mistake at this step, simply glue a piece of heavy paper over the row of holes and start over.

11 Prepare to punch the sewing holes in the signatures. Lay an open signature on the open telephone directory. Do *not* lay the signature in the center crease of the book, but on one of the flat sides. Mark a line along the top of the signature on the paper of the directory. Draw another line $1/8$ inch (3 mm) above the first line; this is the placement line for the cover. You want the signature to be spaced evenly between the top and bottom of the cover, and $1/8$ inch should do it.

12 To punch the signatures, lay an open signature along the lower of the two lines you drew on the page of the directory. Then place the open cover along the top line. You should be able to see the center crease of the signature through the open rectangles in the spine of the cover, as shown in figure 4. Be sure the crease is perpendicular to the horizontal openings. Punch a hole

Figure 5

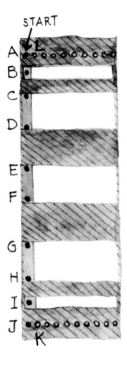

START

A
B
C
D
E
F
G
H
I
J

K

in each signature at the following places: in a top hole made in step 10, in the narrow slit just under the top holes, at the top of the first rectangular opening, at the bottom of the first rectangular opening, at the top and bottom of the second and third rectangular openings, in the narrow slit at the bottom, and in a bottom hole. Each signature will have 10 holes when you're finished. **Note:** If the holes seem too small, lay an open signature, one at a time, in the center *crease* of the directory and re-punch them. By punching in the crease, the awl travels more deeply through the signature to make a wider hole.

13 Position the first signature for sewing. Figure 5 shows the spine of the book, seen from the outside of the cover, before sewing. You'll notice that a single signature is on the inside, pushed up against the left edge of the spine. This is the correct position for beginning the sewing.

14 Thread the sewing needle with approximately 2 yards (1.8 m) of the heavy thread. Use a single strand; do not double the thread, nor tie a knot. Begin by inserting the needle into the top left hole, point A on figure 5 (an arrow marked start guides the way). Be sure to insert the needle into both the cover hole and the top hole of the signature. Pull the thread through, leaving a 5-inch (12.7 cm) tail. Use the paper clip to clip the tail to the back cover for now.

Figure 6

15 Insert the needle from the inside of the signature into the second signature hole. You will come out at point B (figure 5, page 229), which is in the narrow slit. Pull the thread until it is taut. Then insert the needle into point C, which will take you to the inside of the signature. Pull the needle out of the third hole and insert it into the fourth hole.

16 Continue using the running stitch in this way, making sure you pull the thread taut as you go, until you pull the needle out the bottom hole, point J. **Note:** Be sure all stitches are flat and taut, but be careful when tightening them. *Always* pull the thread *parallel* to the plane of the paper. If you pull straight up you may tear the paper.

17 Pick up the second signature and place it alongside the first one inside the cover. Insert the needle into point K, as shown in figure 5, and then into the first *bottom* hole of the second signature. Stitch this signature just as you did the first one. This time, when you get to point L at the top, unclip the tail and tie it snugly to the sewing thread in order to anchor it. Do *not* trim the tail or cut the sewing thread.

18 Pick up the third signature and sew it exactly as you did the others. This time, however, and for all other signatures, do a little scoop stitch before inserting the needle into the next top or bottom hole, as shown in figure 6. This stitch will result in a pretty chain stitch across the top and bottom of the spine. Leaving it out won't cause any structural problems, but it's easy to do and looks more finished.

Figure 7

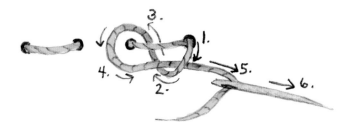

19 Tie off when you finish stitching the final signature. You'll be on the outside of the cover. Insert the needle back into the hole just before the last one so that you are now on the inside of the second-to-last signature. Tie off by sliding the needle under the stitch closest to it and making a little knot, as shown in figure 7.

20 After tying this knot, trim the thread to ½ inch (1.3 cm) and remove the needle. Thread it with the first tail left at the top, and tie it off as you did in step 19 by entering the hole to the right of point A to enter the second signature.

Coming Full Circle

by Shirley Levine

"Suddenly I saw how my skills with textiles and my growing skills with drawing and painting were all part of one big circle."

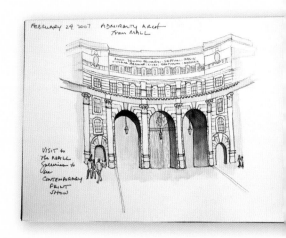

Henry at the Imperial War Museum, London, England. 7 x 10 inches (17.8 x 25.4 cm). Pen, watercolor. Photo by artist.

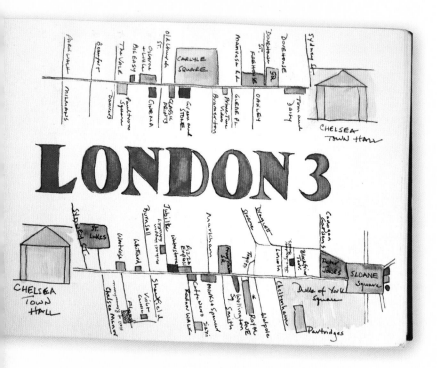

Street Map of King's Road, Chelsea, London, England. 7 x 10 inches (17.8 x 25.4 cm). Pen, watercolor. Photo by artist.

Admirality Arch, London, England. 7 x 10 inches (17.8 x 25.4 cm). Pen, watercolor. Photo by artist.

I keep visual travel journals to document my days and to collect family memories of loved objects, times, and places spent together. I also keep sketchbooks for practicing my art skills, testing new materials, and for drawing in on my frequent museum trips.

My daughter and her family moved to London less than one year after I started keeping a visual journal. When my husband and I would visit them, I would journal every day, and I now have three sketchbooks documenting those fabulous times. The pages are filled with drawings of the children, toys the children wanted me to sketch, drawings of important places in their lives, such as their house and nursery school, sketches of London landmarks, and copies of masterworks from museum visits.

When I partially retired in 2005 from my busy career in internal medicine and hematology as part of a medical school faculty, my interest in drawing and watercolor became my new love.

Full retirement in 2009 was a fabulously happy event because I was so well prepared to add sketchbook art and bookbinding to my lifelong interests in sewing, quilting, and surface design.

Suddenly I saw how my skills with textiles and my growing skills with drawing and painting were all part of one big circle. Now I dye and paint the fabric that becomes the bookcloth for the journals that I make. And the figure drawings I do from live models are becoming a series of small quilts.

Gallery

Andrea A. Peterson, *Penland Sketchbook*, 1993. Hemp, butterfly wing, pastels, and ink. *Photo by artist.*

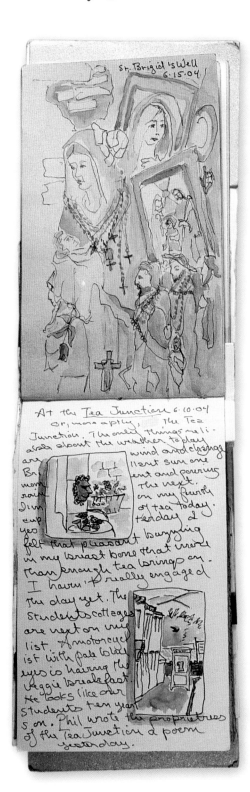

Ann Turkle, *Ireland Journal*, 2004. *Photo by Aleia Woolsey.*

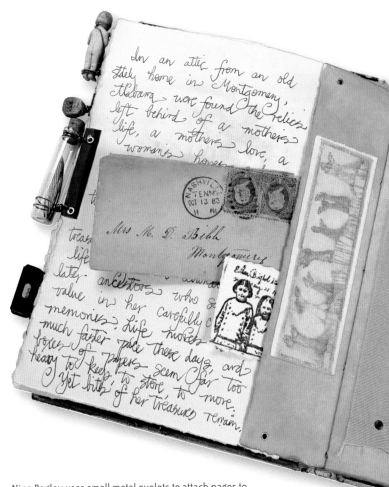

Nina Bagley uses small metal eyelets to attach pages to page stubs and to add elements to pages.

Pat Gaignat, *Untitled Journal Pages*.
8½ x 10½ inches (21.6 x 26.7 cm).
Acrylic, stamps, pen; collage.

Kelcey Loomer, *Untitled Journal Page*. 6 x 9½ inches
(15.2 x 24.1 cm). Watercolor, black ink, sepia pen.

Becca Johnson, *Untitled Journal Pages*. 10 x 27 inches (25.4 x 68.6 cm).
Pencil; taped-on photograph, typed paper, tracing paper, stained paper.

Melanie Testa, *Untitled Journal Page*.
8 x 10½ inches (20.3 x 26.7 cm). Gesso,
acrylic, pencil, marker; collage.

Sandy Webster, *Australia 2005 Journal*. 7¾ x 15½ inches
(19.7 x 39.4 cm). Pen, watercolor.

Sandy Webster, *Australia 2005 Journal.*
7¾ x 15½ inches (19.7 x 39.4 cm). Pen, watercolor.

Kelcey Loomer, 6 x 9½ inches (15.2 x 24.1 cm).
Pen, watercolor.

Pat Gaignat, 5½ x 7½ inches (14 x 19 cm).
Gesso, acrylic, gold pen, letter stamps.

Acknowledgments

From the beginning, my two earlier books on journal keeping, *The Decorated Page* and *The Decorated Journal*, have seemed to me to be one long conversation among many people. And so it has been a great pleasure for me to work with Lark Crafts to combine the two books and bring the material to a culmination through the journal profiles that are new to this edition. I thank Paige Gilchrist, formerly of Lark, and my editor, Linda Kopp, who first championed bringing *The Decorated Page* back into print, and then suggested doing a bind-up of the two books.

The most significant addition to this revision of the two books is the collection of thirteen profiles of journal keepers, which are placed throughout the book. The profilers beautifully demonstrate in their work and in their words a myriad of journal practices. From the bottom of my heart I thank these brave and generous people who sent me their images or let me borrow their journals, trusting me to keep them safe from pets and humidity and the other ordinary perils of my studio for the many weeks that I needed them.

Special thanks for shepherding the book through all the steps of its realization goes to Linda Kopp, who with great good humor added this project to the tottering pile on her overloaded desk and was unfailingly optimistic and fun to work with. Also thanks to Mary McGahren, Travis Medford, and Kristi Pfeffer the book's art directors, who managed to translate my unwieldy cut-and–pasted-and-scribbled-upon mock-up of the combined books into an elegant, clean, and coherent design. Thanks, too, to Stewart O'Shields for his ability to make magic with photography.

As always, I am indebted to my husband, Phil, who took over my cooking night many more times than I even dared to ask, and put up with the expansion of my studio into the dining room, living room, and kitchen for months on end.

Contributing Artists

Laurie Adams 113, 119
Pamela Averick 141
Nina Bagley 71, 119, 213, 218, 233
Bette Bates 33
Coranna Beene 115, 119
Dusty Benedict 27
Jill K. Berry 81, 111, 235
Sarah Bourne 27, 57, 58, 62, 127, 155
Traci Bunkers 78, 101
Benedicte Caneill 34
Justin Cantalini 86
Laura Carter 109, 116, 118, 160
Linda Chaves 104
Tara Chickey 49
Juliana Coles 128, 216
Amy Cook 175
Sheila Cunningham 70
Jane Dalton 83, 102, 144
Wendy Hale Davis 46, 156
Jacob Diehn 99
Clare Duplace 56. 88
Elizabeth Ellison 122, 188
Patricia Gaignat 148, 234, 236
Suan Kaupsinshi Gaylord 181
Jeanne G. Germani 137
Scott Gordon 65
Edie Greene 88, 140
Susan and Jeff Griesmaier 192
Blair Gulledge 108, 182
Megan Gulledge 89
Charlotte Hedlund 84, 143
Dorothy Herbert 112, 116, 117, 120
Aude Iung-Lancrey 100
Dana Fox Jenkins 77
Coral Jensen 44, 217
Becca Johnson 19, 43, 85, 234
Bruce Kremer 9, 117, 164, 216
Laura Ladendorf 18

Eric Larson 133
Shirley Levine 232
Kristen A. Livelsberger 66
Kelcey Loomer 26, 27, 38, 39, 64, 82, 101, 105, 108, 109, 121, 129, 136, 147, 153, 161, 224, 234, 236
Mary Ellen Long 109
Val Lucas 147
Amber Maloy 29
Kore Loy Wildrekinde McWhirter 33, 125
Faith McLellan 91, 151
Miriam McNamara 98
Karen Michel 220
Mary Ann Moss 62, 100
Bobbe Needham 124
Joseph A. Osina 7, 135
Andrea Peterson 47, 106, 152, 169, 233
Nancy Pobanz 96
Victoria Rabinowe 154
Judy Rinks 91
Matt Rogers 30, 89
Susan Saling 11, 112, 205, 232
Janet Scholl 144
Polly Smith 179
Colleen Stanton 45, 48, 49, 107, 113, 114, 123
Ivy Smith 12. 87
Jenny Taliadores 219, 220
Melanie Testa 126, 235
Billie Jean Theide 122
Christine Toriello 40, 107, 117
Ann Turkle 6, 23, 103, 120- 124, 139, 157, 205, 233
Kerstin Vogdes 8, 16, 17, 112, 140, 141, 146
Julie Wagner 25, 154, 221
Sandy Webster 133, 149, 213, 235, 236
Beata Wehr 180
Pamela Lyle Westhaver 100
Jennifer Wing 40

Index